LINCOLNSHIRE AND THE FENS

Frontispiece

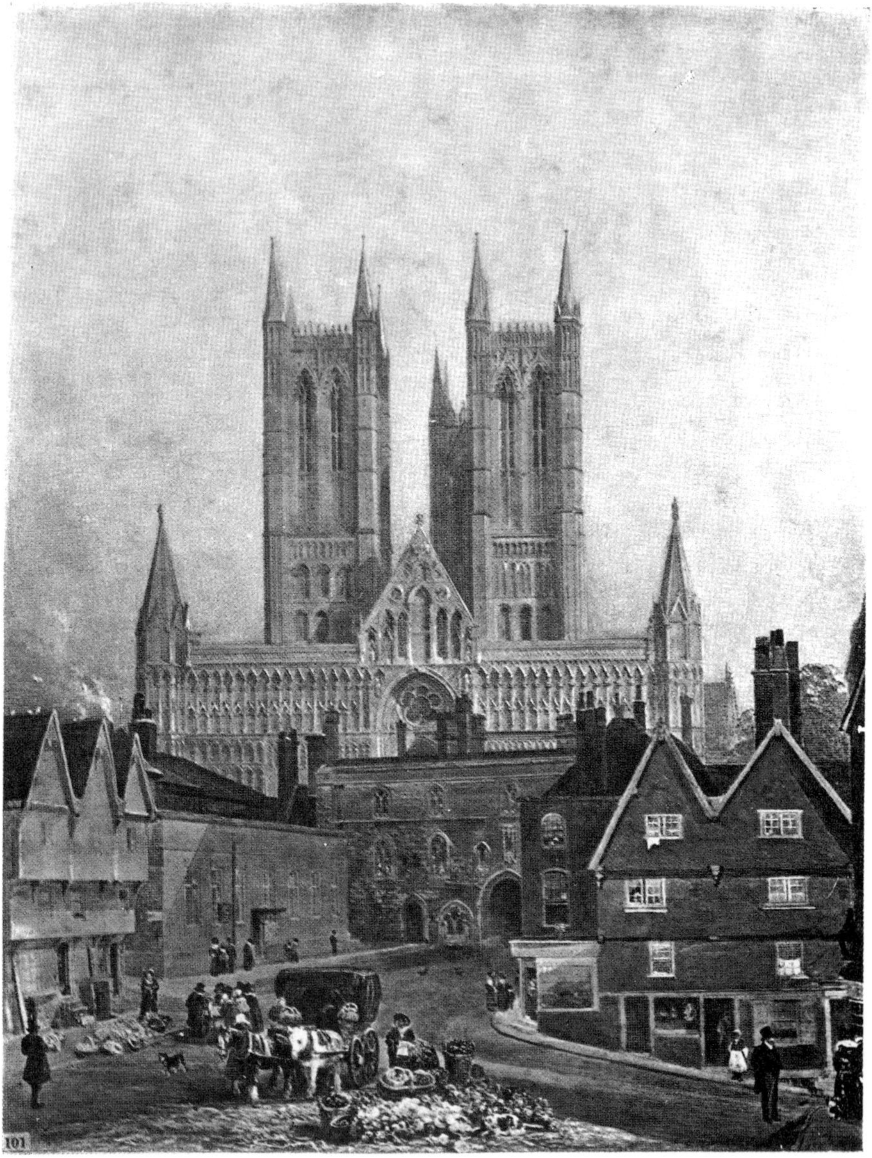

I Lincoln Cathedral

From the watercolour by Peter De Wint

LINCOLNSHIRE AND THE FENS

M. W. BARLEY

Illustrated from photographs by
the Author and Others

With a new Preface by
the Author

Published by EP Publishing Limited, 1972
First published B. T. Batsford, Ltd., 1952

TO
MY PARENTS

Republished 1972 by EP Publishing Limited,
East Ardsley, Wakefield,
Yorkshire, England,
by kind permission of M. W. Barley
and the original publishers

ISBN 0 85409 764 3

Please address all enquiries to EP Publishing Ltd.

Reprinted by Scolar Press Limited,
20 Main Street, Menston,
Yorkshire, U.K.

PREFACE

WHEN Dickens wanted a dreary setting for Lady Dedlock's country place in *Bleak House*, he chose Lincolnshire, and he planted it in a dripping landscape populated only by rabbits, crows, and sodden deer. Scott in *Peveril of the Peak* had Roger Wildrake style himself "of Squattlesea Mere in the moist county of Lincoln". The truth is that Lincolnshire and the Fens are in the driest part of England. One misconception of nineteenth-century novelists has died, but another untruth has taken its place. It is commonly thought that Lincolnshire is flat. The Lincolnshire man's rebuttal takes a double form: first, the county is not flat, and second, if it is flat, that flatness is the essence of its character and particular beauty.

Mr. Harry Batsford's advice when we first discussed this project was that I should not be too much on the defensive. I have not been consciously more so than Cowper was when he wrote:

Scenes must be beautiful which, daily viewed,
Please daily, and whose wealth survives
Long knowledge and the scrutiny of years.

Cowper, Constable, and de Wint found a beauty in the English lowlands which is still there, little altered, for anyone to see who wishes, though it requires a more lively eye than do the highlands. Lincolnshire belongs especially to Peter de Wint, who found a lifelong friend in William Hilton of Lincoln, married his sister Harriet Hilton, and came back time after time to fix for ever the qualities of the Lincolnshire landscape in those wide, low water-colours. George Crabbe, another lowland poet, who belongs as much to that part of the Vale of Belvoir where Kesteven, Nottinghamshire, and Leicestershire meet as he does to the Suffolk coast, wrote of the Fens:

All are appropriate—bog, marsh, and fen,
Are only poor to undiscerning men.

I claim no more discernment than anyone else, but I have enjoyed making the effort to convey in words something of the evolution of this man-made countryside. I have encountered the difficulty that anyone must feel in writing about his own county: one knows at once too much and too little—too much to be able to select, and too little to do justice to one's sentiments. The greatest difficulty of all has been to turn the recollections of unthinking childhood into more substantial form. I am sure that both selections and omissions will call for forgiveness from those who know the county better than I; my hope is that such shortcomings do not spoil the picture of the long partnership of man and nature in this part of England.

I cannot catalogue the names of all those who have helped to make this book. They include relatives, friends of long standing, and those who, as teachers and students, have worked with me in the adult education movement. I must acknowledge my particular debt to Mr. F. T. Baker, who helped me to use the resources of the Lincoln City Library; to my colleagues Mr. W. H. Hosford, Mr. A. Smith, and Mr. A. Champion; and to Mrs. E. H. Rudkin and Mr. C. Brears, who placed their considerable knowledge of the county at my disposal. Mr. J. W. F. Hill found time to read the typescript. It will be plain to those who have read Dr. W. G. Hoskins' *Midland England* in this series that this volume owes a great deal to his; the flattery which is implied could not be more sincere.

M. W. B.

December 1951

PREFACE TO SECOND EDITION

In the twenty years since *Lincolnshire and the Fens* first appeared, a succession of other writers have added to our knowledge of that part of eastern England. In every field of study, from prehistory through place-names to medieval history and the study of farm-houses and cottages, more could be written than was then possible. In general the effect of later research is rather to elaborate the story than to alter it, though of course anyone writing today would wish to change an emphasis here or to qualify a generalisation there.

Correspondents have offered additional material. I have been told that in writing of Lincolnshire food (p. 144) I should have mentioned beans and bacon, and also stuffed chine, which was eaten in May week when young men and women were home from service. Mr. J. A. Prentice, who came to a Fenland chemist's shop in 1904, has written of buying opium by the hundredweight and ten gallons of laudanum at a time; the opium was cut up into small rolls, mostly in half and quarter ounces (p. 123). This makes strange reading at a time of such concern about drug-taking. Some reviewers criticised me for including the Fens — that is, parts of Cambridgeshire and Norfolk — along with Lincolnshire, and it certainly produced an infelicitous opening sentence to ch. IV, but otherwise a rigid adherence to county boundaries would have produced a less complete picture.

The face of Lincolnshire has changed less than that of many counties, but it has become more difficult to pick out the tell-tale features of the past. There are even more bungalows and caravans along the coast; towns like Scunthorpe and Grimsby have spread enormously, and Immingham has now got off the mark (p. 22). Many villages have lost, and are still losing, characteristic farm-houses and cottages, of brick, stone and mud-and-stud; prairie-farming methods have led to the grubbing up of miles of those hedges laid out by inclosure commissioners (p. 177). A writer today would have to depend more on documents and photographs and less on the evidence of his eyes and the memory of living people; this constitutes, I hope, a justification for the reappearance of an attempt to portray part of the face of Britain.

NOVEMBER 1971 M. W. B.

Some errors inevitably occurred in the first edition; overleaf is a list of corrections.

CORRIGENDA

p. 22	*l.*2	John Harrison was in fact born at Nostell Priory, son of an estate carpenter there; he moved to Barrow on Humber at an early age.
p. 35	*l.*7	Norfolk, not Cambridgeshire.
p. 38	*l.*35	There is no *Skegness* R.D.C. The appropriate Rural District takes its name from Spilsby.
p. 43	*l.*38	There is no evidence of a ninth century church at Algarkirk.
p. 66	*l.*4	Ruskington spire was *not* rebuilt, but a porch was constructed from the materials; the date was 1620.
p. 80	*l.*44	Gainsborough Old Hall: the west wing was built in 1480, as a timber-framed structure, and William Hickman cased it in brick in *c.* 1600.
p. 92	*l.*10	For Willoughby, read *Spilsby.*
	*l.*28	For hereditary, read *traditional*; the privilege went with the manor of Scrivelsby, not the Dymoke family.
p. 109	*l.*10	After village, insert *of such small.*
p. 123	*l.*8	For Burroughs, read *Burrows.*
p. 126	*l.*3	The woad mill at Parson Drove was pulled down in 1914. A woad mill at Algarkirk, driven by steam, worked for a few years longer.
p. 178	*l.*27	For Burroughs, read *Burrows.*
p. 179	*l.*20	For High read *Silver.*
p. 116	*l.*27	For Winthorpe read *Ingoldmells.*

CONTENTS

ACKNOWLEDGMENT

THE Publishers wish to thank the following for permission to reproduce the photographs as shown:

Aerofilms Ltd., for fig. 46; Hallam Ashley, F.R.P.S., for fig. 20; M. W. Barley, for figs. 3, 18, 28–30, 36, 41, 42, 44, 45, 57–9, 61, 64, 65, and 77; Ralph Bates, for figs. 60 and 63; Donovan E. H. Box, for fig. 15; the Trustees of the British Museum, for figs. 11 and 12; J. Allan Cash, F.R.P.S., for figs. 27, 49, 68, and 70; J. Chettleburgh, for figs. 56, 62, 66, and 79; G. V. Clark, for fig. 24; the late Brian C. Clayton, for figs. 14, 19, 21, 22, and 32; J. Dixon-Scott, F.R.P.S., for fig. 26; Herbert Felton, F.R.P.S., for fig. 23; Capt. C. G. M. Hatfield, for fig. 74; A. F. Kersting, F.R.P.S., for figs. 5, 16, 25, 33–5, 40, 55, 69, 71, 73, and 75; Northgate Studios, for figs. 7 and 72; The *Nottingham Guardian*, for fig. 52; Picture Post Library, for fig. 53; Dr. J. K. St. Joseph, for figs. 8–10 and 48; E. W. Tattersall, for fig. 39; the late Will F. Taylor, for figs. 4, 47, 50, and 54; Topical Press Agency Ltd., for figs. 2, 6, and 51; Reece Winstone, A.R.P.S., for figs. 13, 17, 43, 67, 76, and 78.

The frontispeice is reproduced by permission of the Trustees of the Victoria and Albert Museum.

Thanks are due to Messrs. Chapman & Hall Ltd. for permission to quote the extract on p. 42 from *Brideshead Revisited* by Evelyn Waugh.

Chapter

I

The Land

"A good prospect alone will ease melancholy."—Robert Burton (Rector of Walesby, 1624–34), *Anatomy of Melancholy*.

IF you wish to see Lincolnshire and the Fens, you must make a special effort to do so. They lie well outside the great ellipse of industrial England, which has London and Manchester as its focal points, and so the main-line railway and the buses carrying people about their daily business do no more than touch the fringe of it. The more easterly of the railway lines to the north, which follows the line of the medieval north road, merely skirts the county. There is a glimpse of the Fens from the carriage windows near Peterborough, not even enough to impress with the tremendous dome of sky, and certainly not enough to convey the man-made wealth of churches and large villages, the solid prosperity and achievement. After Peterborough the railway plunges through the oolite ridge; at its edges there are valleys shut in by short, tumbling hills and many woods; in the heart of the limestone the slopes are longer and from the carriage window you see only the smooth hollow of the valley of the Witham, not the large-scale landscape of the plateau above. At Grantham, the ridge has been pierced, apart from the last outlier on which Great Gonerby stands, and to do it the railway has climbed higher than at any other point between London and the Border. From there the railway (and the north road) runs freely on into the Trent valley, which at this stage, round Newark, belongs equally to Nottinghamshire and Lincolnshire. The last glimpse of Lincolnshire is from the hills near Tuxford, with the whole length of the Lincoln Edge limiting the view east, and Lincoln Minster, visible on all but the worst of days, marking the main break in the ridge.

Travellers on this route have their minds on London or Leeds; many others see another view of Lincolnshire from the windows of the buses and cars that are taking them to Skegness or Cleethorpes. Each sector of the English coast is known best to the millions in the nearest industrial towns, and so Skegness belongs to Nottingham and Leicester, and Cleethorpes to the West Riding. In another sense, as holiday resorts become industrialised, they belong not to the midlands, nor even to England, but to the universalised world of entertainment in which Skegness and Coney

Island may differ in size and situation but not in character. The buses (I counted ninety leaving Nottingham one August morning last year) and the cars are a conveyor belt whose final products are workers reinvigorated by the standardised course in the holiday camp. It is difficult to suggest stopping such a mechanical process, but every writer of a book like this must do so. The appeal was made, rather pompously, in Dr. Cox's *Guide to Lincolnshire*, nearly forty years ago: "to study the picturesque from a motor-car is next to an impossibility; the impression gained is at best but visionary". If you must use a car, make it a means of getting to the Wolds, or the Cliff. Stop anywhere between Lincoln and Kirton-in-Lindsey, or on the Blue Stone Heath Road. Stop and look, and come again to stand; these views change hourly, sometimes throwing up the foreground of villages at your feet, and then drawing the eye into the distance where ridges fifteen miles away, patterned with woods and cornfields, are at last a silhouette against a late sun. In the Cumberland dales, the sun sets long before its time, but in the Fens the sight of the towers of Ely glowing with the last light after the streets below are quite dark is more astonishingly beautiful than the last rays on the pink slopes of Grassmoor. Instead of the anticipation of a completely new view round the shoulder of the next Derbyshire hill, there is the vast panorama with detail enough in it to absorb the eye for hours; as one moves, the elements in the view wheel and turn in a satisfying parade. That is the sensation as one passes the Carltons, and Fillingham, north of Lincoln, or along the chalk scarp above Somerby, and it is felt in the approach to any of the villages of the Marshland fringe, where churches like Saltfleetby All Saints (57) or Croft are seen from every angle before the winding lane, dyked on either side, at last brings you to the churchyard gate. Elsewhere there is a variant of this pleasure—the sight of a church like Maxey in the Fens, or Claypole in the Witham valley, clear and sharp in the spring air, though it is miles away; as the straight road brings you nearer to it, details come into focus and the only change in the view is the gradual magnification. Those who want surprises and to find secret views can go to the Wolds, and particularly to the Somersby valley; they can turn their backs on the commanding view of the Fens from West Keal, and look for Kirmond-le-Mire and Biscathorpe, Scamblesby (47) and Hagworthingham. The names are magnets, and the reward for those who are drawn thither is the sudden drop down the chalk slopes to the lush green of the valley bottoms or the tiny sandstone churches half seen through the hanging woods round Somersby.

The county we are concerned with has as much unity as any human division. Behind the great bow of the coastline, the Trent is the main boundary on the west. Farther south, the land link with the rest of England, the limestone ridge, is crossed by Sewstern Lane, a prehistoric road from the Welland at Stamford to the Trent at Newark. It divides Lincolnshire from Leicestershire; the Romans laid Ermine Street on the southern part of it, and the Great North Road appropriated the Newark end in the thirteenth century; between these two stretches it is still a green road, the only one left in the county, for the ridgeways on the Wolds and the Cliff are now metalled.

Two other areas belong to this book; although they are not wholly Lincolnshire there are good reasons for including them. One is the low ground between the Trent and the Yorkshire Ouse, most of which has always been known as the Isle of Axholme. Though Nottinghamshire claims the southern margin overlooked from Gringley-on-the-Hill, and Hatfield and Thorne took their Moors and Waste into the West Riding of Yorkshire, the villages of the heart of the Isle, Haxey, Epworth, and Crowle, are part of the ancient kingdom of Lindsey. Similarly in the south, the Fens lie mainly in Lincolnshire and no native would hesitate to claim them. In fact the eastern margin belongs to Norfolk, and once over the ancient course of the Nene we must speak of the Marshland, which is a confusion to some, because the same name belongs to the coastal fringe, the salt marshes, and is not elsewhere used of this fresh-water marshland. On the southern and south-western edges of the Fens, settlements on the brink of the low ground have gathered their share of it into the counties of Cambridge, Huntingdon, and Northampton, whose centres of gravity lie on higher ground; Lincolnshire alone has an ancient division, "the parts of Holland", which is entirely fen. The word Holland means land overlooked by high ground, either the Wolds or the limestone ridge; it is curious and misleading that it should be identical with our name for the Netherlands, which has a quite different derivation.

The best way to begin to make the acquaintance of Lincolnshire is to travel north or south, along the grain of the country; there are few parts of England where the pattern is so diagrammatically simple, or where the main roads enable one to see it so clearly. The most ancient way into the county can still be followed, along the spine of limestone which runs from Leicestershire to the Humber. From that ridge you can overlook most of the county, except the Marshland beyond the other ridge of the Wolds, but to see the villages you must drop down from the high ground to the sheltered sites and the more fertile ground where they lie. In south-west Kesteven, the wide and solid limestone plateau is in fact cut by the Witham and Glen valleys, and the sturdy villages of stone houses and small but well-built churches lie on valley slopes, like South Witham, or deep in the woods of the valley bottom, like Easton and South Stoke. Except for Colsterworth, which was made by coach traffic, there are no large villages in the area. As soon as you leave the north road and its garages and "transport cafs", you might be a hundred miles away; Skillington, with its charming church and Jacobean manor-house, is as secluded as anyone could wish. The worst disaster that has struck this part of Lincolnshire is ironstone quarrying; the great ridged dumps form a background now to the view of Colsterworth, and the enormous excavators are eating their way farther and farther into the county. Sited on outlying spurs of the ridge are some good hilltop villages, like Barrowby and Great Gonerby, overlooking the Trent valley and the wide opening of the Vale of Belvoir; or Hough on the Hill, with its miniature square outside the churchyard gate. Better still are the villages from Leadenham towards Lincoln, which cling to the top of the limestone scarp, each with its own steep lane down to the fertile Low Fields. Navenby is a large one-street village, but Leadenham itself, Welbourn, and Wellingore have quiet winding lanes, lined with stone cottages with pantile roofs, or occasionally a brick cottage making a brilliant but harmonious contrast. Behind them is the Lincoln Heath, a name that has lost its obvious significance now that the wide and waterless plateau is growing wheat and sugar-beet, but it is still bleak and devoid of any natural woodland; there is no shelter from the wind except for the occasional plantations of eighteenth-century improving landlords or the hedgerow trees of a nineteenth-century squire. It is not surprising that Cranwell, the first R.A.F. college, was also planted here, though it is sad that Dunston Pillar, put up by Francis Dashwood (best known for his mausoleum at West Wycombe) to light travellers across this lonely heath, has now been taken down because it was dangerous to aircraft.

It is wrong to imply that the limestone area is altogether treeless; the name Kesteven, to which all this southern half of the county west of the Fens belongs, is derived from a Celtic word (*coed*) meaning "wood", and part of it was a royal forest from Norman times until the thirteenth century. The clays covering the oolite on the eastern slopes of the ridge still carry more woodland tha. any other part of the county; this, with the country between Lincoln and Horncastle, and the eastern foothills of the Wolds, has always been well forested. It is not the open woodland of the New Forest, nor the derelict woodland on the poor soil of Sherwood Forest, but woods neat and cared for, on land that is good and highly valued; both the landscape and the villages, such

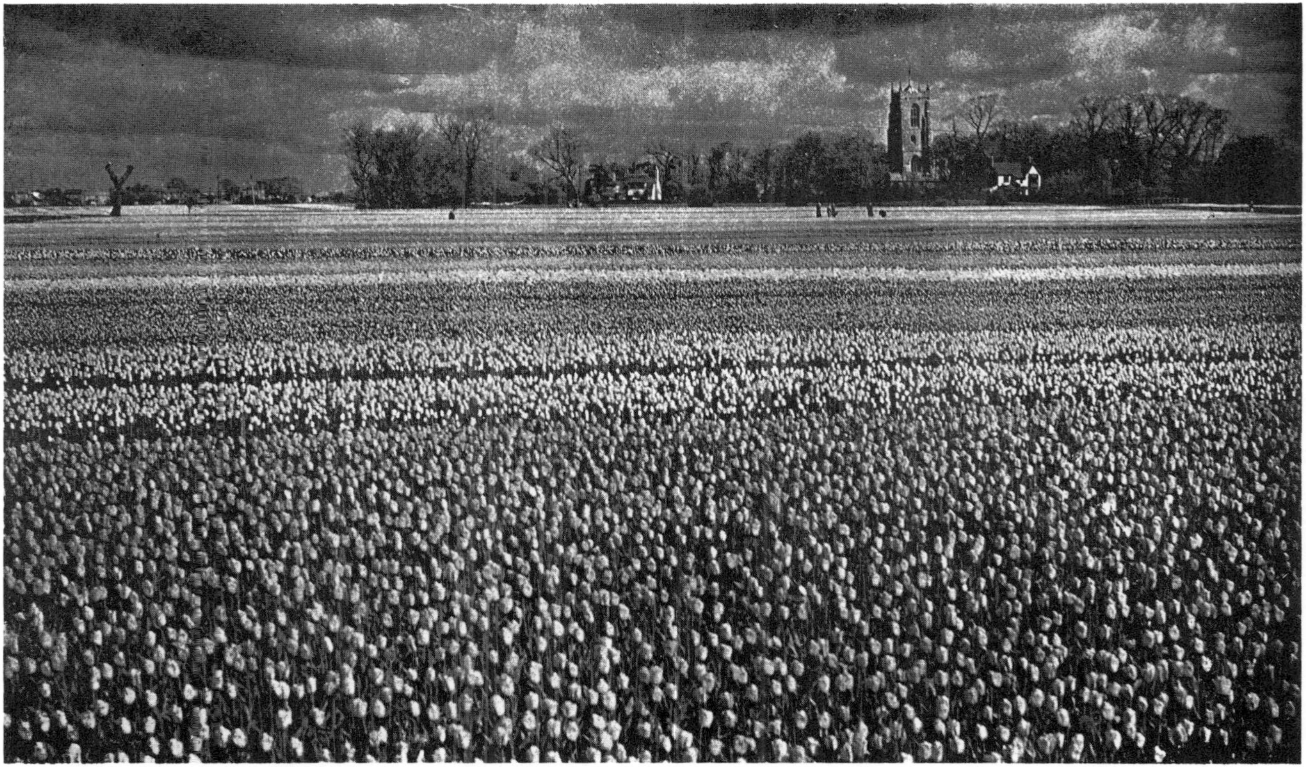

2 A well-known sight round Spalding in spring: tulips at Pinchbeck

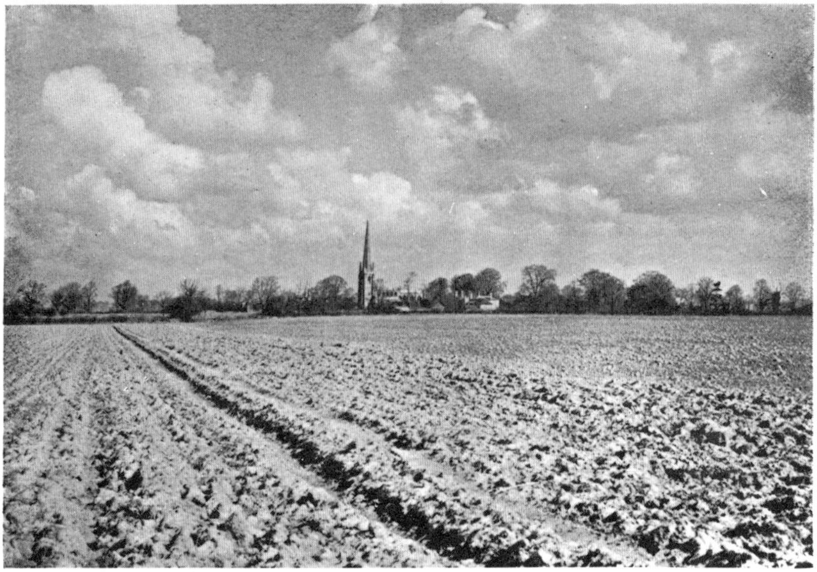

3 The clays of the Witham valley: Brant Broughton in the spring

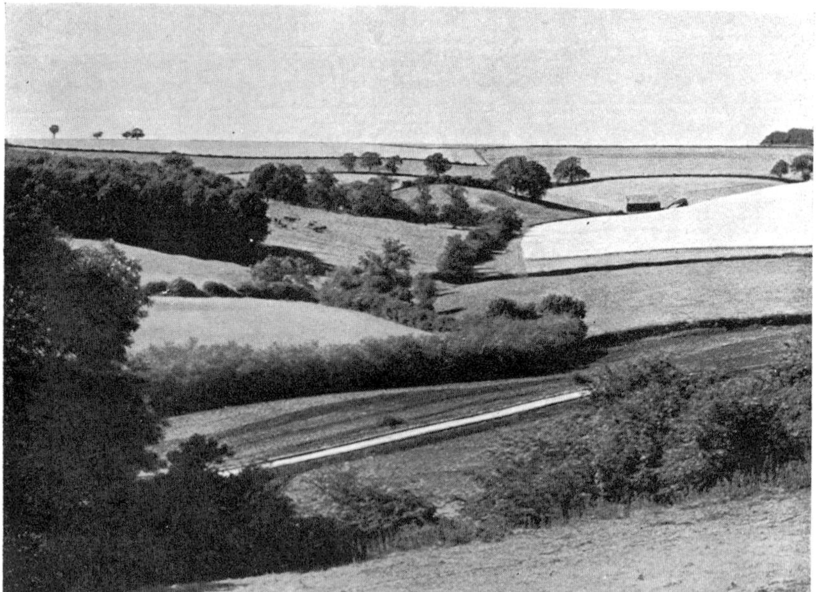

4 The chalk Wolds: Bully Hill, Louth

as Belton or Edenham and Grimsthorpe, reflect the influence of the great houses which made them what they are. Such villages, and there are many in this part of Kesteven, are small and have not been allowed to spread beyond the control of the big house; those that were not restrained, such as Ropsley, Corby, or Castle Bytham, grew in the eighteenth and nineteenth centuries into a generous spread of seemly houses of stone and brick and pantiled roofs. And so in this quarter of the county you can see in a day, in a few hours even, the picturesque seclusion of Holywell, where lanes cut deep into the hillside drop down to the lake, and the only buildings visible are a solitary cottage and the hall glimpsed through the trees; or Castle Bytham, where the great motte of the Norman castle faces the hill covered with a large village of stone houses and roofs of many colours(45).

North of Lincoln the limestone ridge thins out so much that its name, the Cliff, emphasises the steepness of the western scarp and not the plateau; there are no villages on the top; only just room for the Roman Ermine Street to keep a mile or two away from the ridgeway that overlooks the line of villages at the foot of the scarp. These are small villages, each at the bottom of its own lane from the main road; the lanes go on past the villages to isolated farms, nearly all "Granges", which lie half-way towards the next line of villages in the clays; the only road which goes westward in a businesslike way, with its eye on the distance, is the Roman Tillbridge Lane, making for the Trent ford at Littleborough, and eventually for Doncaster and York. It is tempting to stay on the ridge and enjoy the bird's-eye view, but it is worth while to go down, to see a Tudor manor-house and a charming eighteenth-century church tower at North Carlton, a Saxon tower at Harpswell or a great thirteenth-century tower at Grayingham. This scene is best in an afternoon or evening when the light is against you. In the late sunlight the ancient pattern of ridged and furrowed medieval fields comes through the modern diaper work of hawthorn hedges, and two ages of the English countryside are visible at the same time. Kirton-in-Lindsey started, like all the rest, at the foot of the hill, and has climbed to the top; you can look down from the market-place over pantiled roofs instead of green slopes, and the ridge is so narrow that if you turn about the ground drops away immediately into the smooth width of the Ancholme valley backed by the rise of the Wolds, chalk-grey in winter and corn-coloured in the summer. It is worth while to push north past Scunthorpe to the very end of the county, where the limestone dips down below the Humber; the old village of Burton-on-Stather is intact inside a ring of new villas, and Alkborough is an excellent village of stone houses spread spaciously round a handsome church and a manor-house in Jacobean brick. Anyone who penetrates as far as this will be well rewarded by the panorama of Trent Falls. The view is so wide that the winding threads of Trent and Ouse seem thin and shallow streams. Henry Kirke White, the young Nottingham poet, when he stayed at Winteringham in 1804, was happy to watch the view of the Humber and the "hills and receding vales of Yorkshire assume a thousand new aspects". The one thing we miss is the "swelling sail rapidly falling down the river"; and Winteringham and Whitton have lost some of the life they once had when the Humber was a busier river than it is now.

West of the Heath and the Cliff, the valley is filled with clay; it is wide, featureless country between Lincoln and Gainsborough. But the rich land has produced some fine churches; the great minster-like church of Stow(19), or the large churches at Northorpe and Corringham, and the small building at Springthorpe, give distinction to the rather dull villages. Between this line and the Cliff there is room for no more than a hamlet or two, but one of them, Cotes by Stow, still has a church filled with fifteenth-century fittings, including the only complete rood loft and screen in the county. In the clay triangle between Lincoln, Grantham, and Newark there are more surprises: the first is that there, quietly passing the charming villages of bright red brick, is the river Witham, moving modestly northwards, and beyond the river there are outcrops of marlstone on which villages sit a few feet above the cornfields and the meadows. The upper valley of the Witham is worth exploration. It is a different river after it passes Lincoln and slides imperceptibly through the fen; above Lincoln it has enough pace to keep the water clear and the weeds on the move. These villages near the north road were once favourite places for prize fights, for coaches could bring spectators from north and south. Near South Witham is Cribb's Lodge, which was the scene of a match between Tom Cribb and Molyneux, the coloured boxer, which Cribb won; and in Claypole churchyard there is buried Bill Scrimshaw, who in the 1760's was known as a champion wrestler. One of his bouts was with a Derbyshire "don" (the usual word for a man who excelled at any sport or craft); it was celebrated in a ballad which I found copied into a farmer's account book in a Nottinghamshire village:

I

You gentlemen Draw near
And the truth I will Declare;
I will tell you of a Russeller so bold
And he Lives in Lincolnshire.

2

Bill Scrimshaw is his name,
In Claypool Town Does dwell;
He is the Don both far and near,
And he is known very well.

3

On the 21st of November last
This Rustling Match was made
Between Bill Scrimshaw and the Derbyshire Don
Which never was afraid.

4

When these Champions did meet
This Russelling for to try,
"Here's 5 to 1 again Bill Scrimshaw"
The Derbyshire Dons Did cry.

5

John Scrimshaw standing by
And hearing what was said,
Saying "I comd here my brother to back
And your 5 to one I take."

6

Then Haley up and then arose
And he flew into a rage,
Saying "I am come here this Wager to win
Or Die upon the stage."

7

Bill Scrimshaw gave a smile
But nothing he did say;
He soon tripped up the Derbyshire Don
All on the stage he lay.

8

"So now I flung your Don
You Gentlemen you see,
And if you have got a better Don,
Pray bring him unto me.

9

"Bill Scrimshaw is my name
In Claypool town do Dwell;
I am the Don both far and near,
And I am known very well."

10

These Lincolnshire Lads shall wear cockades,
And their Ribbons shall be blue;
Bill Scrimshaw was a tight young lad,
And he was always staunch and true.

Alongside the east side of the Trent from the Nottinghamshire border intermittently as far down as Scunthorpe there is the poorest land in the county: sandy heath with pines and heather, transformed here and there into charming woods with rhododendrons and even made into useful farming land when it was found to be ideal for carrots. There are few villages in it; near Lincoln it is intersected with new straight roads which lead to nothing but chicken farms and bungalows; but near Scunthorpe the sand-dunes and conifers are an unexpected sight in such a well-tamed countryside. Where there are fields, the hedges stand high above their level, for the sand from the middle of the field has blown into the next parish. When Abraham de la Pryme saw the Warrens near Scunthorpe in 1695, they reminded him of "the sandy deserts of Egypt and Arabia, which I had a most clear idea of when I beheld these sandy plains"; a strong wind in dry weather brings sandstorms which choke roads and discommode the traveller. The best-known spot in this kind of country is Scawby, where the peat underlying the sand forms a lake on which black-headed gulls nest by the thousand (7). My recollection of the gull-ponds from childhood was a screaming inferno of wheeling birds, in which one could scarcely tread for fear of breaking eggs or trampling on young. Perhaps that is the usual trick of memory; when I went again last year I found far fewer birds, carefully guarded to nurse their numbers back again after the depredations of human war-time visitors, and I saw more of the rhododendrons and the pines. There is one other stretch of similar country in the neighbourhood of Market Rasen, west of the Wolds, but most of it is conquered; Woodhall Spa has been planted in the midst of a remnant and has made a rather tame pleasance of it.

The Trent in Lincolnshire is a businesslike river, flowing smoothly but masterfully between high banks, built and rebuilt many times, but even now not strong enough when spring tides meet flood waters from Derbyshire and the Midlands. It is too strong for small pleasure boats, and the Aegre at Gainsborough lifts barges as though they were corks; but it is a fine sight to see the strings of barges which go from Newark to Hull inside twelve hours swinging round the curves and past the villages which face each other across the river. These villages are lonely places; the Stockwiths are perhaps the only pair which are still really one with the river as their main street; elsewhere the ferry-boats are rotting or gone because traffic is funnelled across the bridges at Dunham, Gainsborough, and Keadby. Until 1791 there was no bridge lower than Newark, and the river was as busy as a main-line railway, with goods and passenger traffic. It is not surprising that the villages faced the river and throve on it; the two Stockwiths,

Owston Ferry and East Ferry, the Butterwicks, Althorpe, and Burringham are full of eighteenth-century houses and warehouses. It is trite to say they look Dutch, but there is no better word for villages that face a river, and they have all the colours of a Vermeer painting. Although the buildings front on the water, the life in them has turned its back on the river, to the land behind, drained and enriched by warping. This is country which I like best in autumn or winter, when mist hems in the view and the wealth is most visible in long potato clamps and loads of sugar-beet. There are no medieval churches to see, except at Althorpe and Owston; these villages grew up when the Church could do nothing for them, and they were captured by Methodism.

The valley of the Ancholme is a wide plain which scarcely seems to contain a river, only artificial drains; and you realise that the Ancholme is there only if you cross the sluice at South Ferriby, or find yourself at the lonely inn at Brandy Wharf and see barges unloading fertilisers; or if you cross at Brigg, where high and dry ground from either side narrows the width of carr land. "Carr" is the proper word in Lincolnshire for low, peaty ground, and each of the villages on the rim of the valley has its slice of carr going down to the river. Those on the lower slope of the limestone are nearly all tiny, except for Waddingham with its characteristic stone houses and pantile roofs and brick used for jobs that the rubble limestone could not do. On the eastern margin of the valley the chalk scarp gives a good background to a close line of small villages all the way from Caistor to the Humber. Of them all, Bonby is my favourite because I have known it from childhood; I learned there to love the steep climb past the tiny church of chalk and brick up the dusty hill to the Wold top, where you can look past Saxby mill to the Humber and Read's Island. One is drawn to any riverside, and the wooded foothills of the Yorkshire Wolds on the other side look intimately near, but the grey river is wide enough to dwarf the steamers going up to Goole. I like best to stand on the river's brink at South Ferriby; on a winter afternoon the wild geese and peewits rise from the green plate of Read's Island, and the mud takes even better than the water the violets and purples of the sunset. I speak of the mud with something like affection: I have helped to dig a prehistoric boat out of it, and I have watched it loaded into barges to make blacklead for Yorkshire housewives: I have seen it transformed into mother-of-pearl by winter sunlight; it has both use and beauty. Cross the Humber regularly, however, and you will learn respect for it; the banks shift and spread overnight. Henry Kirke White wrote amusingly of taking a small boat across to Hull and getting as near as a mudbank in the harbour; Defoe damned the crossing once and for all as "an ill-favoured, dangerous passage; in an open boat, in which we had about fifteen horses, and ten or twelve cows, mingled with about seventeen or eighteen passengers, call'd Christians; we were about four hours tossed about on the Humber, before we could get to Hull; I was so uneasy at it that I chose to go round by York rather than return to Barton".

Between the upper Ancholme valley and the river Witham—roughly in the triangle between Lincoln, Market Rasen, and Tattershall—is the only part of this large county where there is no clear pattern of villages imposed by geological conditions. There are no large villages except Wragby; only a random scatter of small hamlets lost among the remnants of the forest which once covered the heavy clay. There is a cluster of sites of monasteries—Revesby, Bardney, Kirkstead, Stainfield, Barlings, Tupholme,—close together even for a county which had many small religious houses; here monks in the first flush of enthusiasm could find the seclusion which was already hard to find in the rest of medieval Lincolnshire, and feudal nobles were ready to give them land which few others wished to tackle. Here the roads wind, and winding roads are rare in Lincolnshire, because they are typical of densely wooded country where the men who made them could not see their goal from any distance. The typical Lincolnshire road runs straight until it takes inexplicable right-angle turns; the goal is clear enough to us, but there was some obstacle to earlier travellers that is invisible now. It goes deviously but very soberly, negotiating the layout of open arable fields that have gone: along the side of a furlong, along the headland, and then off again at right angles. It was not made by men travelling far and anxious to get there, but by farmers with their eyes on the ground, on their neighbours' crops; such men would not commit the discourtesy to a neighbour of taking a short cut. Take a party of country folk in a bus (as I have done) and though they may have expressed a willingness to be shown a notable church or a medieval castle, the real pleasure of the men is in the journey itself, and in the chance to admire good crops and feel superior satisfaction at bad ones. Such men made these roads, for their own convenience, and we have inherited in them part of the frame of mind of the countryman.

In the clays that I have described one's eyes are constantly lifted towards the Wolds. South of Caistor the western scarp is not a steep one; the clays mask it and the first sign of Wold as one goes east is clumps of beeches, which are most at home on chalk mixed with some clay. The Wolds rise to no great height—548 feet above Normandy-le-Wold—but high enough to give those enormous views, to which neither pen nor camera can do justice, with Lincoln and Boston Stump, the Humber, and the Wash as their farthest landmark. One eighteenth-century traveller disliked such views because they were "like an embarkment into eternity"; they are more to our taste than his. The Ice Age moulded the Wold landscape into a varied pattern; north of Caistor it is a low, smooth ridge with enough clay mixed with the chalk to make good farm land and suitable ground for Lord Yarborough's miles of plantations; south of Louth the chalk is in places eroded down to the sandstone that underlies it, giving a more broken type of scenery and a quite different flora. Although the ice rode over even the crest of the central Wolds, and left behind Scandinavian erratics such as the blue stone which gave its name to the prehistoric ridgeway, the Blue Stone Heath Road, it left fine swelling uplands above the clay-filled green valleys in which the villages lie. In the summer the expanse of ripening corn "clothes the Wold and meets the sky"; and those who know only the chalk Downs of the south, where there is more permanent grass, ought to see this country in the spring, when there is the subtlest interplay of the greens of young corn and the brown soil over the chalk on the great ranging slopes. Man is scarcely noticed in such a landscape, for the population is thin, like the soil, thinner than anywhere else in the county. The villages are perfectly sited by their streams; some are charming, but many are nondescript, and some are almost squalid, for there is no background of wealth to give the buildings any substance or quality. Many of the small churches had to be rebuilt in the nineteenth century; by the time the Methodist chapels were built Victoria's reign was half over and the chances of a good building gone.

The wealth that made Louth the charming place it is (25), with its great medieval church and its good Georgian houses and shops, came more from the Marshland, on the seaward side of the Wolds; next to the Fens the richest part of the county. The chalk slopes run quietly down into woods, some of them ancient woodland replanted no doubt; some of them new ornamental planting such as the lovely Well Vale near Alford; all the villages at the foot have good streams such as that at Little Cawthorpe, moving fast and clear before they settle down to their slow course through the Marshland. One of the pleasantest roads in the county is down the eastern edge of the Wolds, from Barrow-on-Humber to Burgh-le-Marsh, most of it on the lines of a prehistoric trackway and the last part a Roman road from Lincoln to the coast at Skegness. All the way there is on one side the pale Wold, grey in winter, light green in spring, and light yellow in summer; on the other the constant green of pasture land, and in the distance either the visible Humber or the change in the clouds that denotes the invisible coastline. There is every kind of interest in this line of villages. Barrow-on-Humber was the birthplace of John Harrison, who in the eighteenth century produced the first marine chronometer by which the local time, and hence the longitude of ships at sea, could be measured accurately; his three chronometers are among the treasures of the Greenwich Observatory. Near by is Thornton Curtis, with a good Georgian hall, and the great gatehouse of the abbey, Lincolnshire's finest monastic building; then Brocklesby with the fine Pelham monuments. South of Louth, past Cawthorpe and the water lane down to Legbourne, there are the woods round Muckton, and at Belleau traces of the moated house of the earls of Lindsey, bought in 1650 by the younger Sir Henry Vane.

Anyone who learns to know that road will sooner or later go down into the Marshland. There is little to attract in the stretch north-west of Grimsby, although some may be curious enough to take the electric tram that goes swaying through the fields to Immingham, the Lincolnshire folly. Time has scarcely fulfilled the promise of forty years ago, when the "wondrous and unrivalled dock" made Immingham "a veritable household word throughout the British Empire". The docks are busy, but the building lots laid out enthusiastically are still vacant, and the village has been pulled apart without being made into anything else. Some will go, I hope, to see the Anglo-American monument at Killingholme Haven, on the spot from which the Pilgrim Fathers are said to have sailed for Holland in 1609. The best stretch of Marshland to my mind is that between Grimsby and Mablethorpe, where ancient settlements like Theddlethorpe and Saltfleet proliferated as the salt marsh was drained; there are two Theddlethorpes, two Somercotes, and three Saltfleetbys; once there were two Mablethorpes, but the sea took one. They are young as English villages go, but they made money in time to build fine churches like South Somercotes and Marsh Chapel, Addlethorpe and Winthorpe; great Perpendicular buildings rivalling the Fenland churches. In the spring the pasture land fills up with untidy Lincoln Red cattle, and it is said that they only have to walk round a field to get fat. The Bottom Marsh next the sea has a special visual quality: overhead the Lincolnshire sky at its widest, and below it the dykes filled with flowering rush, yellow water-lily, and water-violet in summer, and the plumed heads of reeds in winter. There are no hedges or fences; only gates at the bridges with a rail at either side to keep in cattle. Clumps of trees hide great farmhouses, some of them standing within medieval moats. Between Mablethorpe and Ingoldmells there is a change; villages like Hogsthorpe stand on hummocks of boulder clay rising out of the silt, and

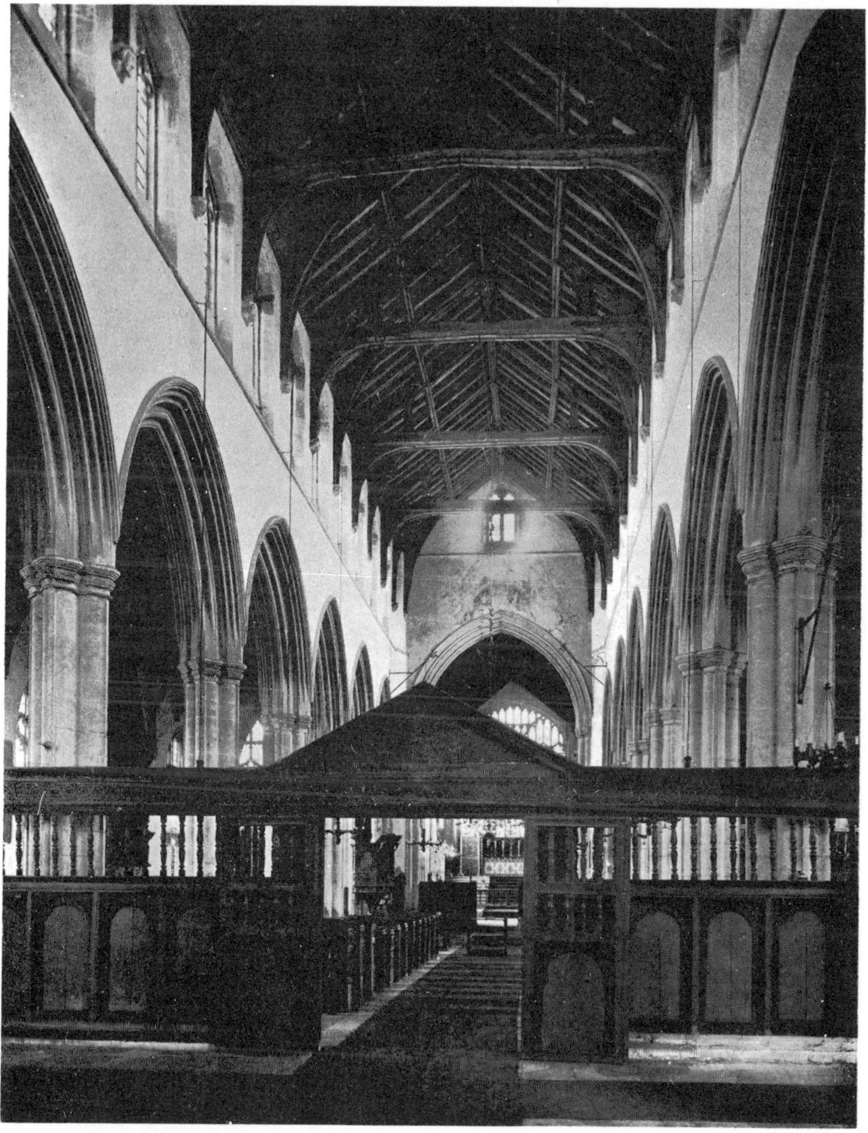

5 A fine church of the Norfolk Marshland:
Walpole St. Peter's fifteenth-century nave and Jacobean screen

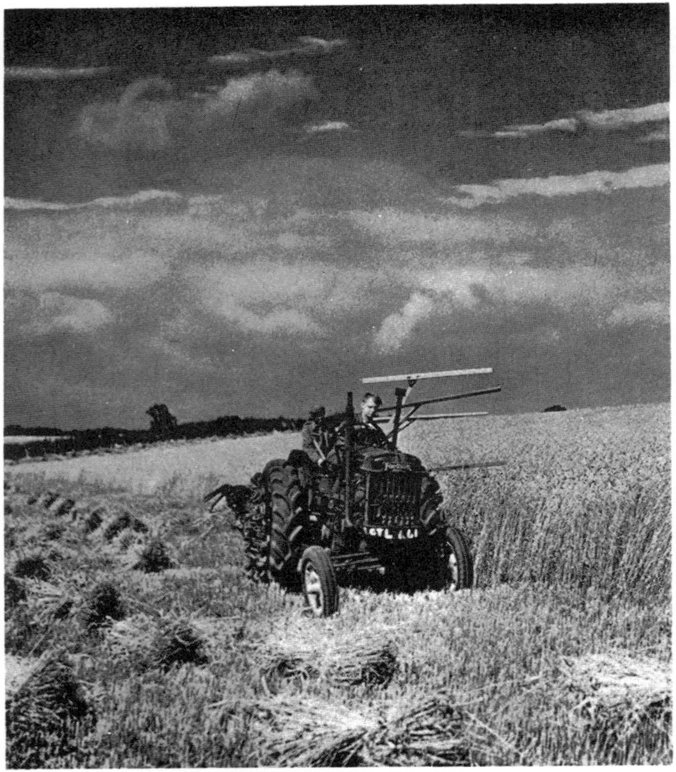

6 Harvesting near Bourne

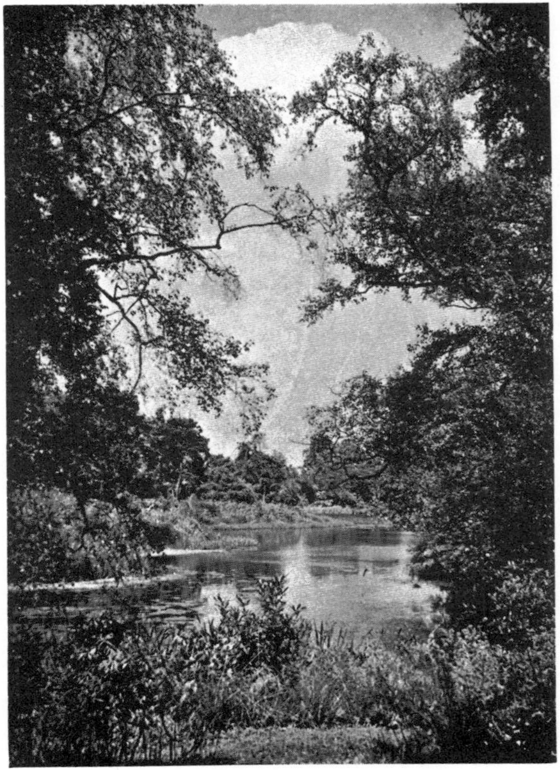

7 Scawby Gull Ponds

round them the undulating country is hedged and ploughed. Then moving south behind Skegness the marsh is level again and passes imperceptibly at Wainfleet into what we call the Fenland. In some parts the farms are spread very thinly: in Wych, an area of about eight square miles behind Ingoldmells, there are only Wych Farm and Pyewipe Hall, and it is a byword locally for loneliness. The "pyewipe" (peewit) is the bird of the lonelier parts of Lincolnshire; it is protected now by Act of Parliament, but was trapped in quantity until a few years ago.

It is difficult to write of the coast without indignation. From Skegness to Mablethorpe the rich grassland has been invaded by a motley crop of the weeds of civilisation—caravans and bungalows, camping-sites and wayside stores. Fortunately the sandhills are high enough to hide most of this from the shore; you can enjoy the clear sun and cool wind with the other thousands, and go home redder than you know. That brilliant poster of an old sailor skipping along the sand ("Skegness is so bracing") has had as much influence as any poster artist can expect, because it promised something which the Lincolnshire coast really can give. Apart from the stretch between Skegness and Mablethorpe, most of the rest of the long line is taken by the Air Ministry, and if you want to see the sand-dunes as nature made them, you must pick your way among the refuse of military occupation and disregard the warnings of danger. There you can sit among the sea buckthorn and marram grass, and watch curlew feeding at the water's edge, or the flocks of dunlins, sanderlings, and ringed plovers motionless on the sandbank, while the summer migrants flit past the bushes around you. The most fascinating spot of all is Gibraltar Point, where there is now a bird observatory, where migrants are trapped and ringed, and remarkable records compiled of the local and migrant bird population. I visited it last in November, and saw thousands of wild geese leaving the potato fields inland to roost on the mud flats, a black stream moving fast across the last light of a wild sky, their gaggling a distant but large mass of sound.

I have left till last the attempt to describe the Fens and the Isle of Axholme, because it is the most difficult part of my task, and also because they need a separate chapter. But I must try to provide a key to the understanding of them. It is land whose potential wealth has always been clear to the eyes of farmers, and from their carefully chosen homes they have brought most of it to bearing. We see only that it is flat; we must learn that the word is relative; the rise of a couple of feet up to a railway line, lifted on ballast to give it a firm foundation in the peat, will be called Station Hill. The pattern of the Fenland villages is a very simple one. There are first those on the outer margin, lying just above the fen on the lower slopes of the western limestone and the northern chalk. They are upland villages; on the western margin they are nearly all stone-built, and in fact the Deepings or Baston are among the best stone villages in the county. They have some of the best churches too; from Ewerby south to the Deepings every one of the long line of villages has a remarkable church. Ewerby's pure Decorated work to my mind puts Heckington into a slightly ostentatious category; Swaton is a text-book of the development of tracery—and so one could go on. This wealth is the wealth of the Fenland; each village has a long slice of peatland to the east. On the northern margin the villages are not so distinguished, but they are very attractive; either they stand on the sandstone foothills, like West Keal, whose church commands an unlimited prospect, or, like Revesby, they lie in the woods on the edge of the clays.

My second group of Fenland villages includes all those which lie in a great arc round the Wash from Wainfleet to King's Lynn; they stand—and this point is essential to an understanding of the Fens—on a band of silt accumulated at the old outfalls of the rivers. Some of them are now six miles from the Wash; on the seaward side of them is salt marsh won from the sea; behind them is peat fen. In this country my definition of the Lincolnshire road does not apply: the main road linking the villages and the roads immediately round them wind as old roads are usually expected to do. On either side the strip of silt, the long straight roads of marsh and fen are the paper projects of modern engineers become reality. The wealth of these villages is spectacular and the best of their churches are very well known, but few people realise that those of the first rank, like Gedney or Kirton, or Walsoken and Walpole St. Peter (5) over the Norfolk border, push into the second rank a dozen others which would be masterpieces in any other setting. That is true of Gosberton, Algarkirk (58), and most of the churches north of Boston.

The link between the uplands and the villages on the silt is my third group of Fenland villages. I mean those perched on islands of clay, either very real (like Ely), or almost imperceptible (like Sibsey and Stickney north of Boston), obtruded through the blanket of peat. Ely is unmatched, but Haxey in the Isle of Axholme deserves to be mentioned in the next, if not in the same, breath; it stands almost as well, and the villages of the Isle of Axholme have a fascinating history behind them, which I shall try to recount later. Now the villages have spread beyond their original centres into the peat fen and the salt marsh surrounding them; the commons which they once shared have been divided out and are under the plough. So Moulton has Moulton Seas End (now six miles or more from the Wash), and farther out still, past Moulton Common, the lonely farms of Moulton Marsh; inland, behind the village, the hamlet of Moulton Chapel is half-way to Moulton Fen, and Moulton Fen is near Crowland, which is eighteen miles from the sea. The isolated farms (Curlew Lodge or Mallard Farm or merely Doubney's Farm) in their circles of sheltering trees mark the last stage of the mastery of this land. A twelfth-century chronicler of Peterborough described the site of the monastery as "so pleasant, so suitable, most fertile and most jocund, abounding in everything and most beautiful, as it were an earthly Paradise offered by God";[1] but this point of view, as I have already said, is rather out of fashion now. If you know the Fens not only in summer, when the churches stand surrounded by miles of ripe corn, or in spring, when the bulb fields round Spalding are filled with Technicolor shades, but at every season, and particularly in winter, the most unlikely of those words comes true.

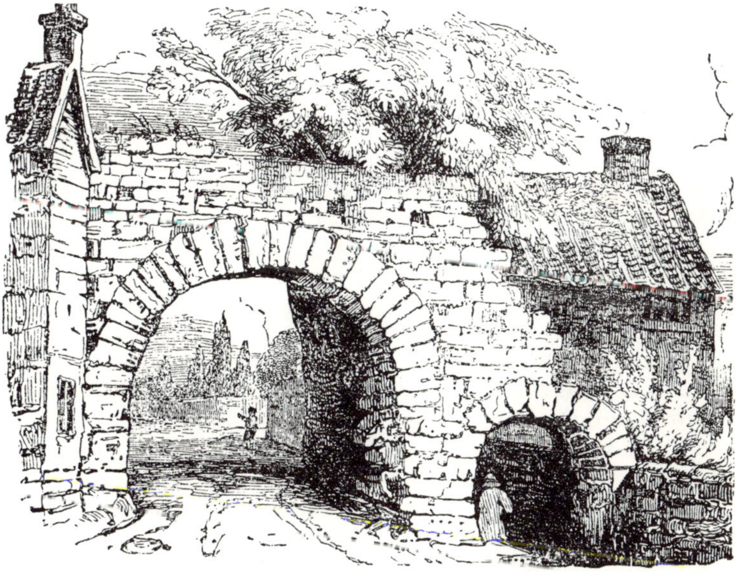

Lincoln: the Roman Newport Arch.
From an engraving after W. H. Bartlett, 1830.

[1] Quoted in H. C. Darby, *The Medieval Fenland*, p. 54.

Chapter

II

THE PEOPLING OF LINCOLNSHIRE

FIVE miles south-west of Grantham on to the top of the limestone ridge, two ancient roads cross, at a farmhouse known as the Three Queens. Two hundred years ago it was the Three Queans, a disreputable inn where highwaymen and suchlike foregathered. Three thousand years ago there were already cross-roads; it was along the route from Leicestershire which here crossed Sewstern Lane that New Stone Age man had come from the focal area of Wessex, bringing with him the essential qualifications for a civilised life—knowledge of farming and stock-raising, and of such attendant arts as pottery-making—to his new home on the Lincolnshire Wolds. We can still follow the tracks of these ancient settlers, although they are now hedged and metalled; the best of them follows the western scarp of the limestone all the way through the county to the Humber, commanding the maximum view over the valley. South of Lincoln it is known as Pottergate, north of Lincoln as Middle Street; it was the Great North Road of prehistoric times, and only the recent changes in the face of the land—the clearing of the valley forests and the cultivation of the clays—have made it a by-road for much of its length. The road south from Lincoln through Sleaford and Bourne towards Peterborough, known as Mareham Lane, is scarcely less ancient. The Wolds have their prehistoric roads: the High Street, running along the western scarp from Horncastle to the Humber, and the Blue Stone Heath Road, which strides along the central ridge close by the Giants Hills long barrow and the other Neolithic barrows discovered by Mr. C. W. Phillips. We cannot easily understand prehistoric farmers' preference for the limestone and the chalk, because the climate is less moist now; the Saxon farmer settled at the foot of the scarp, as he had a plough which could turn over the stiff clays in the valleys. It is in fact the land that we now regard as the poorest of all that has had the most dense and continuous occupation; when the Neolithic and Bronze Age farmers arrived, they found, and no doubt soon dispossessed, primitive hunting and fishing folk squatting on the driest ground they could find—the sandy heaths of north-west Lincolnshire. In the warrens there, at Risby, Crosby, and Manton, or at Santon (Anglo-Saxon "sand farm") the pigmy flints of

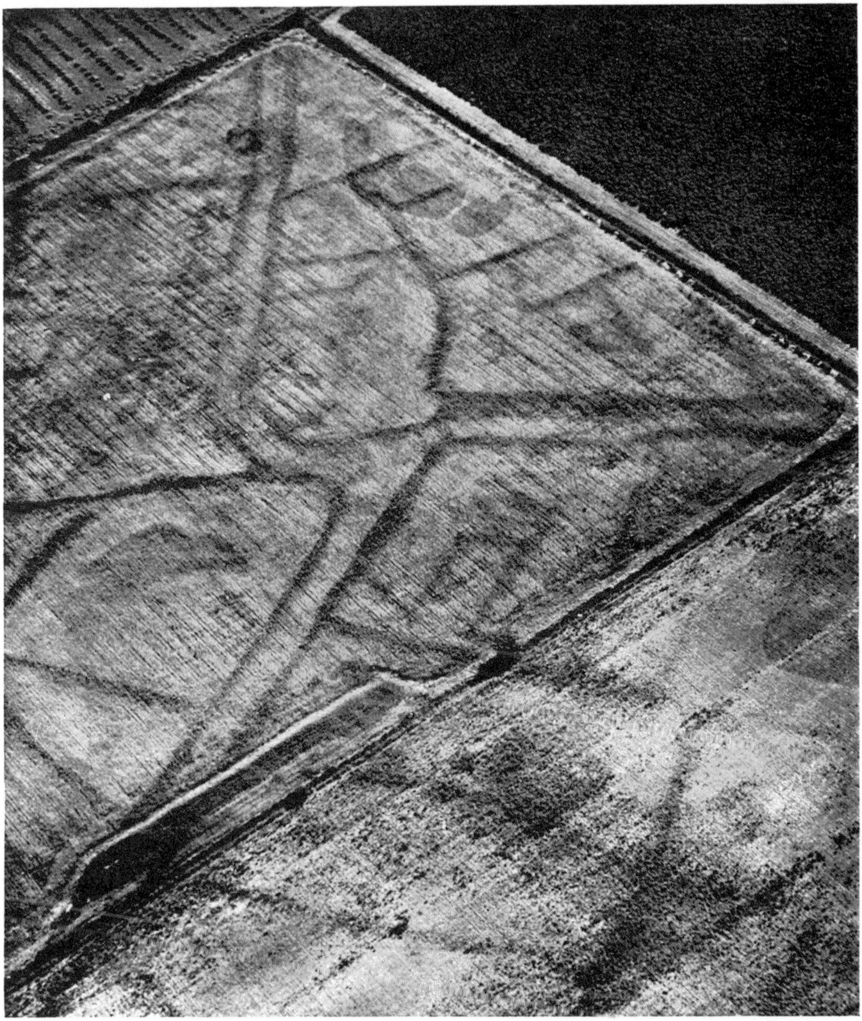

8 Prehistoric Fenland: Celtic droveways and fields visible in standing corn near Spalding

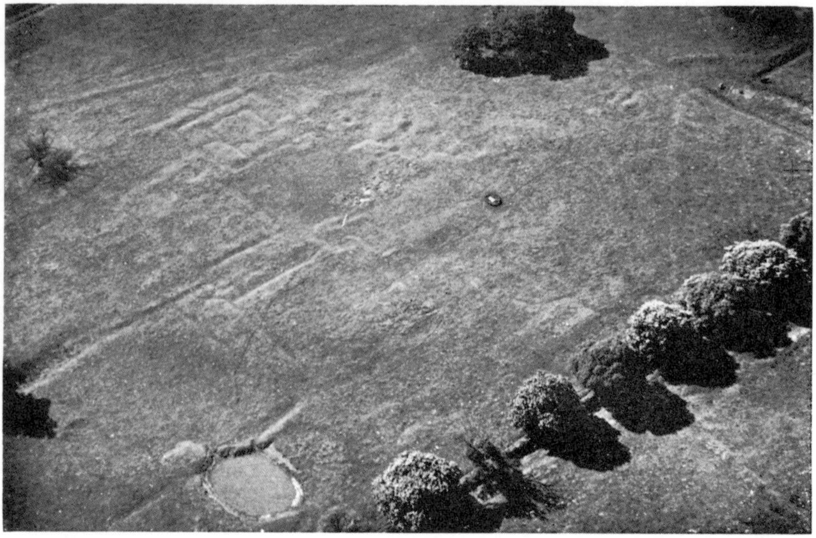

9 The site of Revesby Abbey

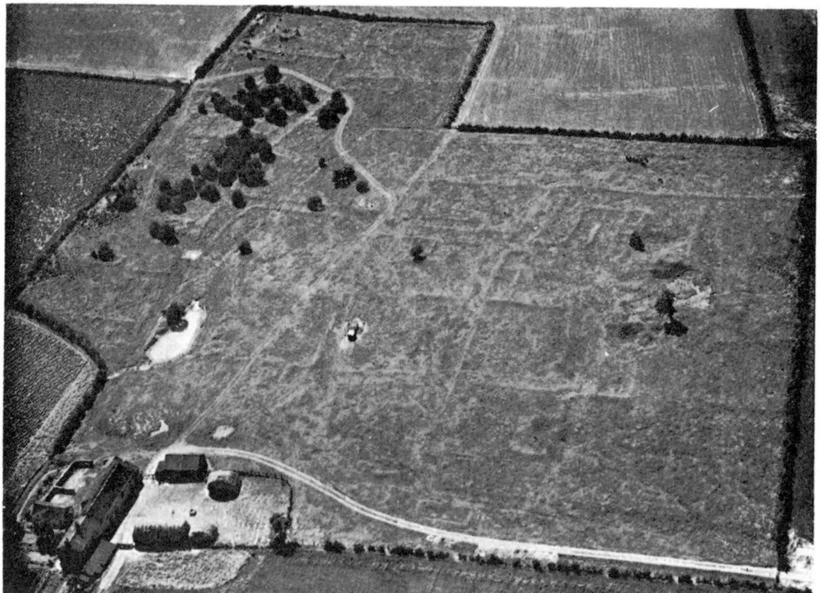

10 The site of the village of Gainsthorpe near Redbourne

Tardenoisian man have been found by the thousand. Bronze Age farmers followed them, and it was possible, a few years ago, to find areas where the blowing sand had exposed the Bronze Age levels, and to pick up fragments of Bronze Age pottery in greater quantity than anywhere else in England. The peat flashes west of Crosby Warren must have been the Tardenoisian hunting-ground; they are now, like Scawby gull-ponds near by, the haunt of the black-headed gull. Another area where the hunters and fishermen could live dry and overlook their hunting- and fishing-grounds was at West Keal, on the southern end of the Wolds; there the sandstone which later was used for building the small Wold churches has decayed into a sandy soil. On the western margin of the Fens, hunters who had acquired the art of pottery-making settled on the gravel round Peterborough, and began the long occupation of that area which lasted into Roman times. Still another favoured spot was the Ancaster gap, where some river—the Witham or the Trent in an earlier phase of the country's history—had cut another passage, only less impressive than the Lincoln one, through the limestone ridge, and left it filled with sand and gravel. Gravel pits there have produced Mesolithic flint implements, Bronze Age pottery and Anglo-Saxon ornaments, and the gravel-getting has destroyed a Romano-British farmstead; the gap was a funnel through which invaders of many different ages found their way from their landing-places on the coast and the rivers to the north midland plain. The finds in the Ancaster gap have been less spectacular than those at Lincoln; men crossing the Witham there lost overboard such masterpieces as the Iron Age shield which is one of the finest things of its kind in the British Museum.

The prehistoric ridgeways developed as links between established groups of settlers; the first paths of pioneers were the great rivers, the Trent, the Welland and Nene, and the Ouse, which were open ways into the heart of lowland England. They were followed by the Bronze Age immigrants who were the first to settle in Lincolnshire intensively, and many centuries later by the English. When the Bronze Age folk came the climate was changing; the impenetrable forests which covered the lowlands were being killed in the Fens and the Isle of Axholme by a subsidence of the land which choked the drainage and buried the trees in a peat bog. The giant trunks are now something for the farmer to marvel at, and often despair of, when he ploughs them up; some of them are as much as sixty feet long without any side-branches; one that grew in an open glade was ten feet in diameter. Off the coast, the stumps are bared at the lowest tides, and the clay in which they grew is occasionally an unpleasant surprise for paddlers(63). On the sluggish and wide streams, such as the

Ancholme of those days, were launched canoes made from these trees. The largest found was the monster dug out from Brigg, which was destroyed at Hull in 1944 by German bombs; it was forty-eight feet long and six feet across. Others nearly as large have been found in the Fens, at Warboys and in Deeping Fen, and no other part of England has produced more of these prehistoric boats. As I write there are reports of still another from the Nene bed in Peterborough to be added to the large score.

Bronze Age man had paddled slowly up the rivers or moved cautiously along the edge of the ridge, where he could not be overlooked. Roman engineers pushed their roads boldly forward; for their large-scale military methods it was simpler to make a new road, duplicating the ridgeway but without its sympathy for the lie of the land. Certainly they had no need for caution; this part of lowland England had no temper to resist. We know all too little of Lincolnshire on the eve of the Roman conquest; there are only a few small examples of those hilltop forts which dominate the ranges of south-western England, and which, as a young officer, Vespasian had to reduce. On the limestone plateau at Honington, commanding the Ancaster gap, is a small camp enclosing not more than an acre within its double ramparts; another, Yarborough Camp, lies on one of the prehistoric tracks on the Wolds and commands the east–west Kirmington gap; but these do not imply any thorough conquest by the camp-building Britons of the south-west. There were connections with Yorkshire, indicated to us by articles of fine metal-work from the Parisian school in East Yorkshire, and coins of the Brigantes of the West Riding. One of the few things we can be certain of is that salt-making was already an established industry on the coast; along the shore between Addlethorpe and Chapel St. Leonards remains have been found of the crude clay dishes in which salt water was evaporated. There is nothing to suggest that Lincolnshire was the home at this time of people as advanced economically or as highly organised politically as the Iceni of East Anglia or the Brigantes of Yorkshire. The fertility of the land of Lincolnshire is in a way our loss; any traces there may have been on the Wolds or the limestone of such prehistoric field systems as those which cover the Wessex uplands have long ago been ploughed out.

If we must give these people a name, we may say that they belonged to the Coritani, who, when the Roman Ninth Legion brought Ermine Street as far as Lincoln and established a temporary camp there, carried their tribute of corn along the new roads and up the hill to feed the occupation forces. Half a century or so later, the soldiers came back, but this time as reservists, members of the new colony established where the fortress had been, and cultivating their allotments north and east of the city. Attempts have been made to see in the pattern of side-roads crossing Ermine Street outside the city walls the regular division or centuriation of the countryside general in Roman times; but the roads in fact owe their regularity to the eighteenth-century surveyor and not to the second-century retired military engineer. In *Lindum Colonia* itself the native Britons, alongside men from every quarter of the Roman world, could enjoy the full range of civilised life. Entering the impressive gates, with their inner and outer arches and vaulted passage between, they could see the magnificent public buildings, now eighteen feet below the level of the Bailgate, one of the buildings topped with a life-size bronze equestrian figure in the full Roman manner. They could see private houses built of local stone but finished with marble and with painted and gilded decoration, standing in their gardens on the hilltop or on the steep terraced slope down to the Witham. They could marvel at the water supply pumped from a spring two miles away, and the system of sewers to dispose of waste. Outside the walls they could watch gilded youth amusing itself with chariot-racing and similar sports. Medieval England spent its resources on churches and monasteries, ours go in aerodromes and atomic energy plants; the surplus wealth of the Roman empire went into secular public buildings, and we cannot conceive from the experience of the twentieth century the generous scale of the provision. Modern Lincoln has little to put alongside its Roman buildings and its medieval Minster. Perhaps the only modern parallel, and a good one as far as it goes, is the Usher Art Gallery, built by the bequest of James Ward Usher in 1927 to house his magnificent collection of watches and clocks and other objects of art. Apart from Lincoln, there were three other Roman towns—Horncastle, Caistor, and Ancaster; although we know very little of any of them, we can say that they were walled towns exhibiting on a smaller scale the same qualities of urban civilisation as Lincoln. Roman Lincolnshire was a wealthy county. Ironstone was quarried, as it is today, near Scunthorpe and Grantham. The coast continued to produce salt; sites like Ingoldmells Point were occupied in Roman times. The mounds which are a feature of marshland parishes as far south as Wainfleet and of many fenland parishes, as the Red Hills are of Essex, are the debris of this industry, though we cannot yet clearly distinguish Roman from pre-Roman and medieval.

The best evidence of the importance of the area to the economy of Roman Britain is provided by the Car Dyke and the Foss Dyke, the only Roman canals in Britain. Much of the Car Dyke is now silted up; its water was used to fill a medieval moat in Pointon, and where one sees it now, at Branston Booths or at Martin, it is only an insignificant catchwater drain. Originally it ran from the Witham just below Lincoln to the Nene east of Peterborough, and was connected with the Cambridgeshire Car Dyke, for which Dr. J. G. D. Clark's excavations near Cottenham have confirmed the Roman origin. Unlike these two, the Foss Dyke, joining the Witham at Brayford Pool in Lincoln to the Trent in Torksey, is still in use as a canal and not merely as a local drain. If the Romans had not cut it, it would have been an obvious project for the canal age of the eighteenth century; after all, it follows a course along which flood waters from the Trent have more than once found their way to Lincoln. But Roman it certainly is, and we may imagine it being made early in the Roman occupation as a route by which supplies of corn from the Fenlands and Lincolnshire could be got down the Trent and up the Ouse to the permanent legionary fortress at York and to the garrisons on Hadrian's Wall.

In the villas which wealthy Britons built for themselves on the hillsides of the limestone and the chalk, the most ornamental features were the patterned pavements, and our knowledge of these would be much the poorer but for the skill of William Fowler of Winterton (1761–1832), who preserved for us a record of the very fine chariot race pavement from Horkstow, part of which is now in the British Museum(11), and many others in Lincolnshire and elsewhere. It is not surprising that he was led to this hobby; he could (and did) start by drawing four pavements from two villas found in his own parish. His engravings could scarcely be bettered now in accuracy or in the pleasure they give to the eye.

Our knowledge of the wealth of upland Lincolnshire in Roman times is only the unfolding of an expected story, but recent discoveries in the Fens are another matter. Stukeley, a great antiquary whom Lincolnshire is proud to claim, noticed traces of Roman occupation there, just as he came to a correct conclusion on the age of the Car Dyke. It has remained for air photography, followed up by the Fenland Research Committee, to demonstrate that the peat lands of the Fens, not then drowned as they were to be later, began to be occupied in the Bronze Age, and that the climax of ancient settlements was in the Roman period, perhaps as a result of an imperial scheme for plantations. Skegness will never alter the name of one of its main streets, but there is no reason as yet to think that the Roman Bank, whether at Skegness or at any point round the Wash to Terrington where it ends, was actually built in Roman times. It belongs almost certainly to a later age when such a protective work was more necessary. In the Fens the archaeologist must look, not for fashionable villas, but for less pretentious (though perhaps scarcely less wealthy) farmsteads and groups of huts in the native tradition. The Britons there lived dry-shod, and their life was not the ague-ridden, mosquito-plagued misery of the thirteenth to the eighteenth centuries. Many of the Roman farmsteads were riverside settlements spread out, for instance, along that old course of the Nene which is still the boundary of Lincolnshire and Cambridgeshire. Whether there were villages, as distinct from individual farms, is uncertain, but our growing knowledge of Iron Age Britain is beginning to suggest that the Celtic Britons did not gather in nucleated villages round some accepted focal point, but preferred the separate farm or small hamlet which is still typical of south-western England.

This story of a peaceful and prosperous countryside is part of the history of the land, but it is not tied to modern Lincolnshire by an unbroken descent and tradition. Between Roman Lincoln and the city to which Paulinus came in A.D. 628, and where his first convert to Christianity was the governor, there are two centuries in which historians cannot place a single event, nor archaeologists provide a clue. The farmsteads and huts of the Britons are found, not underlying modern villages, but away from them (10), and the English farmsteads which have grown into villages must have been planted on virgin territory, by springs where only wild animals had drunk before them and in clearings in the woods which they were the first to make or occupy. We must accept the possibility that the British were allowed to remain, because the small kingdom of the English in north Lincolnshire, the territory of the Lindisfaras, which we know as Lindsey, has itself a British name, and the Roman name for Lincoln (*Lindum colonia*) has descended to us in something much nearer its Roman form than, for instance, the names of Leicester or Ancaster. Among the recorded names of the English kings of Lindsey is Caedbaed, a British name, which suggests the possibility of a marriage in the ruling line with a British woman. There is another curious fact which the reader may ponder on; the shepherd in north-west Lincolnshire, like his fellows farther north, used, until a few years ago, to count his sheep with a set of numerals which were curiously close to Welsh: "Yan, tan, tethera, methera, pimp," etc. Is it a genuine survival or a recent borrowing from Cumberland and Yorkshire?

The place-name experts put us on surer ground when they point to names like Healing, close to the Humber, and Minting, Barlings, Steeping in the Witham valley, and Spalding in the fen. These belong to the most ancient stratum of English place-names, and can be considered along with the heathen Anglian cemeteries found at Elkington in the Wolds near Louth; at Kirton-in-Lindsey close to the Trent, and at Ancaster and Grantham, critical points on the limestone of Kesteven. These ancient names are not common enough, and the cemeteries are not large and rich enough, to suggest that this area was among the first and most attractive goal of the migrants. The long curve of coast was no doubt still inconvenient of approach from the sea by reason of the sandbanks protecting it; the incoming traffic was focused largely on the Humber and the rivers of the Wash, and the inclination of the bands of men whose boats entered the Witham, the Welland or the Trent was to push on, beyond the possibility of clashes with later arrivals, rather than to land on the first piece of suitable ground. But the later expansion of the first pioneers among the English filled the islands of high ground in the Isle of Axholme and the Fens with settlements like Haxey, Ely, and Yaxley, and produced the string of villages along the silt fen from Skegness through Boston to Spalding, Holbeach and Lynn. This movement of younger sons among the later generations of the English settlers also filled in on the map of Lincolnshire the remarkably regular pattern of villages sited at the spring line below the Cliff and the Wold. The men who led these groups saw to it that each had a proportion of stiff clay land and waterlogged peat in the valley—the Low Fields of Coleby and the other villages south of Lincoln, or the Carrs of the Ancholme valley—of hillside pasture and hilltop grazing. Their planning could not be bettered.

Even this thriving and busy community, lifted some way out of its heathen squalor by the work of missionaries like Paulinus, and Saxon saints like Chad at Barrow-on-Humber and Higbald who was buried at Hibaldstow, is not our Lincolnshire. In the ninth century English farmers knew in their turn the danger and destruction that their own ancestors had brought to the Britons; the Saxon monasteries at Bardney, Barrow, and Partney disappeared without a trace, and the wealth of the Fenland monasteries was taken across the sea to be shown off in the halls of Danish vikings on a winter night. At least once the Danes made their winter camp at Torksey, which their long boats could reach with ease, and whence they could move into the heart of midland Mercia. English farmers in Lincolnshire learned to know by sight Ivar the Boneless and Halfdan his brother, sons of Ragnar Lothbrok, the most famous viking of the time, and to fear the exactions of their disciplined armies. The end of the warfare brought not relief for the English, but the division of the land among Danish settlers who took over English farms and villages and made them their own, or founded new alien settlements alongside the old. This process, more than any other single factor, made the Lincolnshire we know. Villages with raw-sounding names like Stragglethorpe or Skegness, or Snitterby; English villages whose smooth names have been turned into Fiskerton, Eagle, and Scopwick; towns where you are as likely to see Kirkgate as Church Street: these reflect the fact that Scandinavian remained a spoken language in Lincolnshire for several centuries after the settlement. There must have been some parts of Lincolnshire, such as central Kesteven (itself in part a Danish name) or the Wold area, where English could seldom be heard, and there is Ingleby—"the farm of the English"—something rare enough for the racial origin of the farmer to be its most distinctive feature. The Fens did not attract the Danes; there are few village names of Danish origin and only an occasional field name, to show that there was a certain infiltration of Danes there among the dominant English. The language of the countryside still shows the source of this element in the population. The word "kirk" has only recently gone out of use in the Grimsby area, and any Dane would understand a Lincolnshire man speaking (as I heard a Fillingham farmer speak in the spring of 1950) of his ancestors as "forelders". On the Trent, names like Marton Rack may well have been given by vikings who knew the Skaggerak; Skitter Haven is first cousin to Copenhagen, and the landing-places on the Trent are "staithes". Not all the new settlers were vikings; men who had actually taken part in the summer campaigns in England were uncommon enough for their new farms to be called Wickenby (the farm of the viking), Somerby (the farm of the summer warrior), or Westlaby (the farm of the west traveller). It was a genuine popular migration of farmers and their wives, but the Danes kept, for defence purposes against the English, a military organisation which is reflected in the forms of social organisation for many centuries after the settlement; the Soke of Peterborough is only one of many such large estates which had Danish lords, a predominantly Danish population, and a remarkably persistent form. The Danes of Lincolnshire produced no sagas of the deeds of the vikings, but there is the Lay of Havelock the Dane, a popular romance composed before the Norman Conquest and written in verse which is saturated with Norse words. Its story of the founding of Grimsby by a fisherman named Grim, out of the reward he gained from sheltering the son of a Danish king, must have been sung round the fire in many a Lincolnshire farmhouse. It reflects the period of two centuries when Lincolnshire belonged to the Scandinavian world of Olaf Tryggvason, the king of Norway who attacked England in the last years of the tenth century, rather than to the England of Æthelred, and preferred the Danish Harthacnut to the English Harold I. It was at Gainsborough that Swein Forkbeard landed in 1013 for his attempt to conquer England, and when he died there the Danish crews of the boats anchored in the Trent immediately put forward Cnut, his younger son, as his successor. It was Norman William's good fortune as well as his political skill and firmness which gave him unchallenged control of his new kingdom; the Scandinavian fleet which sailed into the Humber in 1069, and whose crews were feasted by their compatriots in Lincolnshire, was the last appearance of the Scandinavian long boats on these waters. The tradition of these boats was preserved in the Humber keel, whose square brown sail could be seen, up to a few years ago, on the Humber, the Trent, and the Foss Dyke, passing in their trips with coal and flour the site at Torksey of the winter camp of 872–3, and the Gainsborough where Swein, king of Denmark, landed in 1013.

In spite of this latent loyalty to northern Europe and the kings and warriors of the Scandinavian world, Lincolnshire as a county had by the time of the Norman Conquest been pressed into the same mould of counties as the rest of southern and midland England. But beneath this superficial uniformity in which Lincolnshire on a map is no different from Hampshire or Oxfordshire, lie the subdivisions which reveal the particular traditions and different origins of the parts. To the ancient kingdom of the Lindisfaras was added part of Hatfield, the Isle of Axholme, which Lindsey shares with Yorkshire and Nottinghamshire; similarly the territory of the Gyrwe, an ancient English grouping of peoples, was divided between Cambridgeshire and the parts of Holland. Although Lindsey has survived as a local government area with its own county council, the three ridings into which the Danish settlers divided it have not. Similarly the Danish wapentakes, with outlandish names like Candleshoe, or Winnibriggs and Threo, are lost to all but the curious and will not be found by anyone who looks through a list of local government divisions. The Rural District Council which includes Wragby no longer meets at the burial mound, or *haugr*, of the Danish Wraghi who founded that settlement; and the Skegness R.D.C. prefers to have its office in Skegness rather than by the *haugr* of Calunoth of Candleby. So the ford or *wath* of Kalf of Calceby, the ash-tree or *esk* of Louthesk, the three mounds of Threo (*thrir haugr*) are lost to us, and most of the other places where Danes (and English) met to administer justice and to acclaim their agreement with a brandishing of weapons. One of the few known meeting-places is the Elloe stone, now in a hedge bottom half a mile from Moulton church, which was the meeting-place of the fenland wapentake of Elloe. Any directory will show that the descendants of these men are still to be found; Thorgils has turned into Turgoose, the

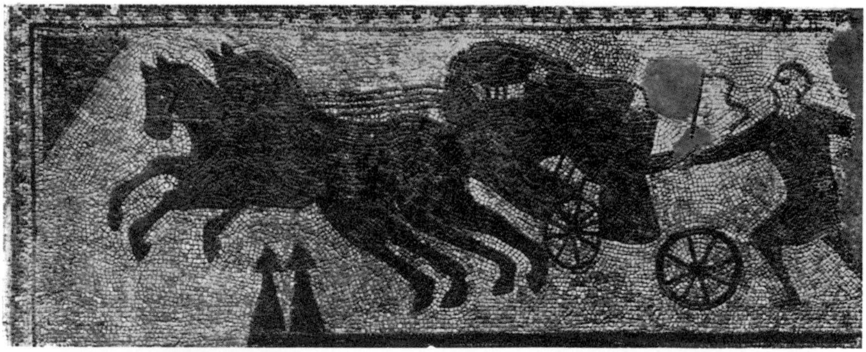

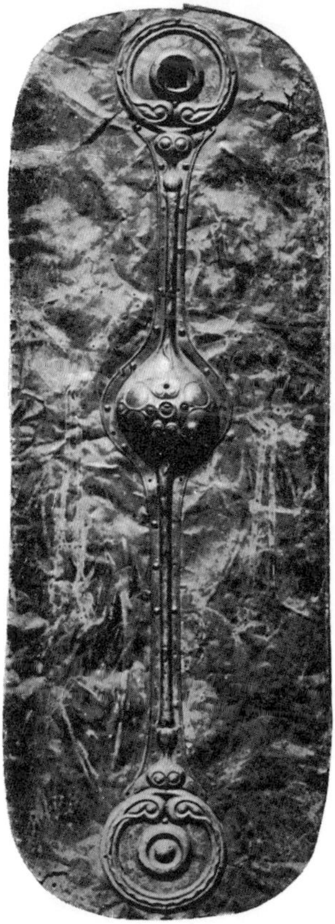

11 Chariot racing on a pavement in a Roman villa at Horkstow

12 Iron Age shield from the Witham near Lincoln

ROMAN AND PREHISTORIC REMAINS

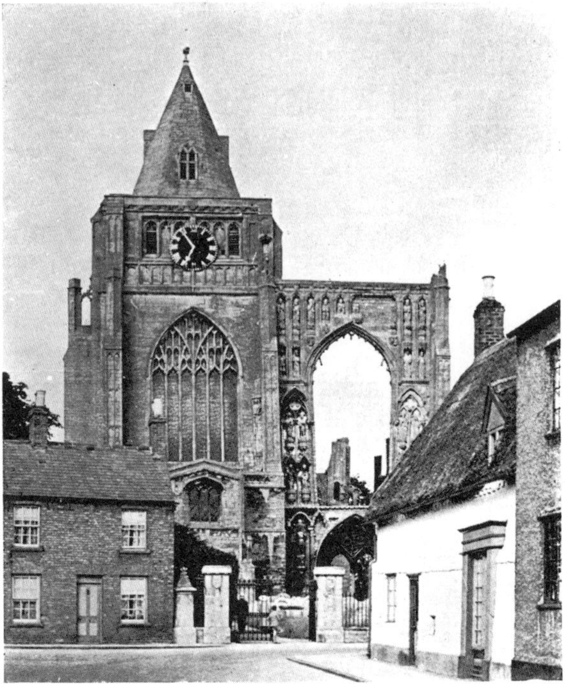

13 Crowland Abbey: the ruined nave and the fifteenth-century north aisle

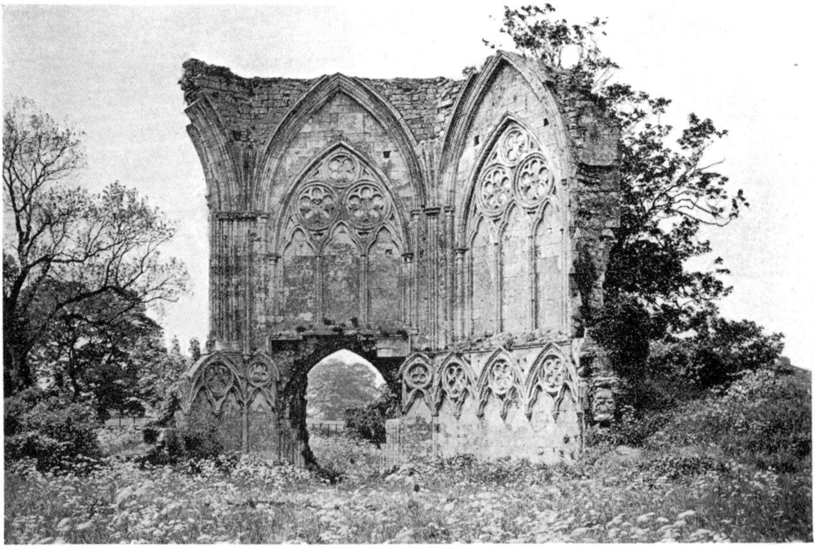

14 Thornton Abbey: remains of thirteenth-century octagonal Chapter House

LINCOLNSHIRE MONASTERIES

Scandinavian *gamal* (old) is disguised as Gamble, and Thorfinnr as Turpin. But the Algers, Danns, Humbles, Spurrs, and Tucks, and the men whose Danish blood is mixed now with English, or disguised under Smith and Walker, still show the same kind of sturdy independence of thought and action which once marked, and doubtless prolonged, the meetings on hilltops, by springs and fords, by the cross or in the clearing, near the new homes of the Danish "forelders" of modern Lincolnshire.

Chapter

III

Churches and Monasteries

"More even than the work of the great architects, I loved buildings that grew silently with the centuries, catching and keeping the best of each generation, while time curbed the artist's pride and the Philistine's vulgarity, and repaired the clumsiness of the dull workman. In such buildings England abounded. . . ."—Evelyn Waugh, *Brideshead Revisited* (R.U. edition, p. 178).

How this Anglo-Danish society in which heathen Danes dominated Christian English became wholly and officially Christian again we do not know. The older monasteries had disappeared in the smoke and flame of the viking raids. Some fenland monasteries were revived before the Conquest, but Bardney lay in ruins until later; Partney and Barrow were never revived. Of Partney nothing whatsoever is known; at Barrow the tradition of St. Chad is still a living one: part of the village is known as Chad, and in the traditional calendar of Barrow before enclosure St. Chad's day (March 2) was the date when the commons were laid, or closed.

The bishops of Lindsey had abandoned their seat (possibly at Caistor), and Lindsey, merged for the first time with Holland and Kesteven, was in the see of bishops who encouraged the conversion of the Danes from the safe distance of Dorchester on Thames, where they remained until William the Conqueror planted the Norman monk Rémi at Lincoln. Some at least of the Kirbys and Kirkbys in Lincolnshire must be so named after churches which the Danes found there when they claimed the land, but we do not know whether the churches were allowed to stand or the priests to minister. It is curious that Lincolnshire has produced no evidence of Christian monuments built or made in the century or so before the Conquest when Scandinavian influence was at its strongest. In the London of Cnut and in the north, craftsmen were carving in a style which blends English and Scandinavian in a vigorous barbaric manner; there is nothing of the kind in Lincolnshire, unless the remarkable spate of church building in the county at the time of the Norman Conquest is evidence of the first enthusiasm and zeal of converts.

Lincolnshire's finest Saxon church is at Barton-on-Humber

(17). It is an out of the way place now to a generation which expects easy and comfortable modes of travel; but in the Middle Ages it was a thriving port and the southern terminus of a ferry across the Humber, which any traveller north and south was bound to use if he chose not to cross the Trent at Nottingham or Newark, or to take a boat on the Trent and the Ouse. So Barton has its two churches, a unique feature now among the small towns of Lincolnshire, and the earlier, the parish church of St. Peter's, was built shortly before A.D. 1000. It is a complex building, its tower base serving as the nave, and having to east and west of the tower a small nave and a narthex or fore-building; the latter survives. At Broughton near Brigg is another Saxon tower which probably served the same function in the original building, as did the tower at Fingest in Buckinghamshire. Broughton and Hough on the Hill, on the western edge of the limestone ridge in Kesteven, both have a stairway housed in a semicircular projection on the western face of the tower.

At Stow there are pre-Conquest remains of a more ambitious type of building—not a parish church, but a minster of secular canons founded by the Bishop of Dorchester early in the eleventh century. Stow's claim to be the mother church of Lincoln, and to have existed in pre-Danish times, cannot be accepted: rather it may represent one of the few signs we can see of a missionary effort among the Danes by the distant bishop. The core of the very imposing cruciform church is Saxon, but it owes its present form (19) to restoration and enrichment by Norman bishops, the insertion of a central tower in the fifteenth century, and enthusiastic restoration a century ago, which vaulted the chancel in the Norman style, although the original vault had not been completed in Norman times.

There are small traces of Saxon work embodied in many parish churches, mainly in the shape of long and short quoins at the angles of naves or towers, and this particular feature survives most frequently in Kesteven—at Ropsley, Cranwell, and Digby, for instance. It may be that the building material was so good that later centuries could enlarge rather than set about rebuilding completely. In the Fens there is no surviving Saxon work, but this must not be taken to mean that no churches were built; there is evidence of churches at Sutterton and Algarkirk in the ninth century. The later wealth of the Fens was too great to tolerate the survival of tiny Saxon buildings. In Lindsey there are survivals of another kind which have interested several generations of students of architecture. These are church towers of a particular type, almost confined to Lindsey, where there are some twenty or more specimens: they are tall and slender without buttresses, of rubble masonry once plastered but now usually bared, with a plain string course at about three-quarters of the height, and having above that a belfry stage lighted by narrow two-light windows. They are familiar to anyone who knows Lincoln or Cleethorpes and there are other groups in the Wolds round Caistor and in the Trent valley near Gainsborough. Some of them are now disguised by later parapets, buttresses and inserted windows. The finest specimens, apart from the two which form such a feature of the lower length of the High Street at Lincoln, are at Bracebridge (now a suburb of Lincoln), at Marton in the Trent valley, and at Rothwell near Caistor; the fine and lofty tower of Clee church, now swallowed up in Cleethorpes, is a good example of the primitive type. Unexpectedly there is a solitary outlier group at Great Hale, on the edge of the Fens in Kesteven. The type possesses both Saxon and Norman features, and must have been built in the fifty or more years on either side of 1066. One is tempted to see these towers as a flowering of religious zeal among the Danish element, especially as in the Grimsby area the Scandinavian element was strong.

In the twenty years following 1072, when the see was transferred to Lincoln, a good deal of the available labour and surplus wealth of the county must have gone in the rebuilding of Lincoln cathedral on the site of the old Minster. The Norman (using the word in its racial and not its historical sense) master mason, whoever he was, gave the new building a west front which is unique among Romanesque cathedrals (1). Its striking quality is now somewhat disguised. The Norman work is framed, as it were, by Bishop Grosseteste's widening and raising of the screen and by the heightening of the towers in the fifteenth century. But inside this frame there is Norman work of two periods; one must disregard the very ornate gables over the aisles, the lower stages of the towers, and the equally elaborate doorways, as well as the band of carving inserted in the façade, to see the grandeur and severity of the original design. The later Norman work was done during the time of Bishop Alexander the Magnificent, after a disastrous fire in 1141. If we recall Alexander's work at Stow, where the chancel was rebuilt and new doorways inserted, and his castles at Sleaford, Newark, and Banbury, we must call him the most energetic and ambitious of the Norman bishops.

Apart from Lincoln, there is little early Norman architecture of note. In some villages it is plain that building operations which had started at about the time of the Conquest went on more or less without a break through much of the twelfth century. Marton, which has one of the best of the early towers, also has a Norman north arcade and chancel arch; at Corringham the west end of the nave, abutting on the Saxon tower, is Norman and at Clee

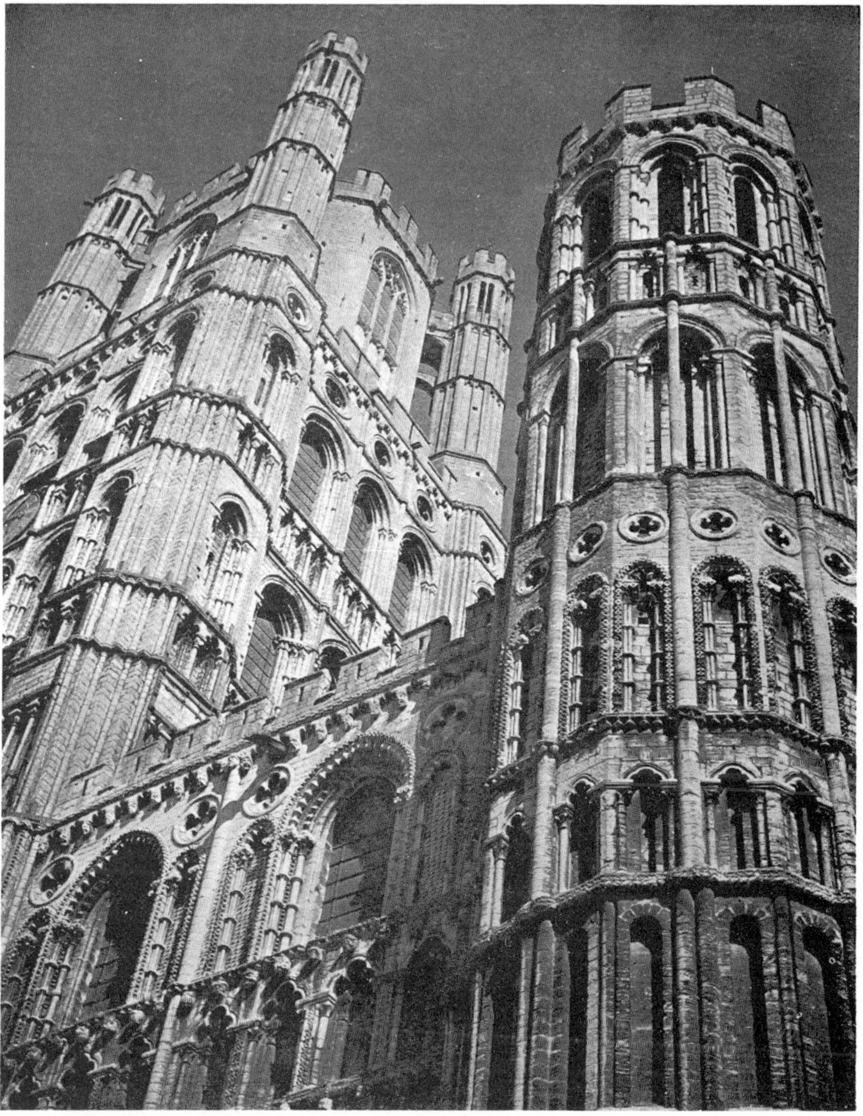

15 Ely: the west transept and central western tower (late twelfth century)

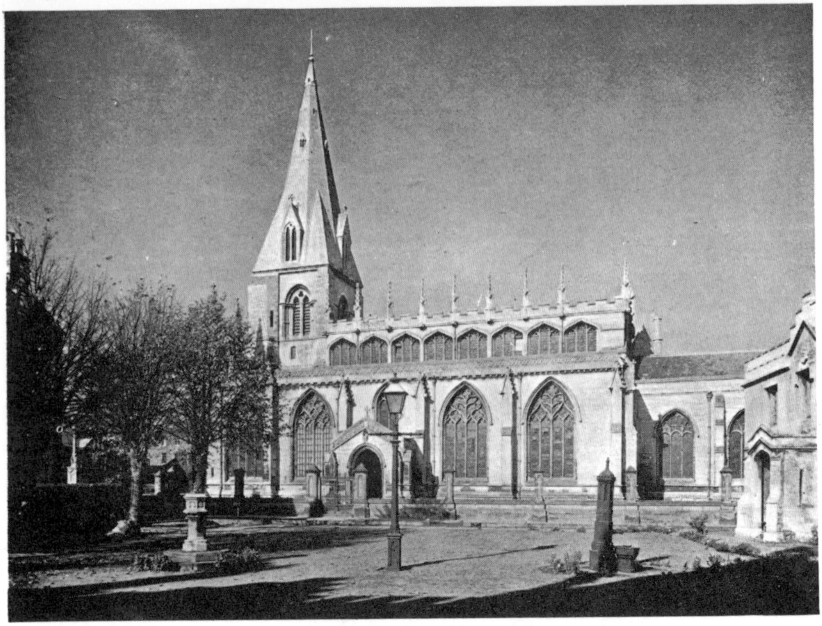

16 (*above*) Sleaford: thirteenth-, fourteenth- and fifteenth-century building

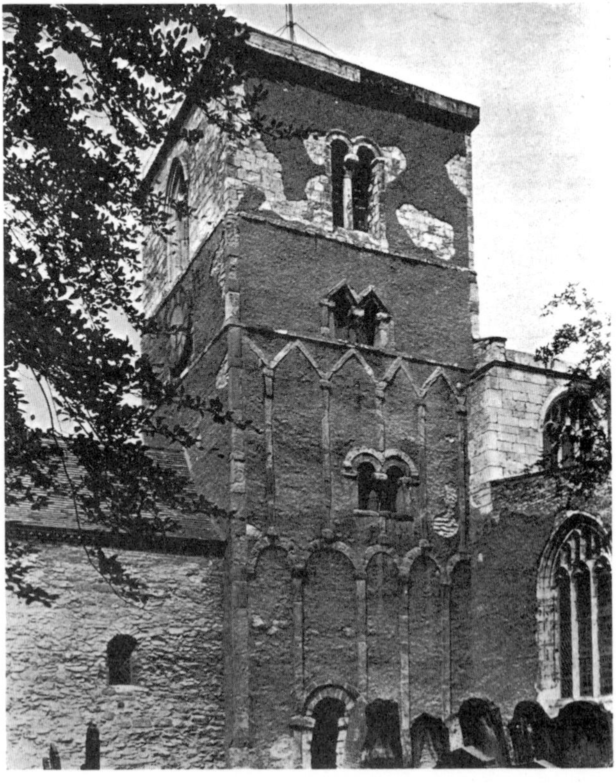

17 Barton-on-Humber: the Saxon tower-nave and narthex, and the fifteenth-century nave and aisles

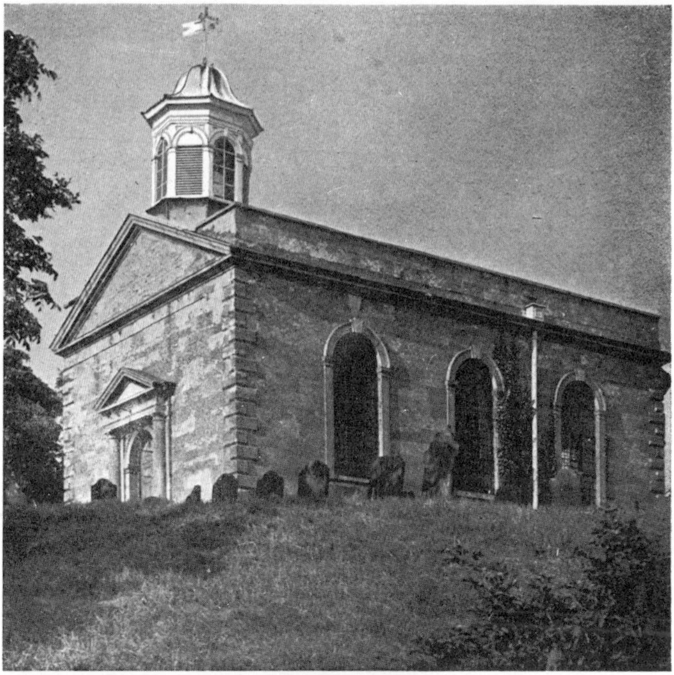

18 (*above*) The Georgian church at Cherry Willingham

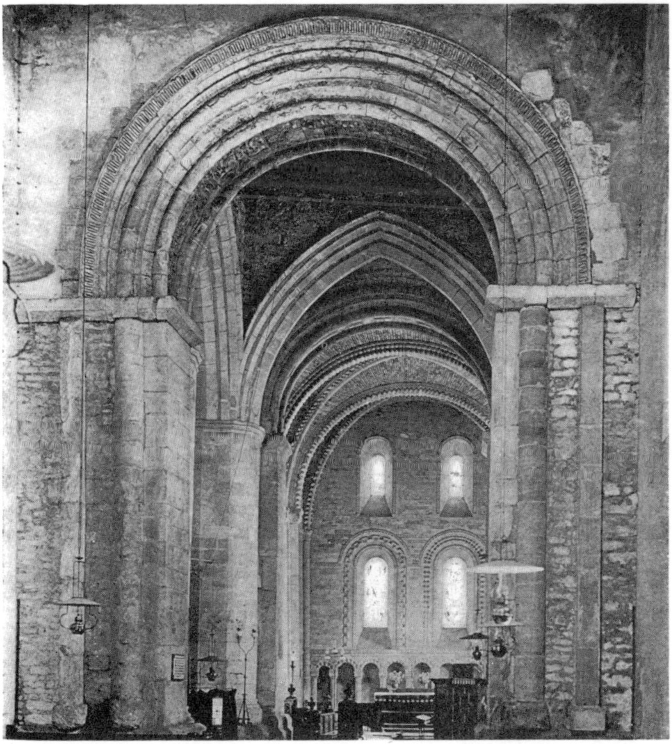

19 Stow: the Saxon crossing, Norman chancel and inserted Early English tower arches

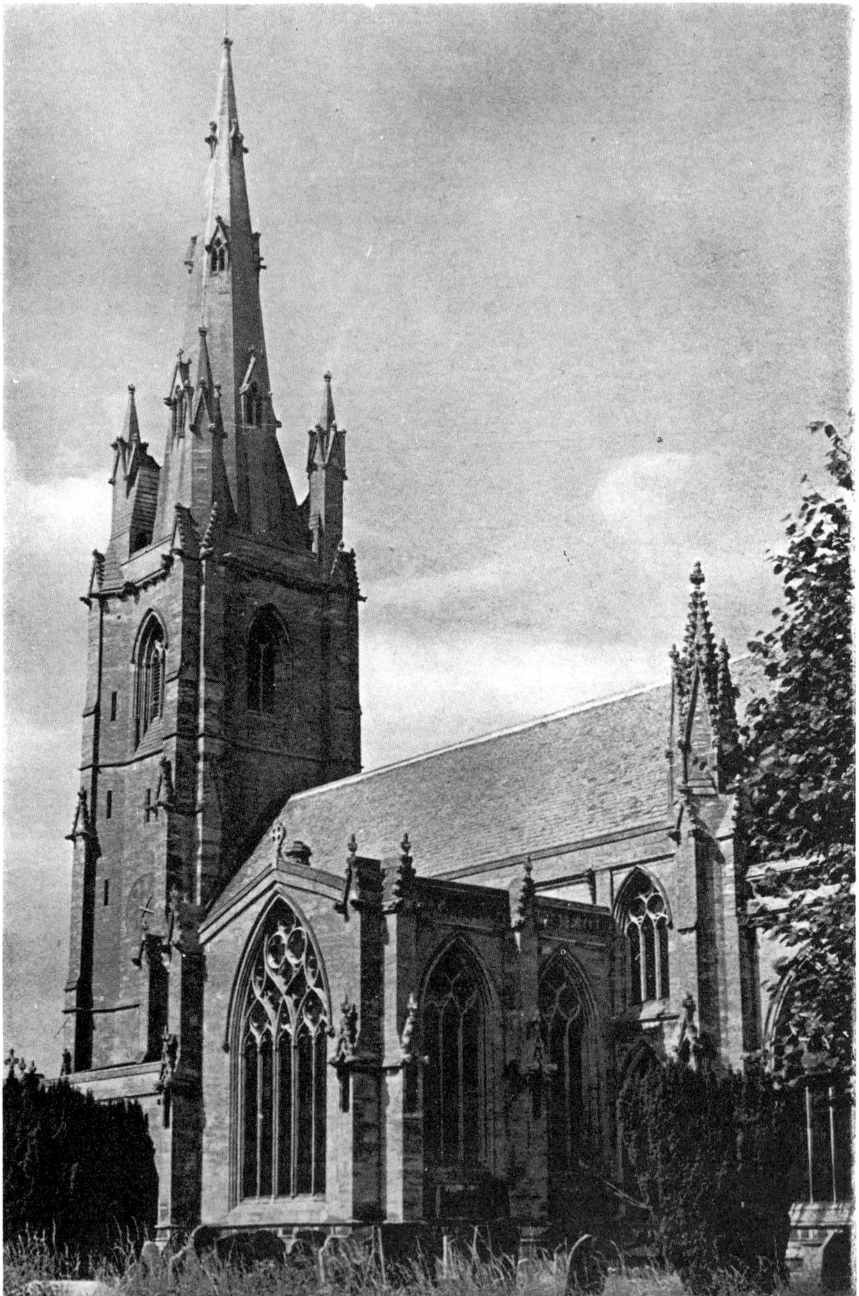

20 Heckington: fine fourteenth-century work in Ancaster stone

the north arcade of the nave is undoubtedly early Norman, and the south arcade later. At Rothwell the aisled nave was built in the twelfth century. It looks as though some communities which had very early added a tall belfry to a small church soon decided to rebuild the church on a scale commensurate with the tower.

Similarly in Kesteven, it is often the churches which have traces of a stone church before the Conquest that in the twelfth century were having aisles added to the nave—for instance at Cranwell and Ropsley—or being otherwise extended. Apart from these second instalments, so to speak, there are a score of places where grand new churches were begun, as generous with stone as one expects of Norman masons. I remember particularly Canwick, Ancaster, Castle Bytham, Cranwell, Syston and Belton. Such building was not confined to the limestone belt; there is good work at Barrow and Irby on Humber, at Rothwell in the Wolds and at Northorpe in the clays of the Trent valley.

The evidence from the Fens is of rather later building activity, but even so it is impressive to note the number of churches planned even in the Norman period on the large scale that we expect there. In some cases it is a tardy, but already ambitious, monastic church of which we have remains today. The nave of the monastic church at Bourne has survived from its Norman first days—more impressive and successful than the incompleted plan for a rebuilding in the thirteenth century. At Frieston, a cell of Crowland north of Boston, the long nave, all that is left of a cruciform church, is mainly Norman, but its west end was completed in the thirteenth century. Deeping St. James was a cell of Thorney, and the parochial nave has a fine Norman arcade. No ordinary parish church was built on quite such a scale as these, but those at Bicker and Horbling are Norman buildings of cruciform plan—evidence of large thinking and no doubt deep pockets. Tilney All Saints, Walsoken, Sibsey, and Long Sutton have large late Norman naves, and Whaplode's long narrow nave of seven bays was begun in the Norman style and completed in about 1200. In the Isle of Axholme, too, there was wealth already: there is a Norman nave at Haxey and tower at Crowle.

There is a great contrast already between these fine buildings, whose original conception was large enough even for succeeding generations, and the small churches such as Greetwell near Lincoln, which later times were unable to expand. But in most cases, here as everywhere, Norman remains are confined to a chancel arch, as at Foston or Dembleby, round which everything else has been rebuilt, or doors thought good enough for re-use in an enlarged building. At Beckingham, the Norman north and south doors are re-set in the aisles which Thomas Sibthorpe, the wealthy parson, rebuilt in the second quarter of the fourteenth century.

It is misleading to describe Norman work in isolation, because it is part of a great phase of activity which lasted for a century or more from about 1150, during which most parish churches took their present shape; later work, except in unusually wealthy towns or large villages, was mainly confined to improving an existing structure. In this grand operation the villages of Kesteven led the way, because of the advantage of good material, and the parish churches took on a pattern which is determined first by that and only second by the economic resources of the area. Perhaps Kesteven's wealth of churches is due in part, as Dr. Hoskins has suggested in *Midland England*, to the fact that the limestone belt with its relatively thin soil was easier to clear and produced quicker returns than the valley clays. Certainly by the last quarter of the twelfth century, to judge from surviving traces of Transitional work, building activity was even more widespread than earlier in the century. There is good work in a score of Kesteven churches, whether it is the tiny north arcade of Stragglethorpe, which, when the double bell gable was added in the thirteenth century, was good enough for later generations; or in the more ambitious work at Grantham. In the Fens building proceeded on the cruciform church at Horbling and on the nave and west front of Whaplode, and a new church was begun at Sutterton; the naves of Market Deeping and Moulton were built and the clerestory added at Long Sutton. But there is also more ambitious work in the clays of the river valleys, at Long Bennington, at Cotes and Willingham by Stow, and at Horkstow and Thornton-le-Moor. In the Marshland from Barton (St. Mary's), or more strictly from Goxhill round to Theddlethorpe All Saints, there are ten or more churches in which building was going on. In the Wolds there are the nave arcades at Hagworthingham, and the tower of Newton-le-Wold; the old church at Walesby near Market Rasen, abandoned by the village which has built itself a new in the valley bottom, is mainly Transitional.

In the thirteenth century the availability of good building stone began to make a marked difference to the development of churches. Transport very easily doubled or trebled the cost of building stone at the quarry face, and we can judge the wealth of the medieval corporations or village communities by their ability to pay for good material from a distance, or their inability to use other than local (and inferior) stone. Many of the Wold villages built in chalk, though it is not very easy to find examples today, either because the chalk walls have been plastered inside and stuccoed outside, as at Bonby in the Ancholme valley; or because they were such poor churches, and the neglect of subsequent poverty-stricken centuries was so great, that they have been rebuilt. The small church at Conisholme is of chalk; it is used at Fotherby along with greenstone and freestone, and at Legbourne near Louth not only the walls but even the jambs of the windows are chalk. In some churches a harder chalk is used for piers and capitals which is creamy yellow in colour, soapy to the touch, and a very effective foil to the dark sandstone of the walls. It can be seen for instance in the chancel arch at South Cockerington, or the piers of West Keal, in much of the interior of Grimoldby, and very handsome it is. In the later Middle Ages sandstone from the southern end of the Wolds was widely used in the Wolds and the Marshland. It is identical with the carstone of the nearest part of Norfolk and with the whole of the Lower Greensand outcrop through Cambridgeshire and Bedfordshire; although known locally as greenstone it has a pleasing range of tone from olive green to a red-brown. One of the easiest quarries to find is at Salmonby where children and lovers have carved initials on the soft face. It is not any better as a material than most sandstones; churches like Bag Enderby look precarious or neglected and the eroded walls are mottled with patches of many ages.

In the Trent valley from the Gainsborough neighbourhood right down to the Leicestershire border, the local lias limestone was used for coursed rubble walling; it may be seen at Marton in the early tower and at Stow, or farther south at Dry Doddington on the edge of Nottinghamshire. The skerry from across the Trent in Nottinghamshire was used to a certain extent; it was quarried at Tuxford and was used for the bay window of Gainsborough Old Hall, which is otherwise timber-framing and brick. On the Cliff north of Lincoln the blue lias gives way to yellow oolitic limestone in the rubble walls of churches and cottages. Lincoln itself seems to be the most northerly point at which the stone is good enough for ashlar work; most of the Minster has come from a local quarry.

South of Lincoln, in Kesteven one begins to meet ashlar masonry, which Dr. W. J. Arkell has described as "the show-flower of masonry". It is the contrast between lavish carved ornament, still sharp and clear, with smooth freestone walling which gives a church like Heckington something of its quality (20). At Brant Broughton the ageless harmony between the Perpendicular nave of 1400 on the one hand, and on the other the chancel rebuilt by Bodley in 1876, has deceived at least one person on first inspection (3). The quarries at Ancaster and Barnack were first discovered by the Romans, like so much of England's good building stone. They were rediscovered by the Saxons and in full swing again by the twelfth century, as witness the Norman arcades of Ancaster and Wilsford. Barnack Rag was the better stone, and the fenland monasteries like Crowland and Ramsey acquired quarrying rights in the Norman period. When Sawtrey abbey was founded in 1147, one of the first things done was to make a waterway from the site to Whittlesea Mere, to link the abbey with the system of waterways on which boatloads of stone for the churches and monasteries of Holland and the Cambridge fens, even for Norwich and Bury St. Edmunds, must have been a common sight. The Roman Car Dyke—or part of it at least—was pressed into use, and many small streams. The building accounts for Tattershall show how in the mid-fifteenth century stone for the church and for the dressings of the castle went by road from the quarries at Wilsford and Ancaster and then by the river Slea to the Witham at Tattershall. In the rebuilding of Louth parish church in the early sixteenth century the same quarries and the same route were used; the churchwardens hired wagons at Coningsby for the long pull over the Wolds. The stone cost them 2/- or more a load at the quarry, and carriage was 1/8*d.* a load. Barnack Rag was worked out by the end of the Middle Ages, and Ketton stone takes its place, but the quarries at Ancaster are still worked. They are worth a visit, whether to see the unchanging methods of stone quarrying, or the unusual flora which has grown up on the hills and hollows of the ancient quarries. The quality of the stone can be seen in many buildings, from parts of Windsor Castle, through the extraordinary Elizabethan Wollaton Hall near Nottingham, to the nineteenth-century railway station at York, and now in the rebuilt House of Commons. The characteristic yellow tone which it retains when used inside buildings is part of the beauty of the famous chancel furniture at Hawton near Newark.

Lincolnshire has two of the finest medieval brick buildings in England—the fourteenth-century gatehouse of Thornton Abbey, a product perhaps of the corporation brick yards at Hull, and fifteenth-century Tattershall castle, built of bricks made on the spot (26). There was less need than in Essex to develop this substitute for stone, but there is more medieval brickwork in the churches of the Fens and the Marshland than one suspects at first. The free-standing tower of Sutton St. James is brick of about 1500, and Bardney in the Witham valley has a brick chancel. Frieston has a north aisle of brick. Terrington St. Clement across the Norfolk border, and Butterwick near Boston have brick clerestories, and at Theddlethorpe All Saints bricks are used in the tower in alternate courses with greenstone. It is difficult to choose between the uniformity of tone and richness of sculptured

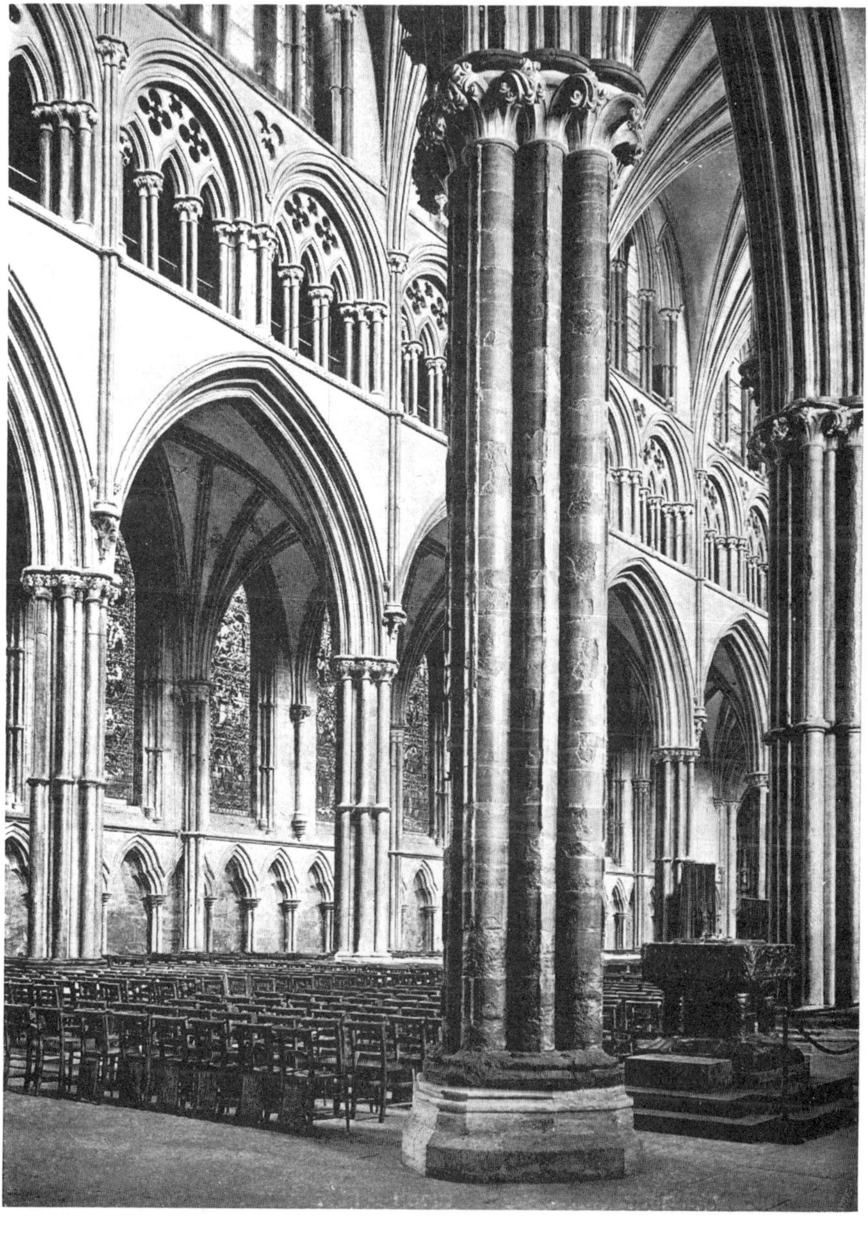

21 Lincoln: limestone and Purbeck marble in the nave (1200–53)

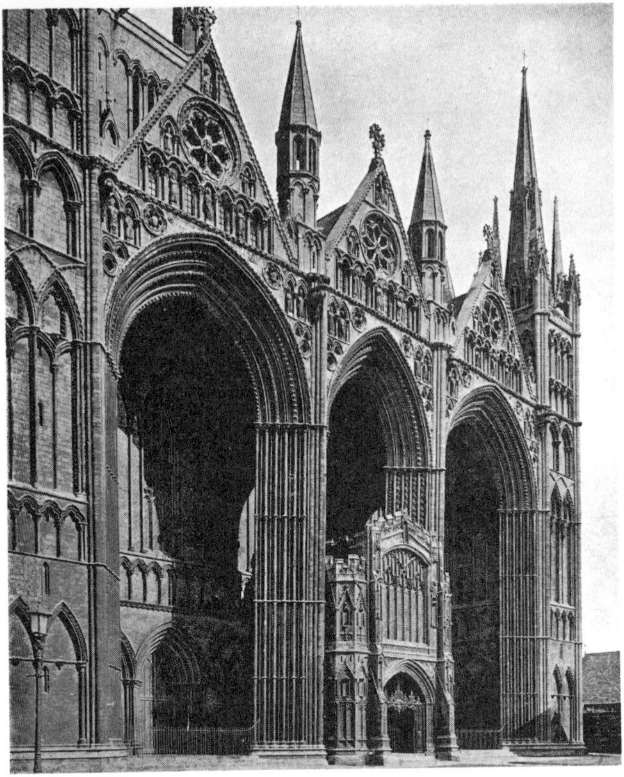

22 (*above*) The Early English west front (1200–20)

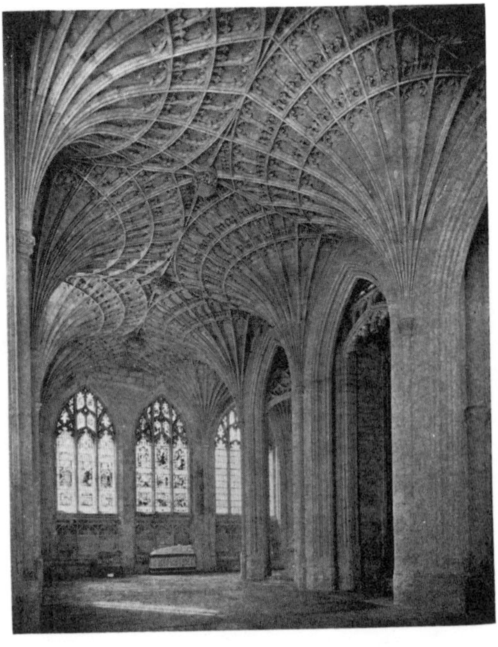

23 The Retrochoir (*c.* 1500)

THE BEGINNING AND END OF GOTHIC AT PETERBOROUGH

ornament of an ashlar building, and the polychrome variety—grey-white or creamy yellow chalk, dark green and brown sandstone, the rosy brown of weathered brick—in the great monuments of the fen and the marsh.

Now, knowing the resources of the medieval masons, we can go in search of the fine churches of the thirteenth century and onward for which Lincolnshire is famous. First and foremost comes Lincoln cathedral (1, 21). I have spoken of the west front, but the view which most visitors see first is that from the south, of a thirteenth-century building; the raising of the towers later improved without basically altering the proportions of the cathedral. Time has merged into one tremendous composition the work of four generations and of an unknown number of master masons. The first of them, Geoffrey de Noiers, was an Englishman, in spite of his name, and for the rebuilding of the minster from the crossing, after its collapse in an earthquake in 1185, he designed the first completely *English* Gothic building in the land (21). In Bishop Grosseteste's time (1235–53) the rebuilding was completed, and the central tower rebuilt a second time after its fall in 1239. Even so the canons were not content, and three years after Grosseteste's death decided to demolish the apse of the choir built in Bishop Hugh's time to provide a fitting home for his remains now that he had been canonised and his tomb had become a place of pilgrimage. The form of the new Angel Choir owes something to the recent work at Ely, but it surpasses anything else of its period in England; architecture and sculpture, rich without a trace of coarseness, are perfectly combined. Again, even before the choir was fully furnished, the central tower was raised—a wonderful climax to more than a century of unbroken effort. Much of the tremendous cost, as I have remarked elsewhere, must have been borne by the small peasant farmers of Danish Lincolnshire.

In the early thirteenth century north-west Lincolnshire comes into the forefront. There are Early English naves at Alkborough and Winteringham, close to the Humber; at Scotter and Scotton, neighbours and no doubt friendly rivals, as so often happened, work on the naves was going on. Scotter has a beautiful north arcade with clustered piers, and at Scotton, in addition to the arcade, there is a north door with dog-tooth mouldings. At Messingham the church is mainly a monument to the acquisitiveness of an early nineteenth-century vicar, who used his position as archdeacon of Stow to fill his own parish church with plunder from many sources; but at least the nave arcades still show what thirteenth-century builders could do. The most beautiful work in these parts is at Kirton-in-Lindsey and Bottesford. Kirton has a good tower, with rich belfry windows, an arcade on the north and a beautiful south doorway; in the chancel the deeply splayed lancets have survived restoration. Bottesford is probably the finest church of this period in the county, with all the features one expects to see still preserved: splayed lancets in the chancel with dog-tooth mouldings, grouped lancets in the transepts, alternate circular and lancet windows in the clerestory; stone seats round the piers of the nave, good furniture in the chancel and transepts and a contemporary font.

In the clays between the Trent and the Lincoln Edge there are a number of handsome and rewarding churches. That is particularly true of the upper Witham valley, between Lincoln and Grantham, a little known but very charming stretch of country. You can start with Marston where the river is for the first time clear of the limestone ridge and flowing, lined by willows, through meadows backed by slight undulations in the clay. At Hougham on the opposite bank there is a thirteenth-century tower; at Westborough, three miles downstream, and one of the most isolated villages in Lincolnshire, there is a lofty nave and large chancel. Westborough church is being restored as I write, after long neglect, never more unfortunate than in the last twenty years; by the time these words are read perhaps the rather startling limewash of the outside of the chancel will have quietened down. At Claypole there is a rich work of the Decorated period, but the nucleus of the church is early thirteenth century. Similarly at Brant Broughton there are lofty Early English arcades, rather thrown into the shade by the wonderful richness of the later work(3). At Beckingham the arcades are early thirteenth century and there is a simple but charming porch of the same date—rebuilt, like the Norman doors, in the fourteenth century.

Farther north in the Trent valley there are small churches redeemed from dullness only by the richness of Early English arcading; at Newton on Trent, where the Trent becomes the boundary with Nottinghamshire, and at Torksey, a small village now and with little to indicate its former importance. In the Isle of Axholme the few ancient villages all show signs of thirteenth-century work in their churches. The Marshland villages reveal that by this time the late settlements in the salt marsh were well established and the rich grazing was beginning to return its wealth. Thornton Curtis and Great Cotes both have fine naves with clustered piers, but of different dates in the early thirteenth century. Farther south Tetney and Conisholme, Humberstone and Mablethorpe, Hogsthorpe and Mumby all have good work of this age, and one may round off this group by including Ingoldmells with its interesting arcades.

In the Fenland it is needless to say that much outstanding building was done in the early Gothic style. In the silt fen there is Benington which has a fine chancel (although the vaulting was never completed) and chancel furnishings. Kirton in Holland still has a dignified nave, although it was wrecked in 1804; is there another case in England of gunpowder being used to reduce the size of a church? Wrangle has a graceful doorway; Weston ranks with Bottesford as one of the most beautiful churches of this period in the county; Wyberton has as much Early English work as was left after the central tower collapsed in the fifteenth century. At Long Sutton there is the remarkable lead-covered spire, with its lead spirelets at the base; it serves as a link between the timber caps of an earlier period (like the candle snuffers of Southwell Minster in Nottinghamshire) and the stone spires which follow. At Frampton the cruciform church was given a broach spire, and at Sutterton the cruciform church was completed. On the inner margin of the Fens there is Coningsby, where restorers have turned the clerestory lancets into the oddest triangular openings; Great Hale with its lofty nave whose effectiveness is sadly diminished by the loss of the chancel in the seventeenth century; Ruskington where the fine Early English church was not improved by the rebuilding of the tower or spire after collapse in 1620. Our heritage would be larger but for such disasters as these. At Deeping St. James the lovely triforium combined with clerestory was built, but at Bourne the monastic resources—even in the thirteenth century—were not sufficient to carry out the planned rebuilding of the nave.

On the oolite ridge the wealth of Early English building is embarrassing to a writer. The churches are not large and in many of them, here as in the Fens, the dignity of the thirteenth-century naves is enhanced by noble clerestories erected later, but they are full of fine workmanship and character. At Stamford All Saints there is lovely carving in the nave capitals; and at St. Mary's the very handsome tower, finished with a spire three generations later. Near by at Greatford is one of the broach spires which along with Frampton, Sleaford, and North Rauceby can be called the earliest examples of this very graceful achievement of the thirteenth-century mason. It is significant that these early spires should be found so close to the Ancaster quarries from which the stone came. The broach spires are in one sense primitive, but they are almost uniformly successful in proportions, and they avoid the problem which beset later masons—the design of the junction of tower and spire—and which few solved with complete success. In speaking of spires it is just as artificial to separate early thirteenth-century work from later as it is to distinguish between Norman and

Transitional; work was going on more or less continuously, and indeed at Leasingham, for instance, the broach spire stands in perfect harmony on the tower which is nearly a century earlier. So the antiquary will find at Ropsley or Grantham distinctions to make; others will find to comment that at Thurlby or Wellingore only the proportions are at fault, which is a rare but unfortunate failing. At Sleaford (16) and Grantham there is immense satisfaction to be found in the effect of tower and spire rising from engaged aisles with magnificent geometrical or flowing tracery in the west windows.

There is much pleasure to be got from contemplation of the exteriors of some of the churches of the last seventy-five years before the Black Death precisely because the variety of effect is so fascinating. At Swaton, one of the loveliest of Lincolnshire's churches, you can see in the east window the first hesitant tracery, and contrast it with the exuberance of the flowing design of the west windows. Similarly at Sutterton in the Fens, or at Navenby on the edge of the limestone scarp, there are windows which in spite of Mr. Harvey's recent urging on us to admire Perpendicular work, still seems as finally satisfying as they did to an earlier generation. There are fine windows at Bolingbroke of this period, at Gedney, Sutterton, Grantham, at Haltham on Bain and Knaith near Gainsborough; exceptionally good ones at Sleaford (16) and the great east window at Ely. There are even whole churches of this period at Brocklesby in the Wolds, Caythorpe, Claypole, Dorrington, Fleet (Fens), Holbeach (Fens), Keelby (Marshland), and, best known of them all, Boston (24), pre-eminent among town churches, and Heckington, famous among village churches (20). Both those are so well known that I prefer to dwell for a moment on Ewerby, not more than two miles from Heckington. The two make perfect foils: Ewerby perhaps finished about 1325 when the rebuilding of Heckington was just beginning, is the less rich in its ornament but the more dignified in its simplicity; it is also superior in design because the Heckington tower and spire are an afterthought, and not a particularly good one at that. Heckington village has lost its character from its willingness to serve the sea-bent tourist; perhaps it could do no other. Ewerby has conceded nothing to the twentieth century and remains withdrawn and quiet, one of the most charming villages in Lincolnshire. But those who admire the whole effect of Ewerby will return to Heckington to linger over the beautiful craftsmanship in the furnishing of its chancel, the sedilia and the famous Easter sepulchre—products of the benevolence of Richard de Potesgrave, the wealthy rector, and of a firm of masons who can be neither named nor located, but whose hand is clear enough here, at Irnham, at Navenby, and at Hawton near Newark.

To complete our picture of the achievements of the century and a half before the Black Death halted building, we need to know something of the monastic churches. Lincolnshire and the Fens had more monasteries than any other part of England, and they included some of the richest, as well as some of the smallest and poorest; but of those fifty or sixty houses the four centuries since the Dissolution have left us very little. There is Ely (15), the wonderful church preserved because from 1109 onwards it was the see of a bishop as well as a monastic church, and Peterborough (22), saved for the same reason because the last abbot became the first bishop under Henry VIII's reorganisation. Ely has more than one similarity to Lincoln: in its siting first of all, and also in the originality of its design both in Norman and later work. The only surviving part of a monastic church now not in use as a church is the small Priory of St. Leonard's, Stamford; the nave, with its excellent west front and north arcade now open to the weather, has simple and beautiful Norman and Transitional work. At Bourne, South Kyme, Frieston, and Deeping St. James, at Thorney and Crowland in the Fens, at Knaith near Gainsborough (Heynings Priory) the parishioners were allowed to keep, or managed ultimately to rescue, part of the monastic church for parish use, and that is all. Very fine these remnants are in many cases: the handsome west front of Crowland (13), a tiny version of Exeter; Deeping with its most impressive interior; the long church at Frieston with its great range of clerestory windows, not more than half the original cruciform building. While the layout of one or two of the larger houses for monks or canons is tolerably well known, we know nothing of the buildings of the small nunneries where the illegitimate, the half-witted, or the merely unmarriageable daughters of the county families lived out their tedious lives. For the rest, we can cross the fields to look at a mere lump of masonry which was once part of Barlings Abbey or Kirkstead; or find, not far away, a piece of thirteenth-century walling which still has the pulpit from which the monks of Tupholme heard readings from the Fathers while they ate; search the back streets of Spalding and find a monastic building now converted into a row of cottages; or see at Ely buildings now housing the school, and other tantalising but imposing fragments incorporated in residentiaries' houses. Only at Thornton Abbey can you see something of the scale of the lost conventual buildings (14). The abbey is most accessible now to Hull and Grimsby cyclists; in the fourteenth century it must have been too accessible to French pirates and rebellious peasants, for the abbey built this great gatehouse in the years following the Peasants' Revolt, and in the next century the long brick barbican was added. The gatehouse has survived only because brick could not be re-used. Torrington, touring Lincolnshire in the 1790's found Crowland, "like Thorney, pillaged to the very bone". His phrase loses some of its edge when one remembers that he "collected" brasses from churches whenever they were loose. A fine tower was standing at Barlings in 1726, but Byng found men daily carting stone away from there and Kirkstead; other monastic buildings had already gone to make roads or bridges (Thornton material made a sluice for the Ancholme at Ferriby); mansions like Lord Clinton's house at Sempringham, and Grimsthorpe, overlooking the site of Vaudey; or to build Cambridge colleges.

The monasteries were at their most flourishing in the thirteenth and early fourteenth centuries, before they began to suffer from the economic changes in the countryside of which they were part, and also from their own extravagance, incompetence and declining zeal. The surviving fragments at Thornton are of a church and chapter house built in the fifty years following 1264. At Louth Park, Bardney, Sempringham, Haverholme, Vaudey, Broadholme, Revesby (9), excavation or inspection of fragments of material shows that major building operations were in hand in the thirteenth century. Of Thornton, Sempringham, Bardney, and Louth Park we know enough to visualise large cruciform churches, as big as Fountains Abbey, larger than Louth parish church. For the rest we must be content to puzzle over green mounds in meadows and parks, or to examine Dr. St. Joseph's aerial photographs; only at Thornton can we walk over Ministry of Works' lawns and see the puzzle explained.

To see the achievements of the last phase of the Middle Ages we can safely leave aside the monasteries and their churches. At Sempringham Priory, where canons and sisters worshipped alongside each other but with an unbroken wall between them, the tower over the canon's church was finished in the early fifteenth century only with repeated cajoling of the faithful and after getting the most potent of indulgences. There was little money to spare from monastic treasuries for the churches they possessed; indeed they had appropriated them on the grounds of their own sore need of the income from the tithes. So in the fourteenth century Sempringham had appropriated Norton Disney and Hacconby, and in many cases they were fortunate enough to take over a brand new fabric, as Bardney did at Heckington. There is only one non-monastic church for which monks can truthfully be given the credit. At Kirkstead, the Cistercian monks built a chapel for lay folks outside the entrance to the precincts, and it remains today, after a precarious and varied history, a most exquisite example of Early English design. Like the chapel at Wykeham in the fens which the prior of Spalding built in the early fourteenth century on one of the granges, it fell into private hands after the Reformation, but it was rescued from ruin some forty years ago. More than one church appropriated to a monastery was allowed to fall into decay while the monks were still responsible: at Humberstone near Grimsby chancel and nave were rebuilt in 1710, and at Whaplode the chancel in 1818, because of medieval neglect.

In the late fourteenth and fifteenth centuries money was more hardly come by, and was concentrated in fewer hands. In the Wolds, and even on limestone, some of the small settlements had begun to decline, in part owing to the pestilence, and in part owing to the decline of mixed farming, and some of the villages disappeared altogether by the Tudor period. In 1397 the vicarage of West Wykeham was united with near-by Ludford Magna; the foundations of the church and the homesteads are clearly to be seen on either side of a little Wold valley sloping down to the river Bain. Similarly Dunsthorpe in 1437 was united with Hameringham because there were no parishioners left at Dunsthorpe—driven away by low wages or killed off by pestilences. The poverty was not universal of course, even in this poor district, and churches like Bag Enderby, Somersby, West Ashby, and Sutterby are charming monuments to the modest standards of small villages. The Fenland and Marshland were exceptional in that the fifteenth-century slump hit them less hardly. The poll-tax returns of 1397 reveal that Holland was the wealthiest part of England. Even here, however, money may have been tight in the first quarter of the fifteenth century: we should not have known that Roger Denis, a London mason, had been engaged on rebuilding the chancel of Surfleet in 1420, and then on the rebuilding of Wyberton after the collapse of the central tower, if he had not had difficulty in getting paid for his work. Apart from such emergency work it is generally true that rebuilding or extension which was not completed before about 1400 had to wait some fifty years. So we find that in that magnificent Marshland church at Croft the arcades are early Perpendicular, the remainder of the fabric and the fine screens and benches much later. At Winthorpe near by the handsome church is the result of an effort that lasted throughout the fifteenth century, and one can envisage the energy that must have gone into the organising of church-ales, the medieval equivalents of bazaars, fêtes, and garden parties. In some of the buildings of this age, the hand of the wealthy individual is not concealed: Great Ponton has a fine tower which looks as if it had strayed from Somerset; it was built in 1519 by Anthony Ellys, a successful wool merchant who built himself a house near by (30). We are told in an inscription on the elaborate porch at Winthorpe that it was paid for by Robert Langnay and William Palmer.

Whatever the effort and however protracted, magnificent churches were built and finishing touches added. There is Barrow-on-Humber side, and Belton, Althorpe, and Haxey in the Isle of Axholme; Bardney in the Witham valley and Saxilby on the Foss Dyke; in the Marshland there are its finest churches at Burgh-le-Marsh, Croft, Hogsthorpe, Marsh Chapel, and Winthorpe. In the Fens there are Friskney, Fishtoft, Gosberton, Quadring; Edenham by its limestone stream and Sedgebrook in the Vale of Belvoir. There are the crocketed spires of south-west Lincolnshire breaking the skyline every few miles along the country between Grantham and Lincoln and the solitary spire of South Somercotes, "Queen of the Marshland". There are the towers at Beckingham and Long Bennington, first cousins to their neighbours across the county boundary in Nottinghamshire at Hawton and Rolleston. There is Gainsborough, its medieval tower married to an eighteenth-century nave and chancel; there is West Keal, looking over the Fens, and the great towers on Humber side at Immingham and Goxhill. In many a church the craftsmanship of earlier centuries is given the good top light it deserves by great ranges of clerestory windows. At Barton-on-Humber (St. Peter's), at Ingoldmells in Marshland, at Frieston and Pinchbeck in the Fens, at Normanton on the limestone and Brant Broughton in the clays you can admire the technical virtuosity and confidence of the culmination of Gothic architecture. In hundreds of churches too there are minor additions and improvements made at this time which are ordinary and uninspired, where technical skill is no more than adequate and inspiration is quite lacking.

I cannot hope to do justice to all the building of this later age; let us linger for a moment with two whose history is well known. Tattershall church was built fairly rapidly in the years following 1440, by Ralph Lord Cromwell, for a time Lord Treasurer of England, and a great builder. His collegiate church was only part of a great conception of castle, collegiate church, almshouses, and school. The church is but a skeleton now that it has lost its medieval glass; the stone pulpitum or screen, the carved wooden pulpit, the brasses of the Cromwells and various members of the college, can only suggest its former wealth. The other church to linger on is the parish church of Louth, where the body of the church was rebuilt in the early fifteenth century, and the spire erected between 1501 and 1515. From the building accounts for

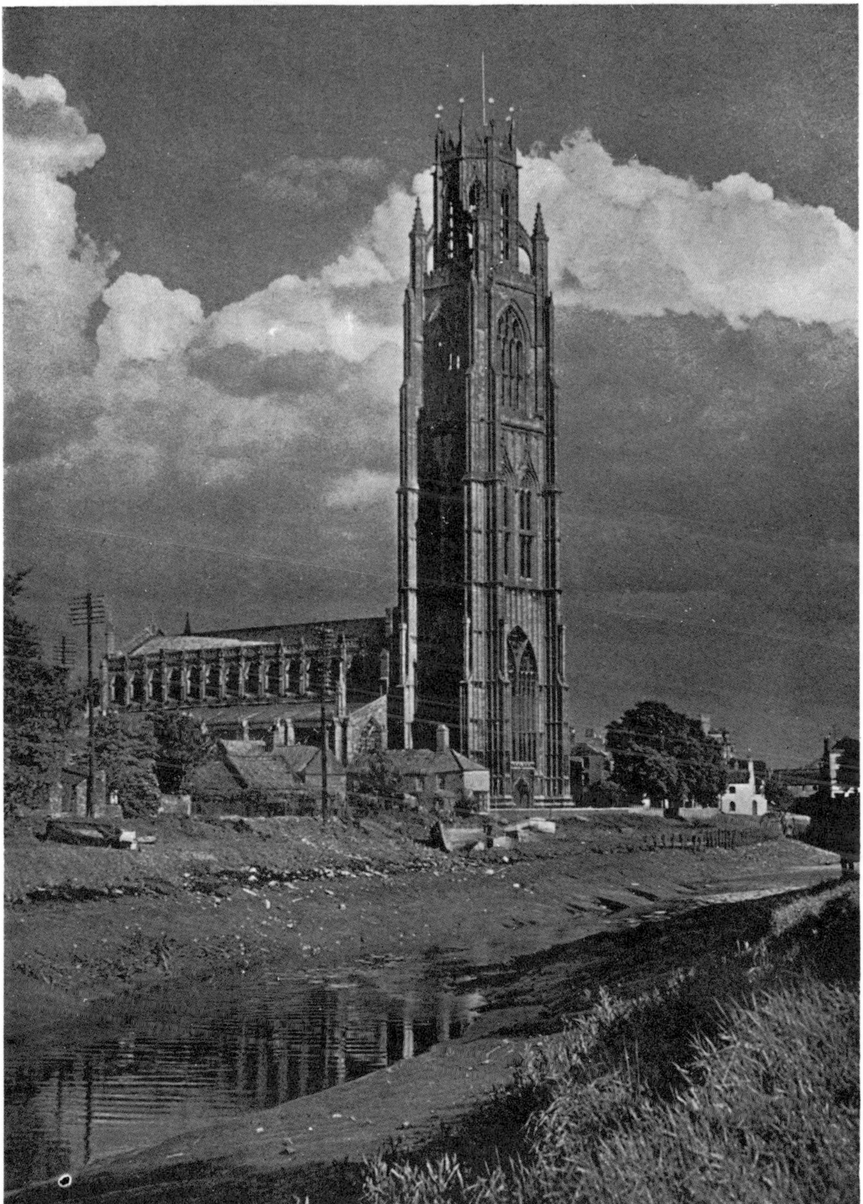

24 A great fifteenth-century parish church: Boston

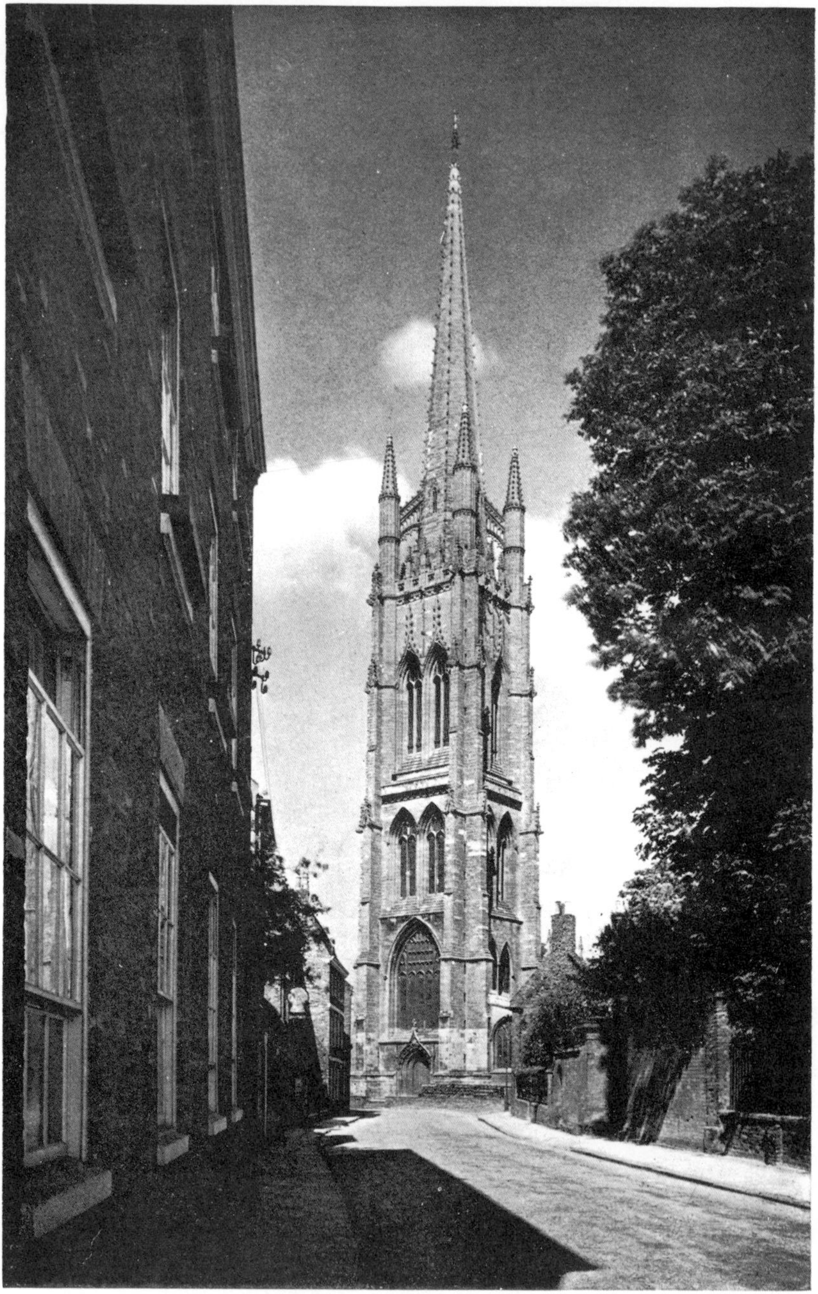

25 The finest spire in England: Louth (completed in 1515)

the latter we know that this, the most perfect spire in England, represents the welding into one glorious achievement of the ideas of two different master masons, backed by all the energies of the small town (25). No wonder that on the day the weathercock was raised, "William Ayleby, parish priest, with many of his brethren priests there present, hallowing the said weathercock and the stone that it stands upon, and then the priests singing *Te Deum laudamus* with organs, and the kirkwardens garred ring all the bells, and caused all the people there being to have bread and ale, and all the loving of God, Our Lady, and All Saints". Louth spire and Boston Stump (24) are two of Lincolnshire's finest buildings, and they both belong to this latter span of the Middle Ages when civic pride had linked itself with religious observances and supplanted enthusiasm for the distant cathedral or even the neighbouring monastery.

After the Reformation there was little urge for church building. The scramble for monastic lands by the gentry was imitated by the village folk: a vestment could be made into a doublet, as it was at Denton, and a stone altar slab would make a convenient table in a new dovecote, as it did (and still does) at Barholme. Some villages could no longer maintain buildings of an earlier age: at Mumby Chapel (or Chapel St. Leonard's as it now is) the churchwardens secured a faculty in 1612 to pull down the south aisle, "the chapel being in ruin and decay, and its size being such compared with the fewness of the inhabitants that some part of it might be demolished". While parishioners sometimes found the maintenance of the nave a heavy burden, more than one rector refused to carry his responsibility for the chancel: the sad aspect of the Marshland churches of Addlethorpe and Ingoldmells is due to the fact that a rector who held them in plurality was allowed in 1708 to demolish both chancels. The roofs had fallen in by 1650 and this was the easiest way out. The chancel of a church was after all regarded almost as private property: there is the extraordinary case of Tattershall, where Lord Fortescue in 1757 gave the medieval glass to Lord Exeter. The villagers objected strongly, and threatened to recruit the help of the Witham boatmen (always a tough and unruly lot) to assist them; but they could not prevent the glass being taken, and Lord Fortescue's steward then defaulted on his promise to reglaze the windows, "as it would only please the people, who have no concern therein, as the chancel belongs entirely to my Lord". The chancel was open to the weather for about fifty years; what is left of its glass can be seen in St. Martin's, Stamford, the parish church of Lord Exeter, the recipient in this strange transaction.

But it is easy to exaggerate the neglect and lethargy of the eighteenth century; the truth is that repairs and restoration were carried out by every generation, as they had to be in buildings that were in continuous use. There is a pleasant Elizabethan church at Carlton-le-Moorland; the tower and spire of Ruskington were rebuilt after collapse in 1618. Much of this work continued to be done in the Gothic style; the nave of King's Lynn parish church was rebuilt, after a storm, but the new work in eighteenth-century Gothic, like the tower and spire at Deeping St. James (1717) has a rather strange look. On the other hand, the oddest thing about the reconstruction of Kirton in Holland in 1804, when all but the nave of the great cruciform church was destroyed, is that the new west tower is perfectly good Gothic—not the self-conscious Gothic of the eighteenth-century revival, but looking like the work of a mason who knew no other way of building. The same is true of Sutterton near by, where the tower and spire were rebuilt in 1787; and at Doddington near Lincoln, close by the Elizabethan house, is a church rebuilt in 1771 which is a creditable copy of its medieval predecessor.

When masons built in stone they kept alive the Gothic vernacular; where brick was the most convenient material, the classical style was inevitable.[1] We should have a much larger inheritance of Georgian churches if the style had not been despised and many of them rebuilt in Gothic in the nineteenth century. All that survives in the towns is the handsome nave of Gainsborough parish church, built by Francis Smith of Warwick in 1745; Brigg had a charming church which was replaced in 1842 by a Gothic corpse; in Lincoln St. Peter at Arches, a dignified building which served as the town church, had to be removed to make room for traffic, and now stands strangely in the middle of a suburban housing estate. In the countryside most of the Georgian churches have gone: Stallingborough, Gautby, Cherry Willingham survive. The most attractive of all is Langton by Spilsby, built in 1725 but described in the Red Guide as "a comparatively modern brick church" because the author could not credit such a pleasant building to the eighteenth century! It stands amid trees in the beautiful Somersby valley and is quite unspoilt. A peal of six bells was hung in the small belfry in the nineteenth century, but as the population was tiny then (as now), a mechanical ringer was put in, on the principle of the musical box, turned by an enormous handle. At Wilsthorpe, near Stamford, there was built in 1719 a small stone church that would be as charming as Langton if it had not fallen into the hands of Victorian restorers who made it a bastard affair. What changes the Victorians wrought can be seen

[1] These remarks on eighteenth-century building owe much to Mr. Howard Colvin.

by looking through the four large volumes of drawings done around 1800 by Claud Nattes for Sir Joseph Banks;[1] the generation of 1835 to 1865 very nearly wiped out the work of the preceding 150 years, as well as falsifying much of the medieval inheritance. On the credit side there are a few well-proportioned buildings, such as George Gilbert Scott's Nocton and St. Nicholas, Lincoln; or St. Swithin's, Lincoln, built by Fowler of Louth in imitation of his own parish church. None of them is alive, brought to life, as medieval churches are, by the loving craftsmanship backed by the reverence, or irreverence, and even at times we should call indecency, of medieval masons. One exception I admit: the Pre-Raphaelite windows at Morton near Gainsborough. There is Gothic stained glass which is not merely striking a Gothic attitude, but that is not enough to show that medieval modes of thought can be recaptured.

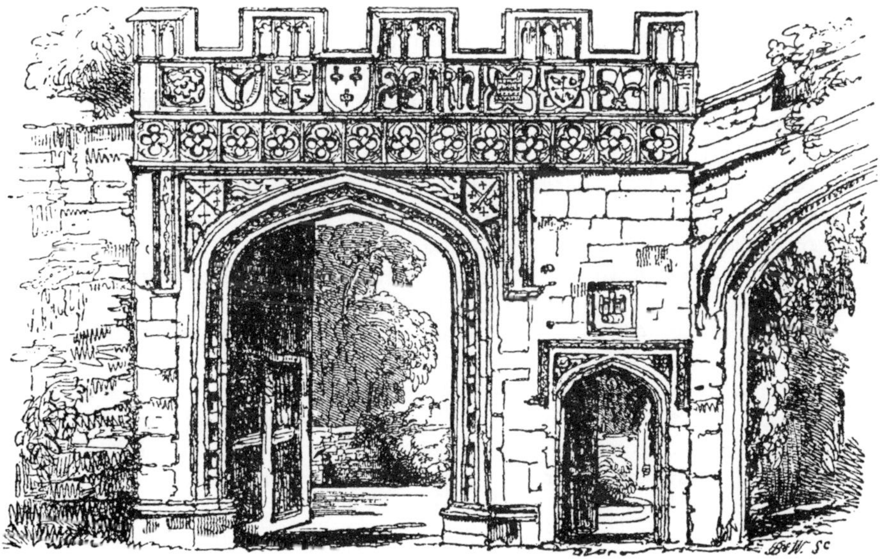

Peterborough: Gateway to the Deancry.
From an engraving after W. H. Bartlett, 1830.

[1] They are now in the Lincoln City Library.

Chapter

IV

Castles and Country Houses

THOSE who go in search of castles in Lincolnshire will find, first of all, Lincoln (27) and Ely: castles of royal origin, key strongholds commanding without rival large areas, and both retaining their twelfth-century character. Apart from them, only Tattershall (26) and Somerton (31) still stand to any extent, and at Folkingham, Castle Bytham, Bolingbroke, and Castle Carlton there are few if any traces of masonry. Bourne, Sleaford, Stamford, and Wisbech once had castles; they are gone. The bishops of Lincoln were among the largest feudal lords of Lincolnshire, and they built their greatest strongholds outside the county—at Newark and Banbury (as well as Sleaford)—and later their manor-houses at Liddington (Rutland) and Buckden (Huntingdonshire); so, for geographical reasons, and others connected with the enduring social makeup of Lincolnshire, the most ambitious country houses of the fifteenth to the eighteenth centuries are elsewhere. Isolated to some extent from the main course of traffic, Lincolnshire has not for that reason been a refuge of feudal lords commanding the loyalty of a simple peasantry, but, because of the wealth of the land, rather a stronghold of free peasants, as wealthy as any in England, among whom feudalism could not find the same foothold as in Northumberland or Cornwall. Similarly the country houses of a later period did not, with the possible exception of Grimsthorpe (37) and Belton (38), rival the great houses of other counties such as Castle Howard, Burghley, or Stowe, whether their owners and builders wished them to do or not. In most cases they did not wish; Charles Pelham, who rebuilt Brocklesby in about 1730, lived unpretentiously among his tenants, and was unique in receiving as a bequest the land and savings of one of his tenants.

The equivalent in Lincolnshire of the house of the grandee is Gunby Hall (now the property of the National Trust) or an Elizabethan house like Doddington Hall, which must have seemed very homely to the eighteenth-century Delavals compared with Seaton Delaval. In addition there are many manor-houses of great character but modest dimensions, not standing aloof in their parks but part of the village they belong to, whether it is a brick village of the Fens or a stone village in Kesteven.

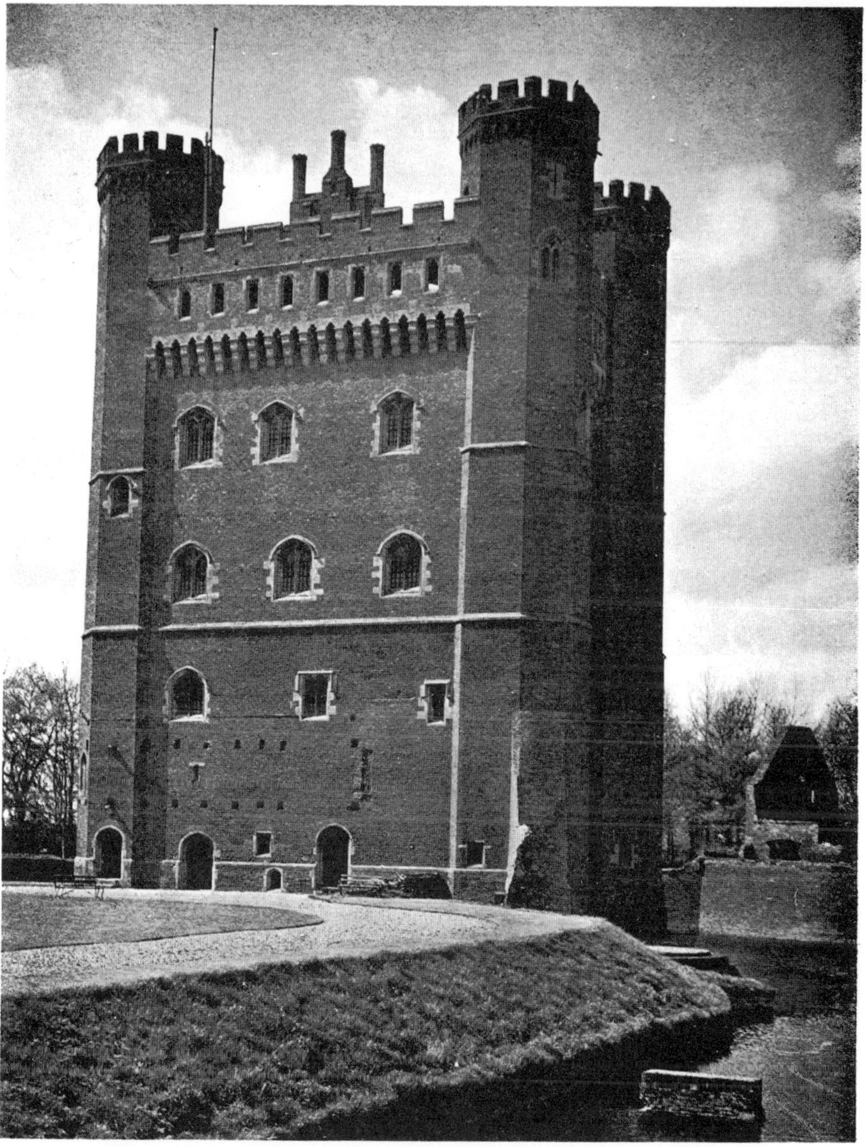

26 Ralph Cromwell's luxurious stronghold in the Witham valley: Tattershall Castle (1433–55)

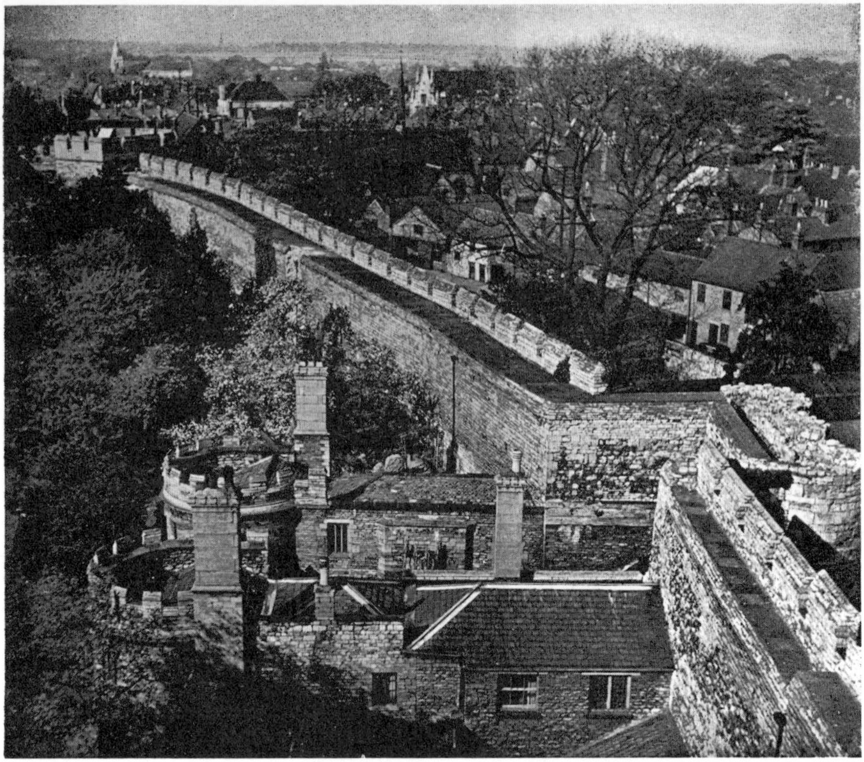

27 The Castle walls and east gate

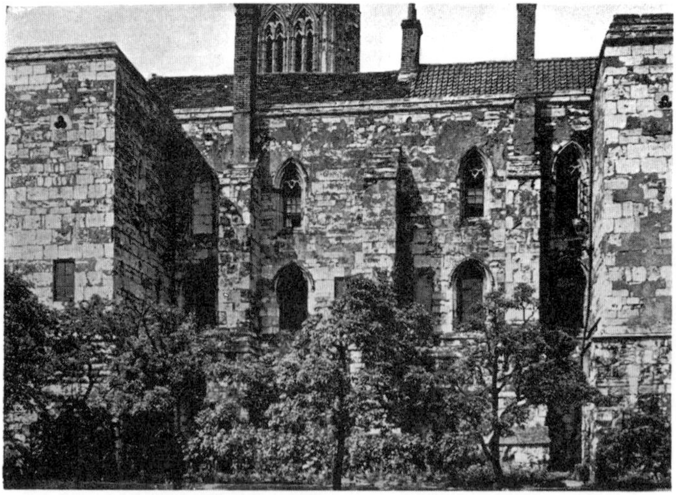

28 South side of Vicar's Court (fourteenth century)

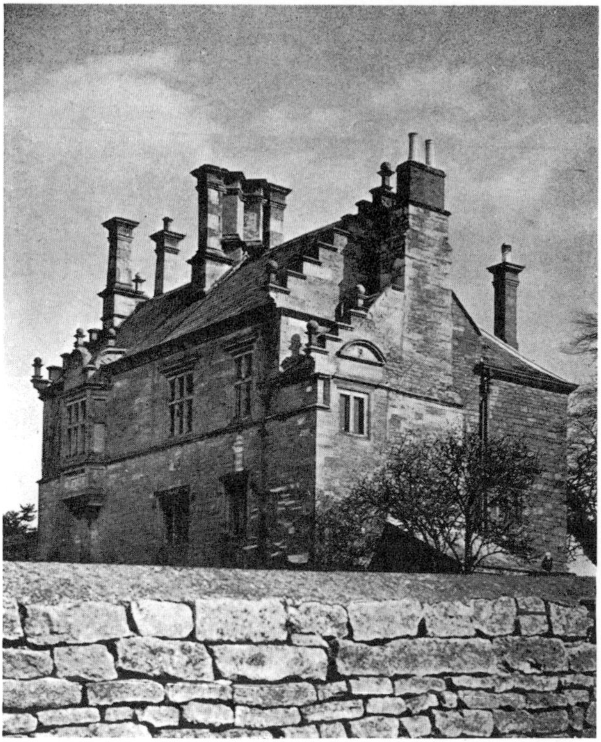

29 Thomas Coney's manor house at Bassingthorpe (1568)

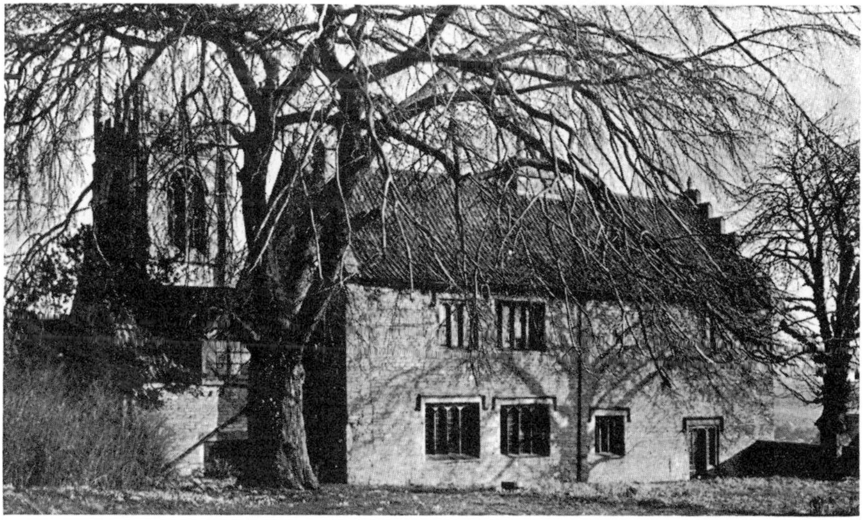

30 Anthony Ellys' house at Great Ponton (*c.* 1516) and the west tower which he built

MERCHANTS' COUNTRY HOUSES

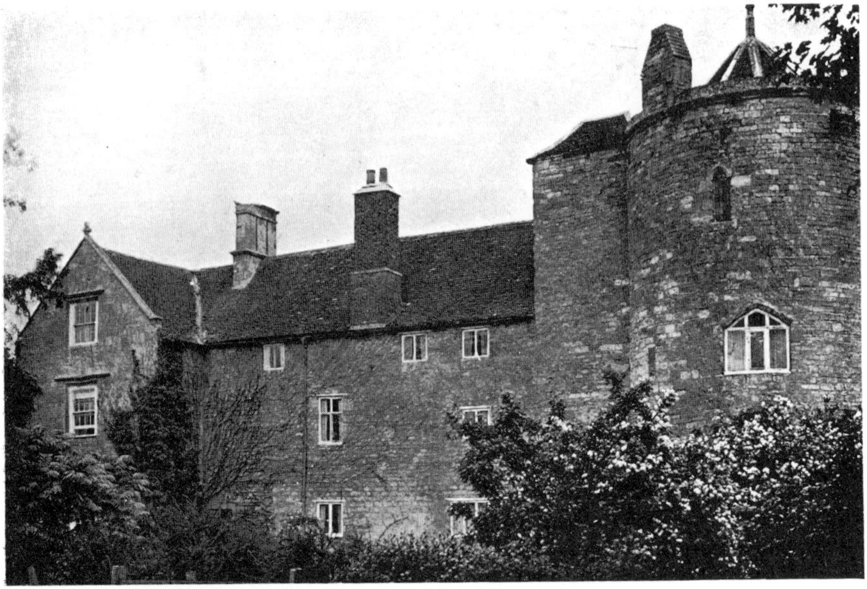

31 Somerton Castle: thirteenth-century tower and Jacobean house

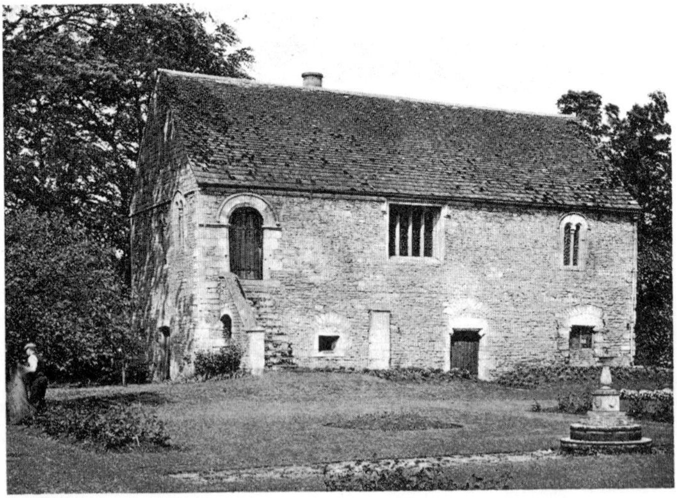

32 Boothby Pagnell Manor House (*c.* 1200)

How many medieval manor-houses have gone can be guessed by the moated sites where the buildings have disappeared and the moats are dry. It was not only the small landowner or squire who in the fourteenth or fifteenth century thought it wise and dignified to surround his home with such defences: Thornton Abbey had its moat, as well as the strong gatehouse and barbican, and of the tiny religious houses in the Marshland, Markby, Hagnaby, and Greenfield adopted the same precaution. Those whose fate or fortune placed them in the low grounds, and denied them the security of a site like Castle Bytham or Bolingbroke, felt they needed artificial defences; in the Marshland, at the eastern foot of the limestone and in the clays between Witham and Ancholme these deserted moats abound. Sometimes the line between a moated manor-house and a castle is hard to draw: by the river Witham near Beckingham a slight natural hill now called Cumberland Hill, has been so strengthened with double ditches at the foot of the slope that it wears a strangely impressive and prehistoric look. It was a fortified manor-house of the Furnivals until the fourteenth century; there is no trace of masonry to be seen now, and local tradition is silent about it. At the other extreme a village like Scredington with its five small moats reveals the unusual form that the manorial system took in Lincolnshire, as we shall see later.

The castle at Lincoln is, as we see it today, a parade of nearly a thousand years of history, from its Norman ramparts (27) to its nineteenth-century Assize Courts; in effect it is nearly two thousand years old, if one recalls that the Norman builders piled the earth rampart over the west wall and rampart of the Roman *colonia*, making a bank twenty to thirty feet high and fifty to sixty yards wide. Archaeologists are tantalised by the thought of the Roman west gate preserved under that great bank of earth.[1] By comparison with Lincoln, the small motte and bailey castle which William built at Ely after the revolt of 1070, is charming but insignificant, and it was dwarfed by the rebuilding of the cathedral church in the following century. Lincoln is unusual in having two mounds (Lewes is the only other example), both commanding the steep southern slope of the hill; that on the south-east, crowned now by the nineteenth-century observation tower built by a prison governor who liked studying the stars (and, incidentally, any attempted escapes), is the older. The second mound, only a short distance away to the west, is one of the finest examples in England of a Norman shellkeep. It was once approached from the inside, like the castles shown in the Bayeux Tapestry, by a drawbridge over its ditch. The Norman east gate on Castle Hill is now

[1] A charming drawing of the Roman gate, as it was discovered in 1836, is reproduced in Professor I. A. Richmond's *Roman Britain.*

somewhat hidden by the thirteenth-century alterations, but on the other side the west gate, not normally accessible to visitors, is quite unaltered. Within the precincts, the old prison with a façade by Carr of York, and the Assize Courts in early nineteenth-century Gothic by Robert Smirke, make a pleasant contrast. The prison has a gruesome fascination to the twentieth-century visitor; it is more interesting to historians as it is to become the repository for all the records of the diocese, the city, and the three ancient parts of Lincolnshire—the finest and largest collection of local records in England.

Lincoln Castle must have been one of the first to receive stone walls on its earth ramparts(27); at Kinnard Castle, by the Trent and guarding the approach from Lincolnshire to the Mowbray domain, the Isle of Axholme, is a large motte and bailey castle which probably never had such defences. Later the Mowbrays moved their stronghold to Epworth. Owston church, like Cuckney not far away in Nottinghamshire, stands within the bailey of the castle. At Barrow-on-Humber the earthwork called the Castles is perhaps another early Norman castle; it has never been excavated, except by a mythical Dane who, according to local tradition came, dug, found what he expected, and took whatever it was back to Denmark with him. It is a curious example of the endurance of the notion of Scandinavian connections.

At Castle Bytham the great mound has reverted to the same condition as Kinnard Castle. It must have been built by Drogo de Bevrere, the Norman lord of Holderness, who raised the even larger motte and bailey there at Skipsea, and Bytham, like Kinnard Castle, is clearly early Norman in date. Henry III besieged it in 1221; it figured in the Wars of the Roses, and was destroyed in a conflagration some time before Leland examined the remnants of its walls. The other Norman castles at Bourne and Folkingham have vanished too: Folkingham was going to ruin when Leland saw it; Bourne is supposed to have been slighted by the Parliamentarians after the Civil War, but there can have been little left for them to destroy.

It is an astonishing and unexpected contrast with such vast works, and knowing the insecurity of the mid-twelfth century (Kinnard Castle was put in order during the rebellion of 1173–4) to be able to turn to a house, in the middle of the limestone country of Kesteven, built a short generation after 1175 without any defences whatsoever. The charming manor-house at Boothby Pagnell makes the usual concession to the times of having its living quarters on the first floor, over a vaulted undercroft(32). The simple layout provides a hall with a fireplace, and next to it a solar without heating; presumably the kitchen was a lean-to building on ground-level. Its nearest cousin in time as well as in space is Oakham, not far away, where the castle defences are later than the ornate hall.

South Kyme, on the edge of the Fens, has not only part of the small priory of Austin canons, but also the tower keep of a mid-thirteenth-century castle built by Gilbert de Umfraville. It is Lincolnshire's only example of its type and age, though in its commanding isolation it suggests comparison with Tattershall and other fifteenth-century towers. The medieval origin of Grimsthorpe Castle is lost to sight under rebuilding, but Somerton and Bolingbroke are interesting examples of later castles, square on plan with corner towers. Bolingbroke became the property of the duchy of Lancaster, and in later centuries the yearly audit for the whole of the duchy was held there; its sandstone walls and towers long withstood the attack of time, and the last remnants fell down only in 1815. At Somerton (31) the good Ancaster freestone has lasted better; one of the corner towers is more or less complete, and remains of another, of rubble limestone from Navenby, are visible incorporated in the farm buildings, and flanking the Elizabethan house which was built out of the materials. It was a small, fortified residence built by Anthony Bek, the son of a Lincolnshire landowner who made a successful career in the Church. He was always much interested in hunting, fighting, and politics, and seized all opportunities for magnificent display. After he was made bishop of Durham in 1283 he built a new banqueting-hall in the castle there, which is now the dining-hall of the university, and endowed a couple of collegiate churches in his diocese. When his overpowering behaviour lost him the favour of Edward I, he tried to appease the king by presenting Somerton castle to him.

The use of Somerton castle as prison for such a distinguished political prisoner as the king of France from August 1359 to March 1360 gives us a chance to see the style which a medieval king maintained even when he was a prisoner, under the pleasant condition of feudal warfare. King John arrived under the escort of William Baron D'Eyncourt and was guarded by forty-four men on the week's journey from Hertford to Somerton. Once established the king used his own resources (eked out by those of Henry Piquart, Edward III's banker, from whom he borrowed largely) to make himself as comfortable as the king of Europe's most civilised country expected him to be. It is difficult to see how the Constable, Sir Henry de Greystoke, and the guards found room alongside John's establishment of chaplains, a doctor, a *maître d'hôtel*, pages, valets, wardrobe men, furriers, grooms, cooks, fruiterer, spiceman, barber, washer, musician, and fool, as well as the purely menial staff; John had already been compelled to reduce his household staff by half. He secured tables, chairs, and forms, no doubt for the hall; for his own room and those of Philip his son and Jean the jester (who came next in popularity, if not in rank) hangings, cushions, and the like. His agents in London, Boston, and Lincoln purchased sugar, powdered ginger, green aniseed, mace, cinnamon, cloves, and lemon conserve; and the usual medicaments —scammony, senna, fine rhubarb, and balsamic syrup. The king's wardrobe had to be replenished, and he ordered from Brussels a suit of marbled violet velvet trimmed with miniver, and another of scarlet lined with blue taffeta. Furs for other garments were bought in Lincoln, and indeed a regular tailoring establishment was set up in the city to supply the royal household. His captivity was not irksome; he was able to spend money on jewellery—a sapphire engraved with a head in intaglio, a sapphire ring enclosing a relic—and silver dishes and cups. His books were rebound, and a new psalter purchased in Lincoln, and even in that cathedral city of medieval England, such French romances as the "Romans de Renart". It was not necessary to interrupt his patronage of painting, and music he could hear on a harp, or on the organ he brought from Hertford. The priest of Navenby came to sing *Ergo Laudes* in the castle chapel and Edward III's own minstrels came to entertain him. His leisure he passed with chess and backgammon. Fortunately for us his household accounts were so well kept that they include even the value of the *cote hardie* which he lost to Tassin, his Lincoln tailor, when they were playing chess; the cost of his falcons and dogs; and of the reward to "one English peasant" who came to the castle with a gift of pears.

In August 1360, for political reasons, John was moved to Berkhampstead; the forty-four armed guards set off again to lead the slow procession of king and royal prince, their staff and twelve waggons of baggage, on the slow journey through Navenby to Grantham, Stamford and the south. Lincolnshire never again saw a medieval household of such a lavish and cultured kind. Bolingbroke, on the other side of the county, was at this time the favourite residence of John of Gaunt, Duke of Lancaster, another great feudal lord who was also a patron of the arts and artists, and here his son Henry IV was born in 1367. At Kettlethorpe, a few miles north of Somerton, only the gateway remains of the moated house of Sir Hugh Swynford, whose widow Catherine was first mistress, then wife, of John of Gaunt. Catherine's sister Phillipa may have been that Phillipa whom Chaucer married in 1366, and it is possible that the poet knew all these three Lincolnshire houses.

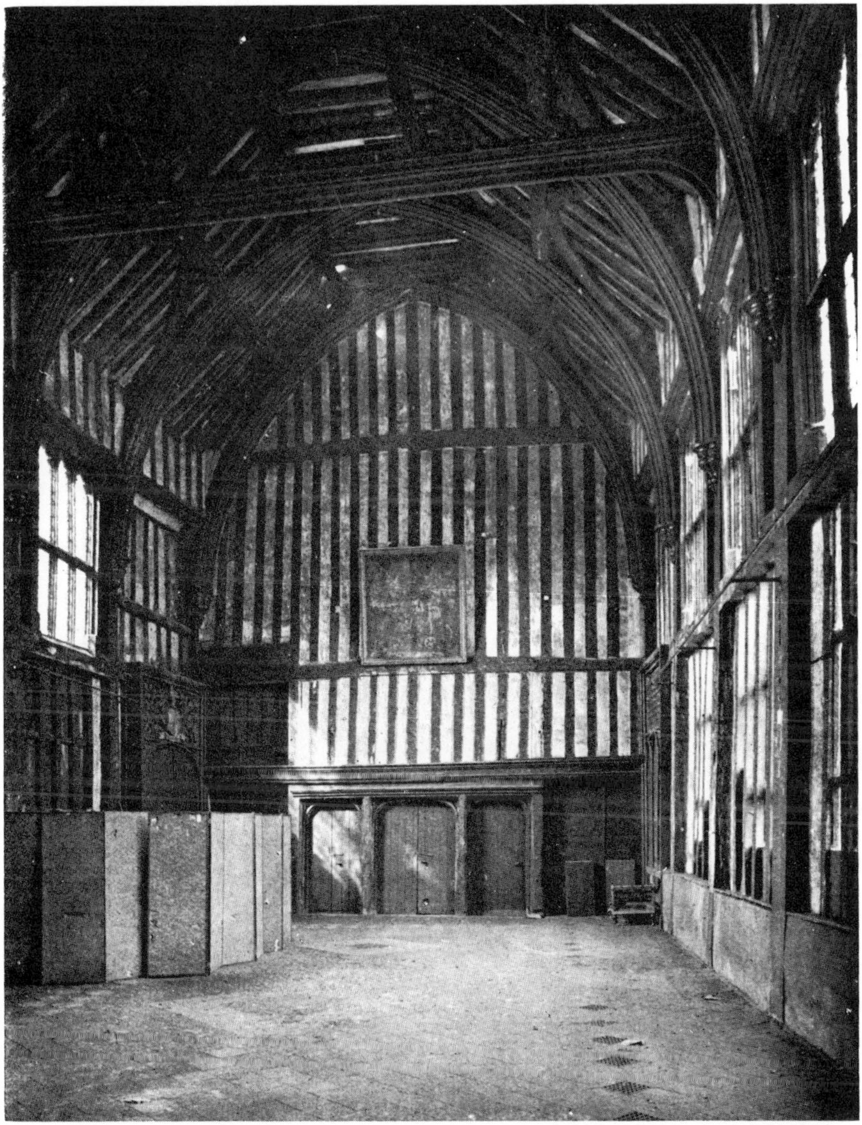

33 Gainsborough Old Hall: the hall, looking towards the screen's end (*c*. 1480)

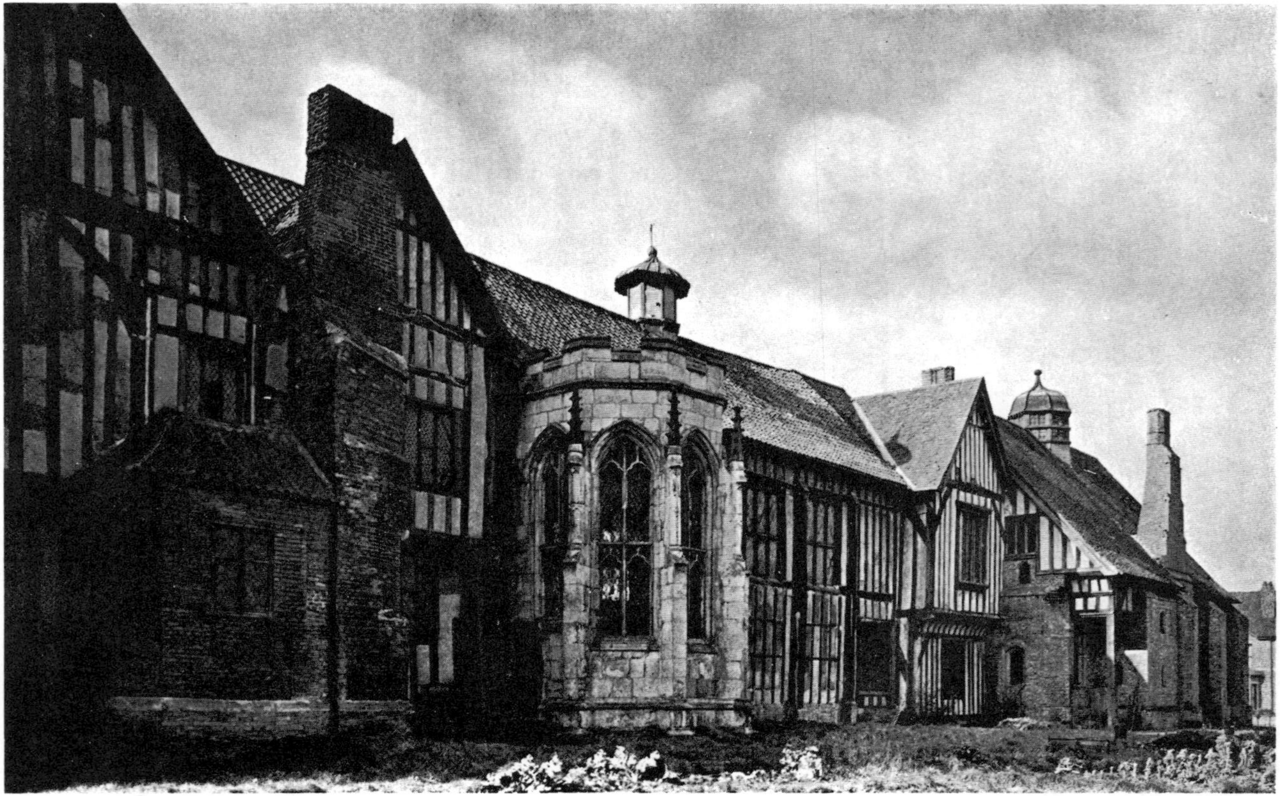

34 Gainsborough Old Hall

Of all the one hundred and twenty or more moated sites in Lincolnshire and the Fens, none is better known today than Tattershall (26). Very few of the thirteenth- and fourteenth-century feudal lords chose Fenland for their homes; there are only two moated sites in the Isle of Axholme, a few in the north-east fen between Boston and Wainfleet, and one or two between Boston and King's Lynn. Nor do we know why Ralph Cromwell should have chosen to build here in such a splendid way, when he had wide estates and resources in Nottinghamshire, whence his family came, and in Derbyshire, where he built South Wingfield manor-house. But it was at Tattershall that he started in 1433, on a site close to the river Witham, where, in the middle of the thirteenth century, Robert of Tattershall had built a modest castle with a curtain wall and angle towers like those at Somerton. Cromwell's scheme was on the grandest scale; it embraced not only a castle suitable for one of the most powerful (and unpopular) men in England, who when he rode abroad was accompanied by 120 mounted retainers; it also included a collegiate church, a school, and almshouses. The scheme was consonant with his worldly dignity and his obligations to God. Such conceptions were in the minds of men like Cromwell at this time; they had before them the example of Henry VI, who was founding his college of Eton, close to Windsor Castle. From what is left at Tattershall we can scarcely see enough to judge either its scale or character; the collegiate buildings east of the church have gone, and the almshouses now standing on the north side were rebuilt later. The castle itself has lost its curtain wall, which Cromwell retained from the previous building; this leaves the tower in deceptive isolation and makes it appear a throw-back to the twelfth-century keep, which it is not. Dr. Douglas Simpson has pointed out that as well as importing a north German mason to supervise the manufacture of the bricks at near-by Edlington Moor, Cromwell also imported ideas developed in Prussia by the Teutonic knights. The most important was the necessity of segregating the unruly and possibly unreliable retainers, who lived in the outer ward, from the lord and his family, who with their more intimate servants enjoyed the comfort and seclusion of the magnificent tower. Tattershall Castle is therefore in one sense a monument to the century when feudalism was disintegrating; old loyalties were dying and new compulsions had not yet arisen. But it is also a magnificent piece of brickwork, and the finest tower built in England since the Norman tower keeps. It was widely imitated: the bishops of Lincoln's palace at Buckden has a close likeness, and nearer at hand there are the smaller copies by local landowners—Hussey Tower and Rochford Tower on the outskirts of Boston, and

Tower on the Moor near Woodhall Spa. The Hussey and Rochford towers have both lost the houses which were once attached to them. It is a pity to have to admit that the Hussey Tower is shamefully neglected by the corporation of Boston; can a municipal body not equal, or at least imitate, the scholarly and thorough restoration of Tattershall by Lord Curzon?

The medieval houses in towns have not fared altogether well. The bishop's medieval palace in Lincoln itself, occupying a magnificent site immediately below the Minster, and arranged in a series of great terraces with the finest view imaginable, has not been rebuilt since the Royalists fired and looted it in the Civil War. The great aisled hall had arcades and window shafts of Purbeck marble similar in style to the great hall of Winchester castle; south of it were the service rooms with a solar over and beyond a kitchen with five enormous fireplaces. East of this original building of the early thirteenth century are later medieval additions and enlargements over vaulted undercrofts, which seem to go deep into the side of the hill. It is a pity that these impressive ruins cannot be properly preserved and made accessible to visitors. Of the smaller houses of the close, only the one which forms the south side of Vicar's Court has kept most of its medieval features(28). At Spalding, Ayscoughfee Hall, built in the fifteenth century by Sir Richard Aldwyn, and later the property of the Ayscoughs, bears now almost no resemblance to the house drawn by Nattes in 1791. Gainsborough Old Hall(34) is a remarkably fine example of a house of about 1480; considering that it has not been occupied as a house for nearly two hundred years its survival is miraculous, but the growth of modern Gainsborough has robbed it of its moat, curtain wall and gatehouse. The house of timber, brick and stone still survives with its magnificent hall and oriel window lighting the dais; behind the dais a wide spiral staircase of wood goes up to the solar and to the gallery in the east wing; at the lower end of the hall the large kitchens are intact. Lord Burgh built it after the previous manor-house had been destroyed by his Lancastrian enemies; a century later the west wing, with its range of chimneys, was added. The Burgh family has gone, and the Hickmans who succeeded them ceased to occupy the house after they bought Thonock in 1714. Now at last the town of Gainsborough is faced squarely with the problem of its inheritance. The house has gone through many vicissitudes, none more curious perhaps than when John Wesley preached there in 1759 to "a wild multitude", but has never in the past lacked the care of its owners.

Gainsborough Old Hall, though it is not fortified, belongs to the Middle Ages, and soon after it was built the changed conditions of the Tudor age brought opportunity to new men. Very few of the medieval families of standing survived into the sixteenth and seventeenth centuries, and those that did came mainly from the second rank. Several families left the Fens for the higher ground. The Copledikes moved from Coupledyke Hall in Frieston to Harrington in the Wolds; the Welbys from Moulton to Denton in Henry VIII's time, and the Heron family from Cressy Hall, Surfleet, to Stubton in the early eighteenth century. At the other end of the county the Sheffield family migrated from Epworth in the Isle across the Trent to the heights of Normanby Park. John Sheffield, third earl of Mulgrave and friend of Pope and Dryden, moved the family monuments from Owston church to Burton-on-Stather. So it was with the Massingberds: Thomas Massingberd of Sutterton acquired property at Burgh-le-Marsh early in the fifteenth century; the family fortunes, built up by skilful farming and judicious trading, were put into land. Sir Thomas Massingberd lived in a moated manor-house north of Bratoft church until he moved to Gunby Hall shortly before 1500. When he died in 1552 he was frugally commemorated by the addition of a new inscription to the brass in Gunby church which had been laid down for his ancestor, another Thomas, a century and a half earlier. In the early seventeenth century Drayner Massingberd purchased Ormsby, the ancient seat of the Skipwith family. Like more than one Lincolnshire gentleman of his rank, he fought for Parliament in the Civil War; he was pardoned at the Restoration and knighted, but remained a confirmed Protestant, and for his known convictions was put under preventive arrest in Hull gaol during Monmouth's rebellion. He built up the family fortune on a solid if not spectacular basis which was to endure into the twentieth century. He enclosed the parishes of Ormsby and Ketsby in 1650, and devoted himself closely to the exploitation and improvement of his estate. The ancient demesne sheep-walks carried some 1,700 sheep; the wool was sold to clothiers from East Anglia and the West Riding. On occasion fat wethers were sold at Smithfield, and sanfoin seed in Cornhill; otherwise the economy of the establishment was purely local. Sheep and cattle were purchased at the many Wold fairs—Partney, Ketsby, Stainton, Spilsby, Horncastle and Louth; sheepskins were sold to a Horncastle glover. Coal was bought at the coast havens—Sutton, Mablethorpe and Theddlethorpe; claret and canary sack at Boston. The ponds were stocked with bream and tench ("bought at Stickford in straw without losing any one"), the garden planted in 1652 with apricot, nectarine, walnuts, pears—Bergamot and Bon Chrétien—half a dozen varieties of cherry and forty apple stocks for his gardener to graft.

This is the careful husbandry of the yeoman, and it enabled his grandson to make a new park and then to rebuild Ormsby Hall in 1752. Another branch of the family, one member of which was an eminent merchant and treasurer of the East India Company, built Gunby Hall, a charmingly simple brick house in the style of Wren.

The Bolle family, from beginnings in thirteenth-century Swineshead and Gosberton, moved up-country, one branch to Scampton, where they built a house on the site of a grange belonging to Kirkstead Abbey, another to Haugh near Alford. There John Bolle was born in 1560, into a world which offered different opportunities from those which had faced his ancestors. He served alongside Essex and Raleigh in the attack on Cadiz in 1596. Among the prisoners was a Spanish lady who fell in love with her captor.

Will you hear a Spanish lady
How she wooed an English man?
Garments gay, as rich as may be,
Decked with jewels she had on.

So the ballad goes, as Bishop Percy preserved it. Some of the jewels she gave him before she retired to a nunnery are dispersed among his descendants, but her portrait, showing her in a green dress, has disappeared. Sir John Bolle served in Ireland under Essex, and died at Thorpe Hall, the house which he had built for himself at Louth. It is much altered now, and the gables of the Elizabethan west side are balanced by a small Queen Anne façade on the east.

Another family which moved from the Fens to the higher ground was the Cust family of Pinchbeck. They had a small estate there (still owned by the Earl of Ancaster) in the fourteenth century. In Charles I's time they were still only substantial yeomen, with an estate of 156 acres, and Henry Cust's solid Puritan convictions were incompatible with the kind of worldly ambition of many of his contemporaries. But Henry made his son Samuel a lawyer—one of the most profitable professions of the time—and so began the process of lifting the family into the ranks of the gentry. Successful marriages led to increased income (£1,000 a year in 1654), the obtaining of a grant of arms, a baronetcy, a house in Stamford, and the grand tour of the Continent for Richard's son Percy. Richard's life looks back to that of his father, the Fen yeoman; Percy was a young man in Restoration England, and when he died in 1699 he left his young heir hopelessly in debt. But this Sir Richard by 1735 had retrieved the position; he married Anne Brownlow, sister and heiress to

Viscount Tyrconnel, and of one-quarter of the large Brownlow estate.

The Brownlow estate was based on one of the largest fortunes made in the law in Stuart England. Its founder was Richard Brownlow, who, as Chief Protonotary of the Court of Common Pleas, had an income of £6,000 a year from his position; he lived at the rate of £2,000 a year and invested the balance in land in Lincolnshire, whence his family had originally sprung. His personal account book (1616–17) has after the figures such sentiments as these: "The Lord gives increase and marvellous are his works, may His name be blessed now and for ever. He raised me from muck above my enemies, holding me in His hands, and placing me among the rich men of the world." I have translated it from Richard Brownlow's Latin, and I am sure the Lincolnshire word "muck" is what he intended by his Latin *stercus*. Brownlow's son John succeeded to an income of £4,000 a year and increased it to £8,000 by judicious purchase; he was made a baronet by Charles I, but was a Parliamentarian by sympathy, and spent most of his time at Belton, managing his large estates with a care and attention to detail which reflect his father's qualities and the yeoman origin of the family. He knew every item involved in the management of his flock of 1,000 sheep at Belton and Londonthorpe, and his account book shows how he hid bags of money and jewellery in boxes and cupboards about his several houses. Naturally, his great-nephew, when he succeeded, proceeded to rebuild the house at Belton (38). The old houses there and at Ringston were pulled down to provide stone; bricks were made on the estate, and the new house, for which Wren is said (without any evidence) to have provided the plans,[1] was completed by 1688. It would be instructive, if space permitted, to compare the contents of the yeoman's house, Croswithand at Pinchbeck, as it was in 1554, with the furniture in the new home; the inventories and many other documents of this remarkable family history were carefully edited by Lady Elizabeth Cust. The carvings by Grinling Gibbons, the fine plaster ceilings, the tapestries from the factory at Stamford patronised by the Cecils and the Brownlows, the family portraits by Wissing, Reynolds, Romney, and Hoppner; all these have been preserved by the good fortune of unbroken male descent through fifteen or more generations. Belton church contains one of the finest series of monuments to be found in the county, to seventeenth- and eighteenth-century Custs and Brownlows. The house cost less than £1,500—a mere trifle compared with the £250,000 lavished on Castle Howard, and it is for that reason typical of

[1] It may have been designed by William Stanton, who was paid £4,921 for stone and marble work.

Lincolnshire where modest origins and the environment engendered a restraint less noticeable in other parts of England.

Such families as the Massingberds and the Custs chose, within their own county, a suitable field for their limited ambitions, and the Fens could not provide it. I have already commented that the larger houses of the gentry are not to be found there, any more than the medieval moated manor-house. This cannot be due to any dislike of Fen scenery; such romantic notions are out of place before the eighteenth century. Hawksmoor early in that century built Panton Hall, near Wragby, on a hilltop; it was rebuilt by Carr of York in 1770. Torrington, when he passed Syston Hall in 1790, spoke of Sir John Thorold's new house there being "stuck in the clouds". On the Lincoln Edge there are Coleby Hall (1628) with temples by Chambers in the gardens; Leadenham Old Hall (about 1700), and Fillingham Castle (1770), all making the most of their commanding position. But Torrington's view that "fens are not the seat of taste and pleasure" is the view of the Age of Taste; the seventeenth-century formal garden and yews of Ayscoughfee at Spalding are just as right there as anywhere, but no Capability Brown could arrange a fenland landscape. Apart from Ayscoughfee, there is one solitary example of a large Elizabethan house in the Fens—Beaupré Hall, near Wisbech; it has been falling into decay for two hundred years, and is now a shattered and roofless ruin. At Thorney, on the site of the monastery, the Earl of Bedford built a small house during the Commonwealth which has been ascribed to Webb because of its similarity to near-by Thorpe Hall. It is not a sumptuous house; it was built only because the earl was compelled for political reasons to live there, and it was his headquarters while he devoted himself to the draining of the Level. Once re-established at Woburn, the earls used the Thorney estate only to produce for Woburn large and steadily increasing supplies of corn, fat cattle, and the typical fenland crops, hemp and cole-seed.

Another family which climbed from yeoman beginnings to the social level of the Georgian peerage was that of Newton of Haydor, which shared ancestry with Newton of Woolsthorpe. At the Restoration Sir John Newton, the first baronet, bought Culverthorpe Hall, a late Elizabethan or Jacobean house, from the Bussey family, and rebuilt a good deal of it. Unfortunately the architect who created the very fine garden front is unknown. A generation later Sir Michael Newton made further improvements at the same time as his brother-in-law, Coke of Norfolk, first Lord Leicester, was rebuilding Holkham.

The Lincolnshire tradition in timber buildings is nothing like as fine as that of the west midlands—mainly because timber was much less plentiful. Knaith Hall, an Elizabethan brick house, was given a black and white front in the last century, and in spite of its charming situation by the Trent, it is a curious rather than handsome house. It is usually said to have been the birthplace of Thomas Sutton, the wealthy Elizabethan commoner who founded the Charterhouse, but he must have been born in an older house somewhere near by. Knaith Hall was built by Lord Willoughby of Parham; his wife was daughter and heiress of Sir Thomas Heneage, who was granted the buildings and lands of the nunnery of Heynings at the Dissolution. Sutton's fortune, made in Durham coal, went after his death in part to Lincoln city, but mainly to the Charterhouse, and he did not build in his native county. A far more handsome building is Doddington Hall, completed by about 1600 by Thomas Taylor, registrar to the Elizabethan bishops of Lincoln; his was another fortune made in law—not in the civil courts, but in the ecclesiastical courts, and no doubt the mark of many a Puritan comment at the time. The brick house is still perfect, and with its small gatehouse is the best Elizabethan building in the county. A few miles away are the ruins of Torksey Castle, a handsome Elizabethan house built by Sir Ambrose Jermyn. His son was a Royalist, and had to abandon his home to the Lincolnshire Parliamentarians. The Newark Royalists burned it on one of their raiding forays, and all we can see is the façade, with the flood water of the Trent lapping its foundations.

Time and change have not been kind to the gentry of Tudor Lincolnshire and their work. Of the dozen parks shown on Saxton's map of 1576, only two—Grimsthorpe and Irnham—remain. They were probably all ancient deer parks, and have given way to the demands of high farming. Of the men who came promptly and as if by right into the ownership of monastic estates, few established lasting properties. Thomas Grantham, a wealthy Lincoln merchant, purchased from the Duke of Suffolk the site of St. Catherine's Priory, on the southern outskirts of the city, and built there a large mansion in which his grandson early in the seventeenth century entertained James I and "kept the old hospitality of England, having a great retinue and a noble table, and [was] a resort of all the nobility and gentry of those parts". The house was pulled down in the eighteenth century. The estates of Lord Hussey in Sleaford passed to Robert Carre, who was, said Leland, "a proper gentleman, whose father was a rich merchant of the Staple". The Carre family have their monuments in Sleaford in brass and alabaster in the church, and in the Grammar School they endowed in 1604; the Hospital which they founded in 1636 stands on the site of their first house. The Carres were at this time among the wealthiest commoners of England; the line died out in 1683. They had come originally from Northumberland, and were only one among many northern families to invade Lincolnshire, where promise was richer than among the dales and fells. Anthony Ellys, a merchant of the Staple, built himself a house at Great Ponton, which still survives, close to the great tower of the church which is his monument. At Bassingthorpe near by, Thomas Coney, another wool merchant and a very wealthy one, built himself a modest house which is Lincolnshire's most attractive Elizabethan home. Ambitious dalesmen like Sir Christopher Wray of Glentworth, successful merchants like William Holles, mercer and alderman of London, and many a Lancashire yeoman's family like Isaac Newton's contributed largely to the new gentry of Tudor Lincolnshire. At the Dissolution of the monasteries the plums fell in clusters into the laps of a few—notably Edward Lord Clinton and Charles Brandon, Duke of Suffolk. The single fruit such men sold again immediately; Grantham of Lincoln purchased St. Catherine's from the Duke of Suffolk; Carre of Sleaford bought Sleaford Castle and manor from Lord Clinton. Much land came by this process to the men whose ancestors had frequently given the land to the monasteries in the first place, who had themselves been stewards to the monastic houses, and no doubt regarded the dispersal of the property as its return to rightful owners. Among such were Sir Thomas Heneage and his brother John; no family gained more than theirs from the suppression. They had owned Hainton since the thirteenth century, and the endurance of the estate into the twentieth reflects the saying of Lord Burghley which Sir George Heneage in 1625 wrote for his infant son's benefit into the family estate book: "He which selleth an acre loseth an ounce of Credit, Gentility being nothing but ancient Riches, so that if the foundation do sink the building must needs consequently follow."

Soldiers and sailors figured among the Elizabethan gentry of the county. Sir William Monson, born at South Carlton, distinguished himself in the attack on Cadiz, and later became vice-admiral of the fleet under the Earl of Lindsey. His elder brother, Sir Thomas Monson, after being master of the armoury at the Tower, retired to South Carlton and passed his old age in teaching young musicians. Another sailor, Edward Fiennes Lord Clinton, built for himself a fine mansion on the site of Sempringham Priory, but work ceased when he died in 1585, and the house was never completed. Marshal Sir William Pelham, younger son of a Sussex family, bought the site of Newstead-on-Ancholme and lived there while buying estates in north-east Lincolnshire, before he died at Flushing in 1587 on the campaign in which Sir Philip Sidney was killed. His son in 1603 built "a very fine stately

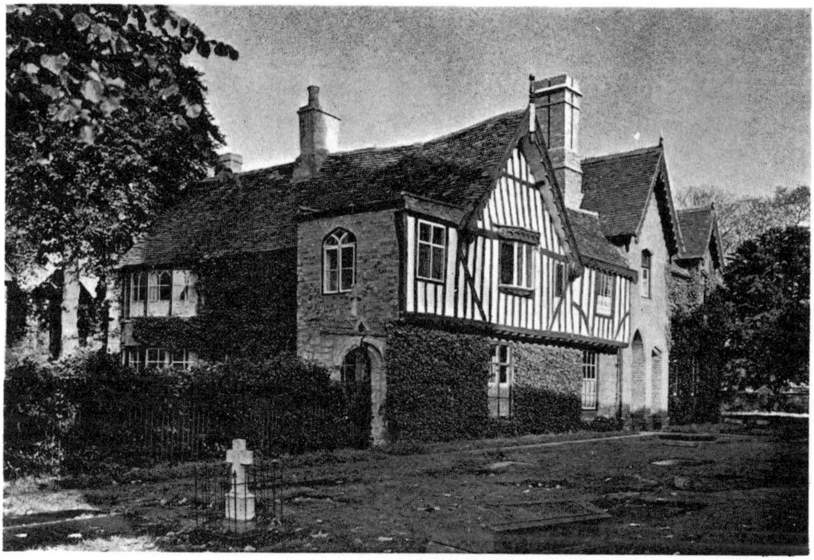

35 Sleaford: the old vicarage (sixteenth century)

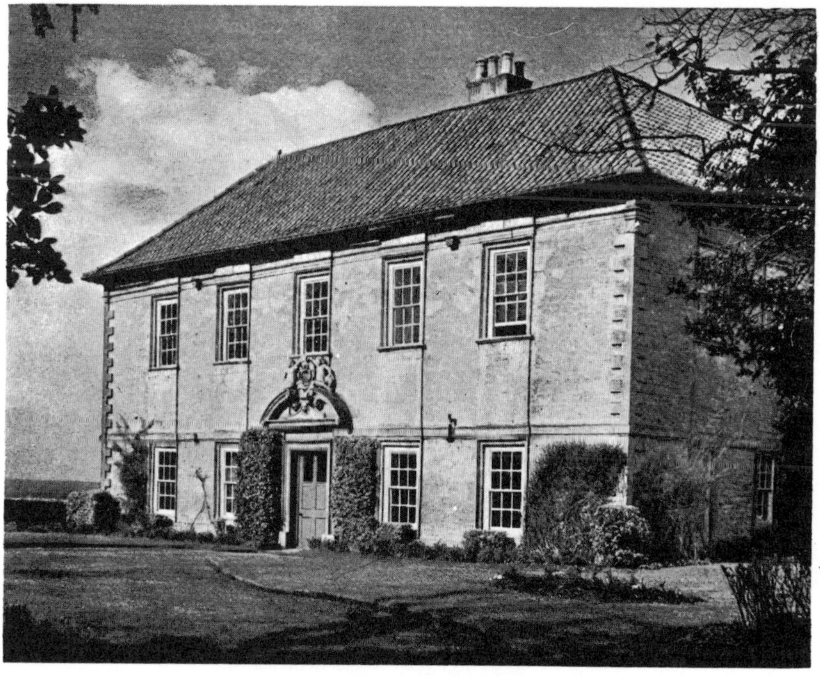

36 Leadenham Old Hall (*c.* 1700)

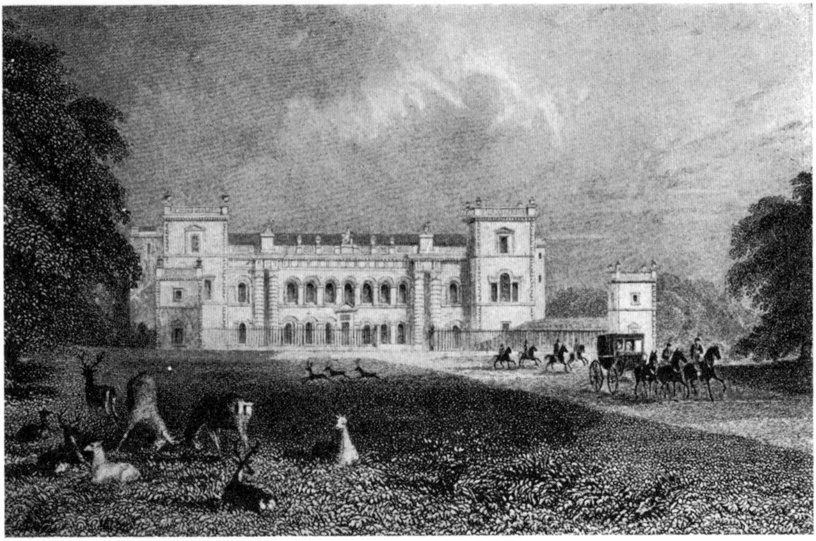

37 Grimsthorpe Castle: Vanbrugh's north front (1723)
From an engraving after T. Allom, 1836

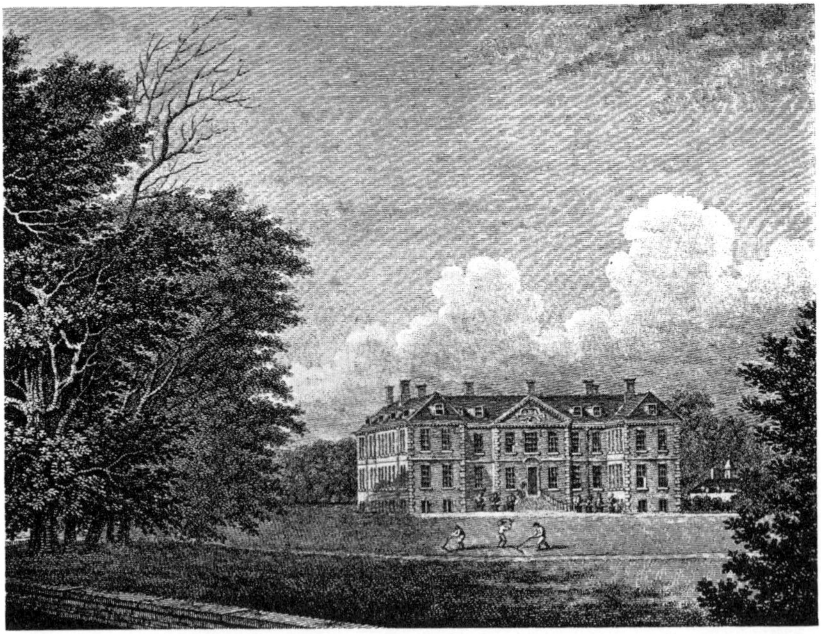

38 Belton House (1689)
From an engraving after C. Nattes, 1794

LINCOLNSHIRE MANSIONS

building" at Brocklesby where the family still resides; the house was rebuilt in about 1730 and again by Blomfield in 1898. The eighteenth-century squires who followed the Elizabethan and Stuart soldiers did not ape the peerage, but contented themselves with enclosing and planting the bare northern Wolds, breeding hunters, and starting fox-hunting in the organised style of the eighteenth century and of Trollope. The thin chalk soil, fit only for sheep-walks, rabbit warrens, hunting the fox, and coursing the hare, has seen more scientific and ornamental silviculture than possibly any other part of England, and the twentieth century has outdone the eighteenth. Brocklesby must be unique in possessing continuous records of planting from 1787—not merely conifers but also mixed plantations which finally mature as hardwoods. Hence the establishment is also noted for the high quality of its beech, ash and oak. Charles Pelham Anderson planted 12½ million trees between 1787 and 1823; the fourth Earl of Yarborough planted more than that before his death in 1936, and the park and the woods south of it represent, as much as the Fens, what changes man can make in a landscape. As a foil to this large-scale husbandry, there is the mausoleum built in 1794 as a monument to Sophia Aufrere, daughter of a Huguenot merchant whom the first Lord Yarborough had met when he was on the grand tour. Wyatt in his design and Nollekens in his statue of her have achieved the most successful monument of the age in the county—small but perfectly sublime. The man who planted and hunted was also connoisseur and patron of such artists as Nollekens and George Stubbs; the house is rich in painting and sculpture of diverse character.[1]

The story of Grimsthorpe Castle, Lincolnshire's greatest country house, and of the county's most distinguished family, is in itself a fabric woven with many of the threads of Lincolnshire's history. The story of the house itself begins, as I have said, in the thirteenth century, but later rebuilding has destroyed the evidence. The present building in effect dates from the Tudor period, when, according to tradition, Charles Brandon, Duke of Suffolk, ran up as quickly as he could a building fit to house that exacting guest, Henry VIII. This is a fitting introduction to an age of extravagant and restless building and rapid vicissitudes in the family history. The manor of Grimsthorpe he had in right of his wife, to whose father, the tenth Lord Willoughby d'Eresby, it had been given

[1] As I write it is announced in *The Times* that the charming baroque group of "Neptune and Glaucus" by Bernini has been purchased for the Victoria and Albert Museum from the present Lord Yarborough. His ancestor bought it at Sir Joshua Reynolds' sale and gave it to his parents-in-law; after their death it returned to the Yarborough's possession and stood for a time in the park at Brocklesby.

by Henry VIII when Lord Willoughby married Mary de Salines, one of Katherine of Aragon's waiting women. The money which the Duke of Suffolk so easily spent came from monastic estates and other properties lavished on a royal favourite—among them Tattershall Castle and the estates of Kirkstead and Vaudey Abbeys. The descent of Lady Willoughby, his fourth wife, carries the story back to Spilsby. The first Baron Willoughby of Eresby was son of a niece of Anthony Bek, the builder of Somerton, and inherited the Bek estates. In the Willoughby chapel at Spilsby there are some of the finest medieval tombs in the county, including an effigy of the second Lord Willoughby d'Eresby, who fought at Crécy, and an unusual brass of *c.* 1400 to the fifth baron and his wife. The sixth Lord Willoughby in the fifteenth century had married Maud Stanhope, one of the heiresses of Lord Cromwell of Tattershall. The seventh and eighth had lost their lives for leading the Lincolnshire rebellion against Edward IV, during which they destroyed the manor-house at Gainsborough which preceded the present Old Hall. Their home, Eresby Hall, stood just outside Spilsby; it disappeared in the eighteenth century and the only link now with this first stage in the family's history is the title of the eldest son of the Earls of Ancaster, owners of Grimsthorpe: Lord Willoughby d'Eresby. The latest memorials at Spilsby are of Richard Bertie and his descendants; he married Lady Willoughby after the death of the Duke of Suffolk. Bertie and his wife were keenly Protestant, and their beliefs drove them abroad during Mary Tudor's reign. The romantic career of Peregrine Bertie, their son, who became eleventh Baron Willoughby, had a fitting beginning, according to contemporary ballads, in a hovel in the Low Countries. No Elizabethan gentleman was the subject of more ballads, owing to the circumstances of his birth while his parents were homeless exiles, and to his tremendous courage in the campaigns in the Low Countries. He fought alongside Sir Philip Sidney at Zutphen, and later commanded English forces in more than one campaign. The portrait of him[1] could not be more what one expects—the pointed beard and ear-rings belong to an age when art and artifice and courage and extravagance were equally commended. Like more than one of his contemporaries, he spent his fortune and his health in the Queen's service.

The life of his parents at Grimsthorpe is revealed in the Elizabethan household accounts; some of their entertainments were homely—a morris dancer from Little Bytham, four musicians and

[1] Formerly at Uffington House, and presented to the National Portrait Gallery in 1929; there is a standing figure of him over his daughter's monument at Spilsby.

a hobby horse for a wedding at Belleau, a juggler with his musician at Grimsthorpe; others were more fashionable—the Queen's players and the Lincoln city waits came in 1562. The Duke of Suffolk's jerry-building is perhaps revealed by the item of brown paper to stop crannies in the chambers when her Grace was sick. Twenty women were employed to weed the gardens and the courts at sundry times at *2d.* the day. The purchase of great quantities of salt fish, barrels of white herrings, and cades of red herrings is a reminder that the medieval observance of Lent was still in force; there is a more modern note in the purchase of 400 oranges, and a London grocer sent cakes of castle soap as well as the usual sweetmeats. The popular sport of the gentry before fox-hunting captured all enthusiasm is shown by the set of rules for coursing the hare, drawn up at Sleaford in Elizabeth's reign, signed by the gentlemen of Nottinghamshire and Lincolnshire, and preserved among the Grimsthorpe muniments. Still another phase of local interest lies in the fact that Peregrine Bertie's son Robert, who was created Earl of Lindsey in 1627, was one of the undertakers of Fen drainage before his death while leading the Royalists at Edgehill.

The castle is best known for Vanbrugh's rebuilding of one side of it (37): his association with it indicates both the standing of the family at the time and the kind of building to expect. He was commissioned in 1722 to redesign a house which had been rebuilt or altered frequently since the Duke of Suffolk's time; only the riding stables now survive from the mid-seventeenth century. Perhaps the Earl of Ancaster found that the architect whose expenditure on Blenheim was more than three times the estimated figure was too expensive for him; whatever the reason, the design published in Colin Campbell's *Vitruvius Britannicus* was never fully carried out. We have only the one façade to show what Vanbrugh would have done in his ripe and quieter old age. It is perhaps the best of all his designs externally; there is a recollection of the daring of Seaton Delaval in the double columns, but they are part of a design in which the recessed front, flanking towers, and small, echoing pavilions have been subdued into a powerful repose. The interior of the wing contains no more than the hall, but it is again the most successful hall that Vanbrugh designed. This part of the building gives character to the great square, the rest of which is pleasant but rather characterless Tudor and Jacobean, smoothed out by nineteenth-century restorers. Last of all, Grimsthorpe has that undefinable asset of being still the home of the family which built it; its pictures—Holbeins, a Van Dyck of Charles I, family portraits by Lawrence and Reynolds—its furniture and tapestries belong here, and are more impressive even than the accumulated perquisites of the office of Lord Great Chamberlain. In Edenham church the story of the Willoughby chapel at Spilsby is brought up to date from Robert Bertie, Peregrine's son and first Earl of Lindsey, to Clementina, Baroness Willoughby and Lord Chamberlain in her own right, who carried those titles into the present Heathcote-Drummond-Willoughby family. Most of the monuments are striking rather than beautiful, especially the life-size figure of the first Earl of Ancaster, in Scheemaker's favourite Roman style, but the whole parade of six centuries of figures here and at Willoughby is a remarkable conspectus of the landed classes of England. In the eighteenth century the owners of the country houses still ruled and shaped the countryside and the lives of its population, managed its political system and graced its society. The Hon. George Hobart rebuilt Nocton church in 1775 conveniently farther away from the hall. Thomas Chaplin of Blankney founded the Lincoln Club there and in 1741 built a clubroom, the Green Man—the building still stands by the roadside; the nobility of Kesteven were members, and races were run on the open heath. Weekly meetings for tea and cards were held at Dunston Pillar, by desire of the ladies and gentlemen of the neighbourhood. Louth in the end of the eighteenth century was one of the gayest towns in the county; society came to take part in the coursing arranged by Chaplin of Tathwell, and stayed for the assemblies and masquerades. Society's patronage gave the Georgian buildings there a grace and polish not always to be seen in a secluded market town. Alford, under the leadership of the Wasteneys of Bilsby and the Massingberds of Gunby, was another resort for the gentry of the Wolds. At the coronation of George IV in 1820, the Dymoke family of Scrivelsby exercised for the last time the hereditary privilege of acting as King's Champion. Young Henry Dymoke, called home urgently from the ship on which he was a midshipman, managed to ride down Westminster Hall and, after issuing the traditional challenge, to back out safely—thanks mainly to the white horse he rode, which had been borrowed from Astley's circus. The way of life to which that ceremony belonged—remnants of feudalism, fortified by new blood in the Tudor and Stuart eras, blown out with ostentation in the eighteenth century—was exploded by the growth of industrial England in the nineteenth century. To its defence came men like Colonel Charles Sibthorpe of Canwick, who as M.P. for Lincoln fought in the Commons to prevent the 1851 Exhibition, and who could be described as "Tory to the backbone" even in an obituary notice in 1855; or Henry Chaplin of Blankney, who before he died in 1923 was described by A. G. Gardiner as "a mirror in which we may see the England of long ago and the

Toryism that is dead". Even the nineteenth century could not build as the seventeenth and eighteenth had done: houses like Stoke Rochford, rebuilt by Salvin in neo-Elizabethan in 1842, or Easton Hall near by, treated in the same way at the same time, are as dead as the Toryism of Sibthorpe and Chaplin. We may regret that Sudbrook Hall, where Peter de Wint frequently stayed, has been pulled down; that Panton Hall is falling into decay, and that Sir Robert Heron's Regency Hall at Stubton has become an educational institution; but there is another side to this change. Sir George Heneage in his estate book described himself as "Lord and Master of Hainton by the permission of God this day". Such a phrase has lost its divine sanction in the eyes of the twentieth century. However gracefully and generously such lordship was exercised, and still is in some places and at some times, we cannot now help seeing that the industrial towns of the West Riding and the midlands were created by men and women who fled from the life dictated by such lords and masters.

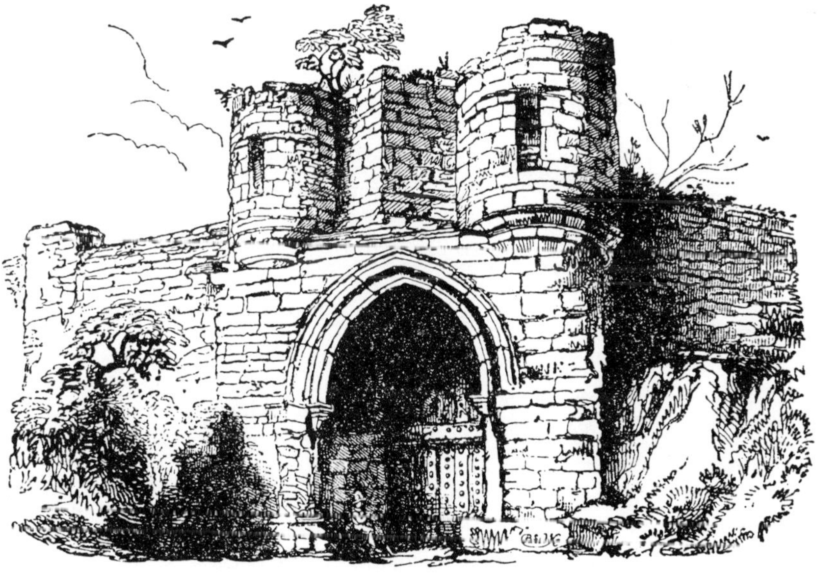

Lincoln: the last Gate of the Castle.

From an engraving after W. H. Bartlett, 1830.

Chapter

V

THE VILLAGE AND ITS PEOPLE

WE have searched the countryside for castles and country houses; in large areas we have found none, and elsewhere far fewer than in other parts of England, and less wealthy ostentation by the grandees of the eighteenth century. Lincolnshire is, after all, typically a county of large villages, and it has been so for as long as history records. One must think of it as a county of working farmers rather than of landowners, and today it is far enough away from the great cities to have been saved from the spare-time farmer and the successful industrialist who decides to balance his large profits in industry by losing money at farming. Good farming land has always meant a relatively mobile farming population; there has been a continual movement of ambitious men to better land. The farming stock has thus continually recruited new blood, yet the villages of Lincolnshire and the traditions of its countryside have shown a solid, enduring character. It was not grounded in economic stagnation and mental inertia; it was a positive quality transmitted from generation to generation of farmers and their wives; a sturdiness of mind which makes Lincolnshire a northern rather than merely a midland, in-between, county. There is the well-known toast which is sometimes thought to be Yorkshire but was certainly current in Lincolnshire:

Here's tew we 'ersens, tew us a'al, a'all on us,
May we niver want for nowt, noän o us,
Nor me naythur.

One very powerful reason for this unchanging Lincolnshire character is the enduring influence of the Danish element in the population. I have picked out of a local telephone directory some fifty current surnames which according to Streatfield's *Lincolnshire and the Danes* are of Danish origin; they include such names as Alger, Basker, Dring, Humble, Kettle, Odell, Swales, and Tovey. I know that I am on uncertain, if not dangerous, ground, in thus proposing the influence of racial differences, but there is plenty of historical evidence to prove the conservatism of the Lincolnshire peasantry for the first half of the past millennium, if not for longer. Lincolnshire, East Anglia, and the midlands were subject to the same immigration, but not with the same intensity, and the three areas have gone different ways.

One characteristic which English shared with Dane was the habit of settling in close, compact groups. You must go to the Celtic fringe of England—to Cornwall, for instance, or, better still, to some completely different country such as Finland—to see that the huddle of farmhouses and cottages round a church, or strung along a roadside, is not something which can be taken for granted. It is not because the population of a country like Finland happens to be much more thinly spread. It is rather that the English and Danish pioneers who first chose a site for cultivation worked together in the initial operation, and co-operation remained the basis of the life of the community until the ties were found irksome and were burst asunder by the gentry. A six-inch map of any village will show what has happened and a pre-enclosure map shows it even better. The village green is not particularly common in Lincolnshire, at least not the green with houses encircling it, except in a case like Market Staunton, where it is not the place for a medieval maypole or a modern cricket match, but the deserted site of an ancient market. It was unusual for a piece of common to lie thus at the centre of a Lincolnshire village. Folkingham, with its very large triangle fringed by houses, might seem an exception, until one realises that a village pond has been filled in and buildings such as a town hall pulled down, to make the open space. Much more often the plan is rectangular, and the area enclosed by the lanes, and given up now to cottages, farmhouses, and the home paddocks, was originally the first furlong of arable laboriously cleared and ploughed by anxious and toiling pioneers.[1] As the community expanded, room had to be found for new farms and dwellings, and it was found, sooner or later, by giving up the adjacent arable, as the present field boundaries very often demonstrate. It was no loss to the community, as it was balanced by the further clearing of woodland on the margin of the parish which the village could accomplish with the strength of its many young men. There are scores of villages in Lincolnshire which reveal this rectangular layout; I will name only Mareham le Fen on the northern margin of the Fens, Goulceby in the Wolds, and Scotton in the north-west. In Finland it is difficult to tell when you are in the middle of a village, because younger sons have gone off and cleared new land away from parents and neighbours; in England, room was found in the back lane for another cottage,

[1] I would not lightly venture to disagree with Dr. Hoskins, but I cannot accept the implication on p. 62 of *Midland England* that this layout of a village either in his county or mine suggests a defensive origin.

and the young man was absorbed in the co-operative routine by which the arable land was cultivated and the commons enjoyed.

In the Fens this does not apply, as the map will show and as history proves. There, on the silt, where the ancient settlements lie, roads wander in any direction out of the village, and throughout the history of this area the young men have dispersed themselves, making first new hamlets like Holbeach Hurn, Gedney Broadgate, or Benington Sea End, and in more recent times farms and cottages strung along the roads or lying snug under the shelter of a bank, miles away from anywhere. The reason is that the open-field system of agriculture which bound together the community on the clay, the chalk, or the limestone never obtained in the Fens and there was no inclination to make room for the young alongside the old. In the Isle of Axholme, on the other hand, the open-field system did obtain on the islands on which the settlements were made, and relics of it have survived at Haxey and Epworth. They are misleading to the student of today because owners of the unenclosed strips are at liberty now to grow any crop they choose, and root crops growing alongside corn on the curving strips are something no medieval farmer ever saw.

The map is now dotted with isolated farmsteads, but you will very rarely find in the buildings evidence of antiquity; the farms are almost invariably built at some date after 1750, when the enclosure commissioners had carved ring-fence farms out of the old open fields, and owners and tenants uprooted themselves from the village community to live and work in isolated freedom. The parson let his glebe farm and the land allotted to him in lieu of tithes; the owners and tenants gave their new houses names which are jocular, or regretful, or pretentious, or merely descriptive. So we find St. Helena, America and Little London, Pyewipe Farm and Cold Harbour, Mount Pleasant and Prospect Farm.[1] On the windy sheep-walks of the Wolds are Bigby Top, Owmby Top and the rest of the Tops; anyone who has climbed those slopes will agree that no other name was possible. Some of the names that appear ancient, like Shifty Nooking and Pasture Lodge, have been transferred from part of the open-field system to the farm carved out of it. There is many a Grange, and it is often impossible to tell whether the farm preserves the site of a monastic grange, long ago abstracted from the routine of the open fields by monastic private enterprise, or merely the pretensions of an eighteenth-century owner who, for want of an abbey or priory, fell back on the next best thing. In many cases it is certainly the former, especially on the Limestone Heath and Cliff. One of the few

[1] There is even, readers with memories of 1950 should note, a Featherbed Farm!

ancient farms is Temple Farm, on the limestone north-west of Grantham, where the Templars undertook the same kind of pioneer development as the Cistercian monks elsewhere. The round church of the Preceptory of Temple Bruer has gone, and all the building except the isolated thirteenth-century tower, where in the summer of 1950 broody hens were sitting on goose eggs, and pigeons murmured above the vaulting apparently oblivious to their Gothic surroundings. But by and large, anyone in search of old farmhouses can afford not to pursue the side-lanes and farm tracks to their sticky end: except in the Fens. There any side-road which leads to a hall—D'Eyncourt Hall, or Blossom Hall, or Cressy Hall—is worth following. Such a search led me the other day to White Loaf Hall in Frieston parish, where there are Jacobean fragments in the later building, and Irby Hall near Whaplode, which preserves some Elizabethan brickwork. Many of them have been rebuilt in recent years of prosperity: Wool Hall near Spalding is the headquarters of a bulb-growing firm, and when I saw it in the spring of 1950 the foreground was paved with one of those patterned carpets of tulip heads which seem a shockingly extravagant form of publicity until one realises that the heads must be picked off if bulb-production, rather than flower-growing, is the object. Other houses have fallen in the world to rural slums—and there are slums even in the Fens—but whatever their condition these ancient sites have something to say about the fascinating history of the Fenland.

This has been a long digression to make a point, but it has revealed one essential phase of the history of rural Lincolnshire. The compact village is no more typical of Lincolnshire than it is of Oxfordshire or Wiltshire, but this widespread uniformity conceals as much as it reveals. Sir Frank Stenton, in a masterly sentence, has described our English forefathers as "free peasants, familiar with life in communities, accustomed to discussion in popular assemblies, and deferential to kingship as part of the natural order of things". But in the critically insecure centuries before and after the Norman Conquest that freedom was lost, and over much of midland and most of southern England the descendants of those free peasants became unfree villeins, tied to a particular lord and his manor and subject to inherited obligations and services. That sentence, written of seventh- and eighth-century England, remains true of the centuries that followed with the simple but critical omission of the one word "free". Only in Lincolnshire, and to a lesser extent in the adjacent counties, where descendants of the rank and file of the Danish army formed more than half the population of many of the villages, did this manorialisation not take place in any general way. Hence in the twelfth and thirteenth centuries while the bulk of the rural population of a southern village performed with mute resignation the customary but onerous labour services required by the lord of the manor—several days' work each week through most of the year, without pay, but with a dinner of bread and herrings—many Lincolnshire peasants proved their freedom by granting part of their small estates for the endowment of a near-by monastery, and had friends and relations witness the gift or sale in charters no different from those made by the highest in the land. Thus we know that in 1176 Ketel Dumping and his son Odo gave land at Saltfleetby to Lincoln, and Hugh and Oggrim, the sons of Aluerun, endowed the minster with two of their few acres. Nowhere else in England is there such evidence of the large degree of freedom enjoyed by the medieval peasant. These men were no wealthier than their counterparts in the south, but the freedom they had they clung to, and they thus paved the way for generation after generation of free farmers, right into the twentieth century. In the later Middle Ages when feudal society was in solution and lawyers were writing about forms of tenure, because that was a subject which mattered to a growing number of men, it was recognised that socage tenure was the best available. That was the form *par excellence* in Lincolnshire; its advantage was that while it was nearly always free of services, the money rent was usually very small, and it was free of the incidents of knight service such as wardship, which could be disastrous to an estate in conditions of medieval insecurity and was at best irksome until it was abolished in 1660.

To the tidy-minded Norman clerk many a Lincolnshire village must have been a great puzzle; Domesday Book records that the village of Killingholme consisted of six manors, and Keelby of seven. The village united in one manor was unusual, and this condition is perpetuated for us in the fields around the village of Scredington; the five-moated manor-house sites there must be more or less of the same period. The village, rather than the manor, was the economic and social unit, and was the repository of the custom of the village—or the commonwealth, as it frequently called itself in the seventeenth century. In Elizabethan times, the people of Barrow-on-Humber committed to writing the customs of the place; the small paper book in which they were written out again in 1713, after the original had no doubt become dirty and tattered from constant reference, is still in the church chest there. There were three manors in the village, and the villagers laid down their obligations: "the Down Hall, Westcote, Besby Manor and George Marriss' Farm are every one of them to keep a common bull and a common boar for the service of themselves and the town, and also the town is to provide a bull for its own service". The Down Hall paid the vicar each year 14 quarters of barley, and Westcote provided three waggon-loads of straw for strewing the floor of the church. Such customs are nothing unusual; the point is that this statement makes no distinction between the duties of the lord of the manor and those of the village neatherd. Both served the commonwealth of the town. Very probably by the sixteenth century these manors meant no more than those services to the village; many small manors must have disintegrated early, because there was so little profit in maintaining them. Then the sokeman was free to climb, and the villein after him. Not that conditions were always favourable to the able and ambitious. The villein of the Middle Ages, tied to one manor and one lord, and without any ultimate right to whatever wealth he could accumulate, was the ancestor of the Tudor peasant who, whether rich or poor, was usually quite free, but occasionally found the arm of the law unexpectedly long. At Long Bennington, in Queen Elizabeth's time there were two brothers, Thomas and Robert Gilbert, who were wealthy farmers by the standards of their times. A rapacious courtier or Crown official discovered that they, and others in the village, were by blood bondmen, descended from generations of villeins, and their fortunes therefore the property of the Crown. The brothers paid about a third of their fortune to buy their freedom; the poor villeins who had "Nothinge to live uponn" could not be bled, and were left in their nominal bondage.

The large sokes of Lincolnshire, large scattered estates attached to a central manor like Caistor, Bolingbroke, Horncastle or Grantham, have been broken up; but one of them in Northamptonshire—the Soke of Peterborough—has survived, because its lords, the abbey before the Dissolution and the Cecils afterwards, were powerful enough and near enough at hand to preserve the rights that belonged to them. Some of the Lincolnshire sokes had non-resident lords who were too far away to check peasant ambitions or whittle down peasant privileges. But the court of the soke went on meeting, and it is a memorable thing that for a thousand years the tenants of lands in Denton and other villages round Grantham, the centre of one of the sokes, met at Grantham regularly to conduct the affairs of the villages to which they belonged.

The key to an essential part of the history of these village communities lies in the surviving buildings, because they are likely to belong to the period of greatest prosperity or development. Lincolnshire today is the county where you will most frequently see modern farm buildings, although in fact they are less like farms than food factories. In the Fens the lofty glasshouse in which seed potatoes are sprouted has become part of every farm. The isolated farmsteads, if they are not survivals of the enclosure period, are likely to belong to the mid-Victorian era, the last time that English farmers were prosperous before the present decade. The village itself, as it stands, is mainly a product of the two centuries from 1660 to 1860, and not much more has been added since the latter date than has survived from before the earlier. How, when, and why the village came to be rebuilt is the result of the subtle interplay of many factors—farm rents and food prices, the cost of timber and brick, the wages of unskilled and skilled labour—which varied from place to place and time to time. Some of these factors are hard to weigh, but much is clear.

There is no black and white building in the west midland style, and even houses with a simple timber frame are uncommon. Oak was scarce by the seventeenth century, and much of the timber used for houses before and during that century was in less durable timbers.[1] Perhaps it is for this reason that there is not a single cruck cottage to be found in the county, as far as I know. We can safely say that the only mud and stud houses to be found today are built of oak and few are older than the seventeenth or even the eighteenth century. They are to be found here and there in clays of the Witham valley, on the Wolds, and in the Marshland. Usually they have a central chimney stack, the normal arrangement in the seventeenth century, and the staircase either winds up alongside the fireplace, or mounts straight, and sometimes open, on the end wall of one of the two rooms. The straight staircase is probably only a recent improvement in the place of a mere ladder. Such houses required no professional builders in their erection; nothing but the skill of the village carpenter, and the knowledge possessed by many folk in the village of digging the clay and puddling it. A brick chimney, however, required a bricklayer. In 1676 Drayner Massingberd of Ormsby noted in his account book:

> Sellars, Robt. I told him I would build him a brick chimney this summer, he serving the mason at his own labour and charge.

In 1683 he resolved to build a new house for one of his tenants in Tetford:

> 11th Dec. Mon. "I have this day agreed with Samuel Edwards of Ormsby to take down the chimney in the house in Tetford which I have let to William Howard and put up sparrs instead of it, and build a New House in that yard which shall be two bays with a chimney in the midst of the whole building to be 30 foot long the

[1] Harrison commented in Elizabeth's reign: "In times past men were contented to dwell in houses built of sallow, willow, plumtree, hard beam and elm . . . but now all these are rejected and nothing but oak in any manner regarded."

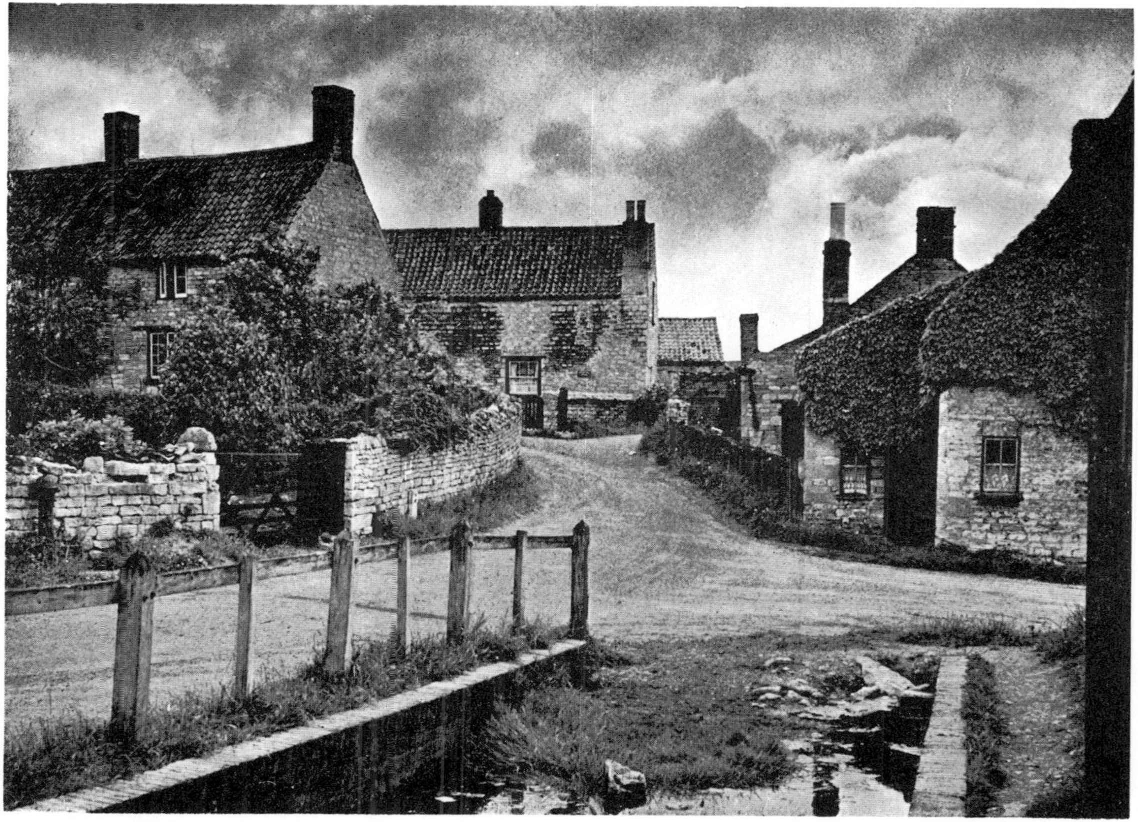

39 A village on the limestone: Newton's Woolsthorpe

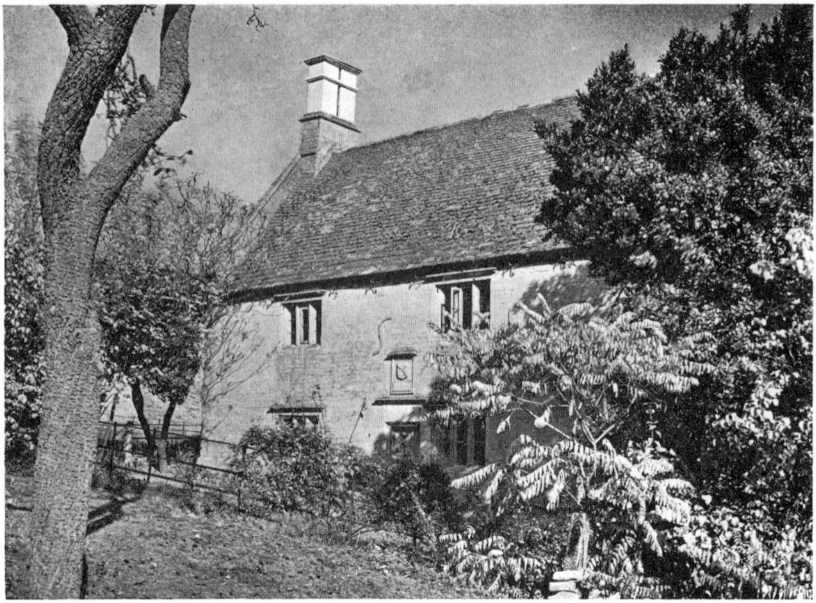

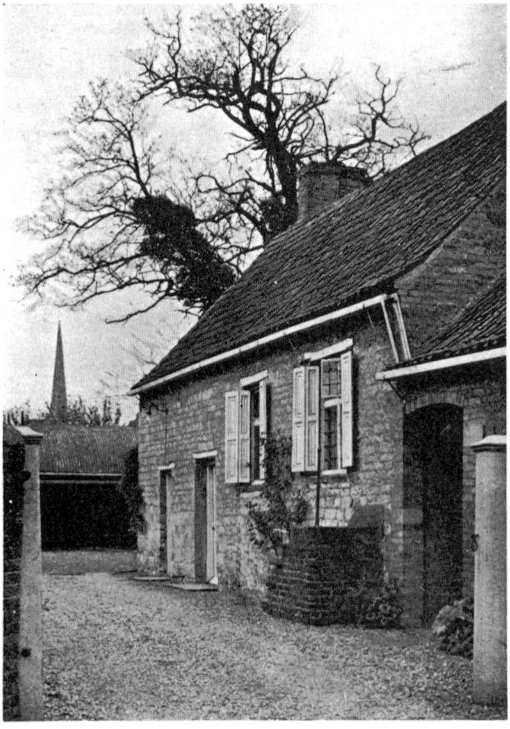

40 (*above*) Woolsthorpe Manor, birthplace of Sir Isaac Newton

41 The Friends' Meeting House at Brant Broughton (1701)

post to be 7 foot high at the least and to take timber for it growing in the house closes, the bancooples sparrs windbeame and side winers and post Armes to be all of sawne timber the middle sparrs Poules [i.e. unsawn poles] and he is to finish it with dores and all things necessary for carpenter's work before 1st April next for which I am to give him 14 pence a foot counting one end and one side in length as usual.

W. MASSINGBERD
S. EDWARDS

Mem: I must carry bays stones [on which the main timbers were to stand] to it and ye Poules and help him with horses and draught to hayle the wood timber to it and cause my tenants in Tetford to help him to raise."

Using wood from the home closes in this fashion was not an economy that he forced on his tenants but disregarded in his own affairs; he was at this time having the hall rebuilt, and except for finishing bricks for the front brought from Hull the bricks were made in "brick kiln close". A labourer's house could be built in 1688 for less than £15; that was the cost of a cottage built at Saleby, and the price included £1 18*s.* 6*d.* "to Goodman Young for the earth making and the house walling and the chimney" (also of earth in this case), and "1 dozen and a half of bread and 3½ dozen of ale spent when we raised the house". Arthur Young, in his report on the state of agriculture in Lincolnshire, published in 1797, could still recommend farmers to build new cottages of mud and stud, because that could be done for £30, whereas new brick cottages in the enclosed fen cost £50 each, or £84 for a pair.

In these circumstances, it is clear that the rebuilding in brick which went on, particularly from about 1680 onwards, has something to do with rising social standards and pretensions, as well as with the rise in the price of timber and the fall in the cost of bricks. A study of some of the many thousands of probate inventories preserved at Lincoln among the diocesan records shows how the process took place, and suggests the reasons for it. The lists made by four neighbours of all "the goods and chattels, moveable and unmoveable" of the deceased person reveal with intimate clarity all the ranges from the barest poverty to the most surprising wealth. They reveal most of all not only a certain improvement of standards (whatever the allowance to be made for rising prices in the Tudor and Jacobean periods), but also the increasing differentiation between rich and poor. The average Elizabethan who made a will, whether townsman or villager, died leaving house and goods worth about £17; the corresponding figure for the time of Queen Anne is four times as high. But such an average is misleading; among the Elizabethan inventories there were few men whose goods were worth more than £100, but after 1660 this was true of three men out of seven who made wills.

For ordinary folk the improvements within their means consisted mainly of minor enlargements, such as the addition of a kitchen to the existing house of one, two, or three rooms. The majority of the Elizabethan houses had no more than three rooms —usually the hall and a parlour, the third room being sometimes a kitchen or a chamber, but sometimes only a buttery or milk-house. To this building another bay could be added, or an outshot made at the back, or a chamber contrived over hall or parlour by boarding over. After 1660 that kind of piecemeal enlargement went on, but rather more radical rebuilding became common. A comparison of inventories for the period from 1570 to 1700 shows that up to 1660 there is a steady growth in the size of the average house, but that by 1700 there is a more marked increase in the number of houses with five, six, or seven rooms, which suggests that these are new houses. Such perhaps was the home of James Neesby, a Gainsborough plumber who died in 1703 possessing goods worth only £22 19*s*. 6*d*.; his home consisted of the "house" or hall—the term "house" is almost universal in the seventeenth century for the hall from which all other rooms had been developed, and which was still the living-room—the little parlour, the little chamber to the street, the little chamber to the yard, and the great chamber, as well as the cellar, the brewhouse and the garret. More typical was the house of John Fowler of Manton, labourer, whose status was about the same as Neesby's; his house in 1706 had a house "or fore-room", a parlour, a house chamber, and a parlour chamber (that is, chambers over those lower rooms), a bakehouse and a buttery; or the home of George Kitching, a blacksmith of Burton-on-Stather, which had a "house", a best and a little parlour, chambers over house and both parlours, and a buttery. Even in 1700 the kitchen was not an essential part of a home; the cooking utensils—the "gallows" from which pots and kettles hung over the fire, the "brandreth" on which they stood when not in use—are listed under the furnishings of the hall of Kitching's house. The chambers are occasionally used as bedrooms, but only as secondary ones, for a large family; the parlour, and even the hall, contained "poyll beds" or "trundle beds", and the chambers were store-rooms for goods which must be kept dry —corn or malt, wool or hemp. Sometimes they were used for storing cheese, which most farmhouses made, and occasionally they were filled merely with odds and ends not worth listing separately—the "old huslements" of seventeenth-century Lincolnshire.

We can trace the growth of the house of the Newton family of

Woolsthorpe, and indeed furnish the homes of Isaac Newton's ancestors, for the inventories have been published. His great-grandfather, John Newton, who died in 1562, was already a well-established yeoman farmer, and it was he who bought an estate at Woolsthorpe; perhaps as a result of a fortunate marriage with another well-to-do yeoman family. His home, however, consisted of two rooms only—the hall and the parlour—and though he died possessing goods worth £93 4*s*. 4*d*. (well above the average) most of this was made up of farm stock and gear, and his household goods were worth only about £18. It was Sir Isaac's grandfather Robert who bought the manor of Woolsthorpe in 1623, and with it the well-known manor-house, which must have been a new building at the time(40). It is a T-shaped house, with hall and parlour and behind them a wing containing dairy and kitchen. All these rooms were chambered over, but the chamber over the kitchen had an outside stone stairway to it, and was used as a granary. When Sir Isaac's father died in 1642, the house was very simply furnished: one misses the tables, forms, and cushions, and the painted clothes on the walls; the pewter is not itemised and there is none of the silver that one might expect in the house of a yeoman worth £459.

Item in the hall two tables 2 cuberts and other things	02	13	4
Item in kitchen one leade with brewing vessell and other things	02	10	00
Item goods in the dayry	00	10	00
Item uponn bond	15	00	00
Item in the parler 3 bedsteds with furniture one presse two chestes with other implements	10	00	00
Item ten paire of flaxen sheets five pair of hempen sheets 3 dozen of napkins five paire of pillowbears five towells and six table cloths	09	10	00
Item in the chamber over the parlour one bedsted one chest with other implements	01	00	00
Item in the chamber over the butterie two bedsteds with furniture and other implements	06	13	4
Item goods in the chamber and the hall	01	10	00
Item in brasse and pewter	06	00	00
Item goods in the butterie	01	10	00

Newton's father, like the most enterprising of his contemporaries, was able and willing to lend money to friends and neighbours; hence the £15 "upon bond". In this century, before the establishment of banks, and away from London and the facilities provided by goldsmiths and scriveners, it was the yeoman or the successful shopkeeper who provided that service in the village community and accumulated still greater wealth in the process. A Horncastle ironmonger in 1644 left behind him a "large debt book of good debts £317"; "in the same debt book debts that are desparate £47"; "debts upon specialty £65", and was owed altogether more that £1,000. Francis Hodgson, yeoman, of Gayton-in-the-Marsh, "had lent abroad in bonds and bills and other debts £360". Such men would have been called *kulaks* in post-revolutionary Russia, and condemned in modern India, but it is not for us to judge them.

Brickwork earlier than about 1660 is very rare in any Lincolnshire village. There are houses in Coningsby and Hagworthingham of about this date, with ornate pilasters and arcading in moulded brick, echoing faintly the Renaissance styles of the towns, and mixed naïvely with surviving Gothic features. Here and there are curved gable ends, as, for instance, in the small manor-house at Little Cawthorpe dated 1673, or a house at Newton on Trent dated 1693. One builder's device of Dutch origin which was widely adopted was the practice of laying courses at an angle in the gable end, in a series of triangles, so as to secure a smooth coping for the gable which rises high above the steeply pitched roof. We expect an old house in Lincolnshire to have gables higher than the level of the roof, because the builder's problem was less to keep out the rain than to prevent the wind from lifting the thatch or tiles. The earliest example of this brick "tumbling", as far as I know, is in the almshouses at Tattershall, which are said to be 1486, but are probably later. Whatever the date at which the device was borrowed from Holland, it came into general use throughout most of the county and lasts into the nineteenth century. It was used in a great variety of ways; one of the most pleasing is the brick wedges in the gables of rubble limestone cottages at Waddingham, Kirton-in-Lindsey, and other villages at the northern end of the limestone belt. Apart from that strictly practical device, the only ornament usually to be found is a string-course of two or three protruding courses above the first floor; the oversailing courses beneath the eaves, with bricks laid denticular fashion, or later, diagonally, breaking the transition from wall to roof, are one of those many bits of building technique in which one cannot distinguish use from ornament.

The normal cover for a mud cottage was thatch—occasionally reed, but much more commonly straw, even in the fens and the marsh. Occasionally you will find round thatched cottages; there is a charming example at Langton near the Georgian church (64), and there are others at Sutterton in the Fens and at Anwick near Sleaford. They are delightful affectations of improving landlords of the early nineteenth century, taken straight out of some book like Papworth's *Rural Residences*. In the Marshland thatched roofs are nearly always half-hipped. Not many brick houses were thatched originally; at the time when they were built, the usual roofing was pantiles—again an importation from Holland. Lincolnshire villages, and even more towns like Louth or Market Rasen, owe much of their attractiveness to the effect of light on pantiled roofs.

It is as wrong to imply that these cottages and farmhouses were the product of one building operation as it would be to say the same of most parish churches. Mud and stud cottages have had the mud replaced by brick, or have been encased with brick as they stood. One must remember that the easiest improvement or rebuilding was that which could be done over the heads of the occupants.[1] If you are puzzled by the deep eaves of a brick and pantiled cottage in marsh villages such as Maltby or Strubby, the explanation is that pantiles have been laid over thatch. It has been left to the twentieth century to cover decaying thatch with corrugated iron—not only in poor cottages in sad Wold villages like Skendleby, but even on a handsome seventeenth-century manor-house at Grimoldby. Inside many a plain Victorian cottage you can find a winding stair by the fire, or a heavy beam still visible above a modern grate, revealing the ancient core of the house; there may be pairs of crucks to be found, as I have found them in Nottinghamshire, a butt still protruding outside covered with hollyhocks, and the rest to be traced inside behind modern kitchen and tidy parlour.

There is, for me at least, no tiring of the variety of tone and texture to be found in these brick villages, if you give yourself a chance to see them in every kind of weather and to learn what best to look for. See them on a dull winter day, when there is no break in the great width of grey sky, and the dark brown of the early brickwork is dull enough, in the Stockwiths along Trent-side, at Laceby in the beginning of the marsh, or in Crowland deep in the Fens. On a spring day, or late on a summer evening, the pantiles hold the bright light and even the brickwork has a rich texture against clear sky and fresh green. For sheer brightness I know nothing to equal the really glowing colour of bricks in Brant Broughton and the villages near by; I can find no name for the colour, and in any case I should not like my recollection of it to be vulgarised by Technicolor terminology. If you want to see variety in brick-making look closely at the villages lying between Lincoln and the foot of the Wolds. The oldest brickwork (early

[1] This has been vividly demonstrated in the Trent valley village where I now live. In the year 1948 an early eighteenth-century cottage with low roof and dormer windows was formed into a modern villa without disturbing the occupants except by builders' dust. A single course brick wall went up round the old walls, and the occupants lived downstairs while the roof was raised, the staircase and bedrooms remodelled, and, of course, a bathroom put in.

eighteenth century) is a dull brown, but there is no monotony because of the pleasing variety of hand-made bricks laid in Yorkshire bond. Later eighteenth-century bricks are lighter in colour; they range uncertainly from a brown-pink to a pink-cream, and now that Flemish bond is the usual thing, they are sometimes used with red headers. The same variations can be seen in Ely; the bricks of seventeenth- and eighteenth-century houses are pink or cream; what is different here from Lincolnshire is that there are no pantiles, but roofing of small flat tiles of a dull green, covered with moss and lichen. In the nineteenth century, alas, builders could obtain a yellow-grey brick which was clearly thought to be superior, because it imitated stone, and so it was used in the 1830's for rebuilding the churches at Searby and Wragby, and the almshouses in the latter villages. The colour is unfortunate, but much more the unhappy effect is due to the uniformity of size and colour of machine-made bricks. As a matter of course the roofing for such a brick was Welsh slate; pantiles, like local red bricks, were despised because they "glowed with a coarsely ruddy aspect", as Archdeacon Trollope, worthy Lincolnshire antiquary, put it in 1858. Victorian England, if not refined, was at least respectable, and one way for a building to avoid coarseness was by not being anything at all except a few thousand grey bricks.

In the Wolds bricks were disliked long before Archdeacon Trollope was born—not for any moral judgment which called them coarse, but just because they were *wrong*. There must have been a good many chalk cottages once, although I have seen none except in Swaby. When brick was used in place of mud or clunch, it was very properly whitewashed, to give it the same finish as all the other houses. Here shows the strength of the village community. No one wanted to stick out; the horrors of suburbia are due to the fact that everyone wants to find some way of being different, whether it is green pantiles, or a false Tudor gable, or, if all else fails, a fantastic or pretentious name on the gate.

All Lincolnshire is not brick, however. It is not well enough known by those who admire the Cotswolds that all the features which delight the eye there can be found in Kesteven, and even, thinning out perceptibly, north of Lincoln to the Humber. Along roads whose wide verges have the characteristic yellow-green tone of grass on limestone, past fields bounded by dry stone walls, you come to village after village whose stone houses are built of rubble limestone from the near-by quarry. In southern Kesteven in villages like Barholme the roofs are usually Collyweston slate, but farther away from Northamptonshire the red pantiles are just as effective. In west Kesteven clay was easily got for tiles, and even within the span of the stone belt there are quite old brickyards. It is a good thing that English brick- and tile-makers did not follow the Dutch habit of producing glazed pantiles. They can be seen occasionally in the Vale of Belvoir and they give a very puzzling impression of being wet on a sunny day. One difference between Kesteven and the Cotswolds is that they have more sixteenth- and seventeenth-century building. Houses like the Tudor Old Hall at Wilsthorpe or the Old House, Leasingham, with the date 1655 in the central gable, are relatively rare. That is to say that there are not usually more than one or two examples in each village, manor-houses, or the homes of substantial yeoman. There are exceptions, of course; Caythorpe has at least three houses dated between 1660 and 1690, and the Hall Farm, with its curved gables, belongs to the same period, but the bulk of the building is eighteenth century. In southern Kesteven, the rubble limestone building spreads out into the Fenland, and in fact the finest stone villages in the county are perhaps the Deepings, following the Welland for two or three miles, and Baston, alongside the straight road into Deeping Fen. The most charming of them all, however, is Castle Bytham (45). The core of the village lies on the hilltop, overlooking the great Norman earthwork, and the houses are ranged round the church down the steep hillside and along the valley at the bottom. Near the church is a lovely early seventeenth-century house with a stone roof; on the other side the church is the manor-house with pantiles of a magnificent orange-yellow colour, growing a green lichen. The rest of the village has good thatch, old and new, and pantiles of the usual colour. I have never seen a village with such a range of colours in old buildings, and all the materials are local. The yellow pantiles, and probably also some green ones, were made at Little Bytham, two miles away, and not less than a century ago. On the western side of the limestone ridge there are still other variations to be seen, this time in stone. At villages like Caythorpe and Hough on the Hill it is ironstone of a warm brown, sometimes used in alternate courses with yellow oolite, and still farther west the blue grey of lias limestone. Long Bennington is a very handsome village, with a good deal of grey limestone used for walls and paving, but predominantly an eighteenth-century brick village. The older cottages are near the church, where the village started, but the eighteenth-century building was alongside the wide north road, so that the occupants could sit at the parlour window or stand at the front gate and see the coaches pass, every hour or two, at a rattling good pace. Cowper understood such a frame of mind when he wrote of the man

that deems his leisure well bestowed,
In contemplation of a turnpike road.

All these effects, in stone from grey to brown, in brick from dark brown to the most glowing red, in roofs, from thatch to yellow pantiles, were got from materials taken from the earth on which the village stood. It is a commonplace that such local products will harmonise with the landscape in which we view them, but it is not always realised that such local self-sufficiency did not spell monotony of effect, but might, in a limited area or even within the length of a village street, have a remarkable range of compass. Socially, the community which expresses itself in this unself-conscious but beautiful building included everyone except the lonely man who had withdrawn himself to the depths of his park or the mansion on the hilltop. The lord of the small manor certainly was part of the village; at Foston, or Allington, or Barholme, or a score of other villages, the manor-house is different only in scale, and that not considerably. The lovely stone manor-house at Allington, with its Baroque gables, is not much larger than many a brick farmhouse of the eighteenth century (42). The village parson certainly did not protrude as far as his house was concerned. I have read through a great many of the terriers among the diocesan archives at Lincoln, and they frequently describe in detail the home of the seventeenth- and eighteenth-century parson. He was no richer than most of his farmer neighbours, and poorer than some; his house differed little from theirs. It too had been reared from the soil of the village; out of some eighty terriers dating from the period 1600 to 1660 which mentioned the material, three-quarters speak of houses "walled with earth and thatched with straw". Only one was of brick—Skirbeck near Boston—and some thirteen were "rough stone"—the rubble limestone of the Heath and Cliff. The vicarage at Epworth from which young John Wesley was rescued in 1709, when the islanders set fire to it over his father's head, consisted of "five bays, but all of mud and plaster, the whole building being contrived into 3 stories, and disposed in 7 chief rooms; kitchen, hall, parlour, butterie and 3 large upper rooms, and some others of common use". That house was larger than the average, because the living was richer; it was probably not a very old house. Most country parsons in the seventeenth century lived in houses with six or seven rooms, including the dairy (or milkhouse as it was called) and buttery or pantry. Usually those rooms were the hall (still the main living-room), parlour, kitchen, and chambers over those rooms. Not more than one in ten of them had a study. The floors of the upper chambers were often plaster, but very frequently they were laid with earth, and sometimes with boards. Plaster floors can still be found in bedrooms and attics of many farmhouses and cottages of Lincolnshire; obviously the oldest of them are Elizabethan.

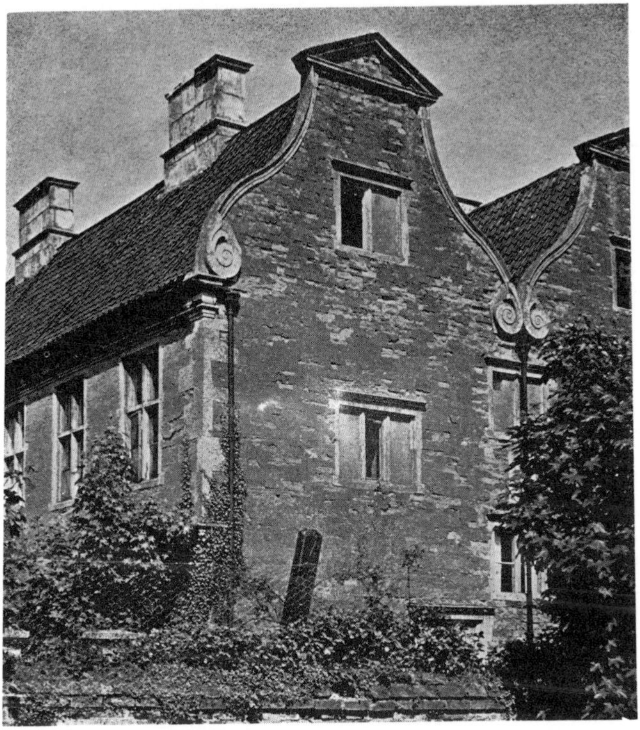

42 (*left*) Allington Manor House (*c.* 1660)

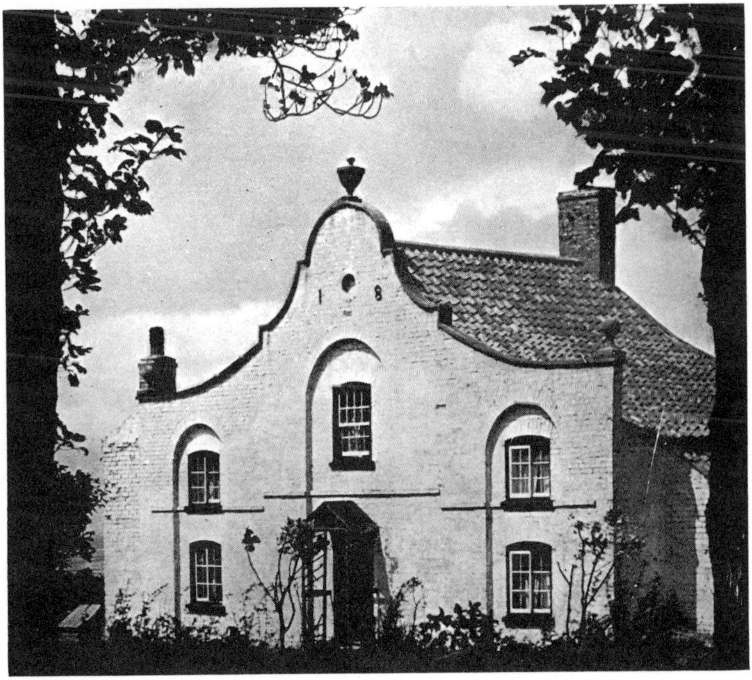

43 A Georgian version at Asterby

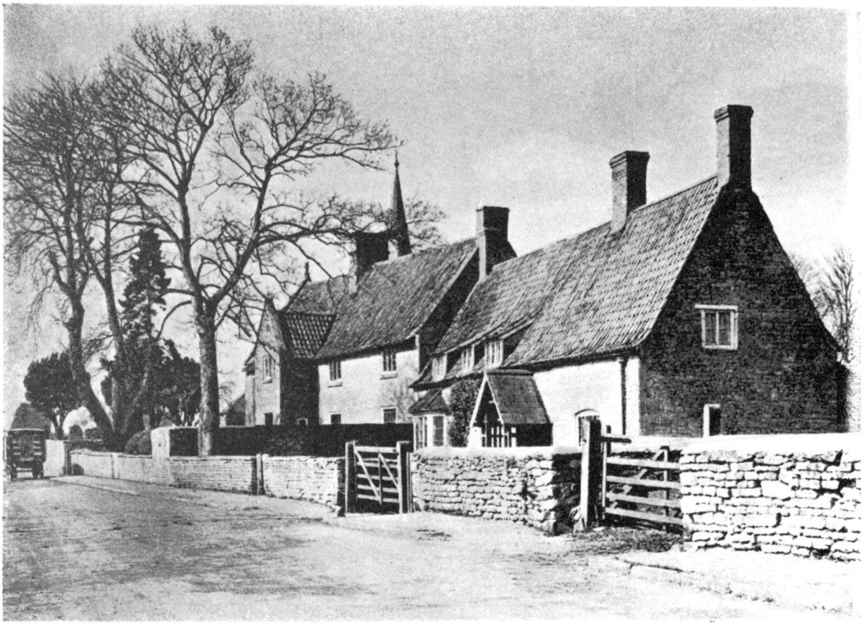

44 Seventeenth-century cottages at Kelby

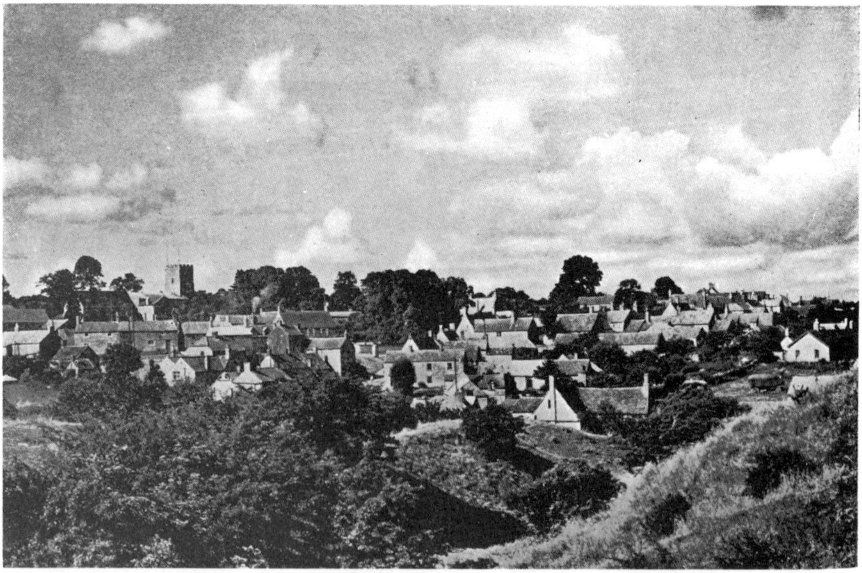

45 Castle Bytham: the village from the ramparts of the Norman castle

Plaster was cheaper than boards for flooring, and perhaps a better protection from fire. Some of the smaller houses, if we can trust the description in terriers, had no kitchen, and that room is sometimes described in terms which make it plain that it was not yet regarded as a normal part of the house. At Bratoft the kitchen was "distant from the house upon the east". We can envisage clearly the kitchen at Low Toynton in 1611, which had "a chimney in it with a great oven in it to bake bread and a little oven for pies or manchet, with a chamber over it having a little chimney in it". At Ulceby the parlour and kitchen had "earth floors not covered" and this may have been true of many other houses. Of Wickenby we are told in a terrier copied in the register that "the old parsonage house consisted of one parlour, a butterie, an hall, and a little kitchen at the entrie thereof. But now the first of May, 1617, a new house hath from the ground been newly and strongly built. It hath now a double chimney, a handsome kitchyn, a prettie hall, a faire parlour." It is a far cry from such a modest house (in spite of the happy adjectives) to the house which was built early in the eighteenth century for the vicar of Sutterton, or the enormous Georgian vicarage at near by Pinchbeck, but no doubt those and a good many other large Georgian houses were built out of private means rather than the income of the living. Many of them, like the rest of the village, were rebuilt in the century and a half following 1680. At Wyberton in 1687 the incumbent was granted a faculty to rebuild the old mud and stud house "in brick and tiled after a more curious and commendable manner, with kitchen, parlour, a large staircase in the midst at the entrance of the great door below, two chambers, a large study and small closets on the second story, and garrets, and a large porch with steps ascending to it at the entrance".

This village community not only built its own dwellings but satisfied most of its own daily needs from its own resources. The parish registers of Beelsby, a tiny village in the Wolds. show that before the nineteenth century it has a weaver, fuller, tailor, miller, carpenter, blacksmith, and a dish turner who made the wooden platters and bowls once found in every house. Tudor and Jacobean inventories show that there were few houses which did not possess the means of making food, drink, and clothing. Those small stone mortars which are so common in the countryside, and are sometimes put in the church by an enthusiastic parson and labelled "old font", are really for grinding mustard or malt. In many a house there was a spinning-wheel, and a few pounds of flax or hemp yarn stored in one of the upper chambers, to be handed over to the weaver to make up into sheets or clothing. Sugar came from the hives of bees in the garden. Salt, made near the coast, at a hundred places between Grimsby and Boston, could be bought from pedlars or at the fair. The wealthier visited the shop in the market town. A mercer at Horncastle when he died in 1570 had a most exciting range of articles; canvas, linen and fustian, linsy worsted and English worsted by the ell, as well as Flanders satin, black velvet and taffeta, tawny-flowered damask, black and crimson chamlet, buckram and bustian; remnants of sayes and mockadores; bolt cloth and feather-bed tick; silk fringe and Spanish stitching silk; broad and narrow ruffles, silk hats, mole hats and taffeta hats for women.

The village, without outside help or inspiration, without inspectors, organisers, or grant-in-aid, managed also to look after the less material needs of its members. One of the most enduring village institutions has been that intended to help those who in emergency require it. In the past two centuries it has been the village friendly society; farther back it was the village guild. We know best the religious activities of the guilds—the altars maintained in the parish church, the procession arranged, the miracle play performed. Unhappily no Lincolnshire village has preserved its guildhall, where regular feasts were held, though there is evidence that many had one—Manby and Ormsby in the Wolds, for example, and Fishtoft and the Deepings in the Fens. I shall say something later of the guilds in such towns as Boston and King's Lynn. The fourteenth-century regulations of the guild at Killingholme show that if any member lost a beast, had his house burnt by mishap, or broken into by robbers, help would be given, as of course it would in the case of death. Moreover, "if any brother or sister has a friend at home, for love of whom he does not wish to go to the guild [meeting] and if there is no retail tavern in the soke where he dwells, he may send for a gallon of the best ale to the Bailiff of the guild". In 1819 a Miss Hatfield, author of improving works like *Letters on the Importance of the Female Sex*, penetrated into what she rightly called the "Terra Incognita of Lincolnshire", and commented in letters to her brother on the nobility and wisdom of the peasants of the Humberside villages. She found that each had a cow, and "should any disorder or accident deprive them of that generous animal, its value is advanced by a contributory club instituted for that purpose". Thus the "common and middling folk" of the villages shared their resources and their burdens, their pleasures and their ills.

Only thus could the commonwealth survive, for it was subject to constant attack. Like all great achievements it was not easy of attainment, and its civilisation was as precarious a thing as ours seems today to us, who use the word "commonwealth" with a wider meaning, but no deeper content. It was subject to plague and famine, flood, and fire, but men knew then, as we know today, that nature is much easier to control, and most natural ills easier to cure, than the activities of man. It was to such attacks that the village felt. Villages have vanished from the map; Gainsthorpe near Kirton-in-Lindsey (10), West Wykeham and South Cadeby in the Wolds, Sempringham on the edge of the limestone, are no more than grass fields where the run of the village street, the foundations of houses, and the boundaries of the crofts can be faintly discerned as irregularities in the surface; of others such as Thoresby and Osgodby there is no trace on the ground of the work of ancient pioneers. Some of these, no doubt, were wiped out by pestilence, in 1349 or later, but I suspect that man destroyed more than did the Black Death. The first onslaught came from the earliest large-scale farmers of the Middle Ages—the monks. Sometimes, as at Thoresby, near Revesby Abbey, the initial gift of land for the foundation of the house involved the displacement of "rustics". In a number of cases these lost villages in Lincolnshire, as in Yorkshire, were sites of monastic granges; the story is no doubt that the monastery acquired land by gift, and by purchase rounded off an estate which could be withdrawn from the routine of the open fields of which it had been part. Where monks showed an example, the gentry of the fifteenth century onwards followed. In 1631, the list of "depopulators" who had been dealt with by the Council included the names of Hussey, Ayscough, Whichcote, Carre, Wray, Rossiter, Tyrwhitt and Bussey—the best-known families in the country. In 1637 when the new vicar of East Wykeham arrived for his induction, he found that "there was no question as to where we should stay, for the village consisted of one house". Where the village had gone, sooner or later the church followed. Beelsby, a large village of about two hundred people at the time of Domesday Book, has never been as large as that since the Middle Ages, and the church has lost its tower, both its aisles, and half its chancel. At Kirmond-le-Mire in 1690 it was said that the village consisted of one farmer who rented the whole lordship, and eight or nine cottages; the farmer would not, and the cottagers could not, maintain the church.

The fabric of the church reflects the vicissitudes through which the village community passed, and some of the actors are there perpetuated for us to see their station in life, the careers they made for themselves and the kindly verdict of their successors on them. At every age from the thirteenth century onwards there was good stone and good money for monuments. Lincolnshire is rich in memorial brasses; they have no local flavour, and were no doubt made in the larger workshops of London or Norwich, but they are worth examination. At Croft and Buslingthorpe (60) there are two of the earliest brasses in England; half effigies of knights in chain mail. There are fine brasses to members of the feudal nobility at Spilsby (Lord Willoughby d'Eresby) and Tattershall (Ralph, Lord Cromwell the founder of the collegiate church and builder of the fifteenth-century castle). At Broughton and Irnham there are knights of the fourteenth century, and of the Lancastrian age at Laughton and Gunby; there are ladies of their time at Gedney and Spilsby. There is a medieval judge at Gunby; at Tattershall as well as the magnificent Cromwell brasses there are memorials to some of the clergy of the collegiate church. The new merchant class is well represented; besides the well-known brasses of the Brownes at All Saints, Stamford, there are those of other wool merchants at Algarkirk in the Fens, at Lynwood, and at Winthorpe; at Barton-on-Humber there is one of Simon Seman, the London vintner, with his feet resting on wine barrels. There are memorials which bear witness to the close connection between the ports of the Wash and the other side of the North Sea: the great brasses at King's Lynn to Robert Braunche and Adam of Walsoken, which were engraved in Lübeck or some such Hanseatic town, and the slab at Boston to a Münster merchant who was buried in the Grey Friars there. The brasses of the later period are often thought inferior, but they are sometimes portraits as well as memorials: I recall the brass at Scrivelsby to Sir Harry Dymoke (1545), a very old man with a long beard who had acted as champion at the coronations of Richard III, Henry VII, and Henry VIII; then the lame Robert Palmer (1515) at Winthorpe, with his crutch by his side, and Edward Nayler (1632) at Bigby, "faithfull and painefull minister of God's word".

Of the great monuments of the Tudor and Stuart gentry the county has a fair number; the churches at Old Somerby and Belton (the Brownlows) Brocklesby (the Pelhams) Hainton (the Heneages) Spilsby (the Willoughbys) South Carlton (the Monsons) and Burton-on-Stather (the Sheffields) are almost appropriated to the memories of families still eminent in the county. Elsewhere, often in a small church such as Haugh near Alford which might seem scarcely worth a visit, you can see the figure of a vigorous Elizabethan sea captain, Sir John Bolle, portrayed in quiet alabaster; or see the raffish bust of Sir Richard Earl (1697) at Stragglethorpe, the fat curls of his wig dusty with time, and pompous self-assurance in the eighteenth-century figure of Richard Welby at Denton. But there are hundreds of more modest memorials than these. I think of Somerby, where now there is no more than a small church half-way up the slope of the Wolds, an eighteenth-century hall, and a farmstead near by.

In the church there is an inscription to Sir Edward Rossiter, who fought in the Civil War for Parliament and built the mansion-house in 1660; next to it another to William Weston, whose father rebuilt the hall in the 1750's and who died "at Mootajill upon the Ganges", after serving assistant to the East India Company's Resident at the Court of the Nabob of Bengal. Outside in the churchyard there is a stone to Joseph Willmore who died in 1882 after being "for more than 70 years an esteemed and faithful servant" at the hall. They are all there, the knight and the peasant, the Parliamentary soldier, the Georgian empire-builder, and the Victorian coachman, their bones turned over and mingled many times by church restorers and village gravediggers, until they are actually as well as metaphorically part of the soil of Lincolnshire. "When a whirle-winde hath blowne the dust of the Church-yard into the Church, and the man sweeps out the dust of the Church into the Church-yard, who will undertake to sift those dusts again, and to pronounce, This is the Patrician, this is the noble flour, and this the yeomanly, this the Plebeian bran."

Chapter

VI

The Fens and the Isle of Axholme

A GOOD deal has already been said about these parts, but they are so foreign to the rest of England, and their past so incomprehensible to many, that it is not enough to gather them into generalisations about Lincolnshire. The greatest difficulty is the lack of a scholarly and comprehensive history of the Fenlands, although Professor H. C. Darby's two volumes on *The Medieval Fenland* and *The Draining of the Fens* go far to fill that need. What is certain is that for most of the past thousand years the Fenland has been the home of one of the wealthiest, if not the wealthiest, agricultural communities in England. Two things have obscured this to observers. One was the recurrent floods and the disastrous occasions when, for a time, the perpetual effort to control the rivers and protect the land broke down. We can remember the most recent occasion in 1947 (51) when the press had dramatic photographs of attempts to strengthen the banks of Cowbit Wash, and then to close the gaps through which flood waters poured over the most valuable farming land in England. In 1948 two large areas of salt marsh were reclaimed from the Wash: one of them at Wainfleet and Friskney, north of Boston, the other north of Spalding near the mouth of the Welland. That too was a dramatic struggle; it was a question of whether the new banks, each enclosing about 1,500 acres of land which would be worth nearly £100 an acre when won from the sea, could be closed before the autumn high tides and winter gales, and whether they could withstand the first onset of the sea before they were grassed over and consolidated. The victory was never really in doubt, but journalists helped to keep alive the feeling that farming there must be a precarious business. Perhaps it is, but in no part of the world are people to be deterred from living on land which is liable to flood. Nearly every year we see photographs of flooded villas in the Thames Valley; and avalanches in Alpine valleys remind us that Swiss farmers have their own disasters to guard against. The Trent has broken its banks many times; the breach in 1947 at Morton, near Gainsborough (52), was not the first at that point, and the Trent-side villages from Newark northwards are always conscious of their danger. The Saxons and Danes who founded the riverside settlements had a sharper eye to the risk than the enclosing landlords of the eighteenth century, building farmsteads on their new allotments, or the speculative builders of the twentieth, putting up country residences for townsmen. When the Trent broke at Spalford in 1795, and the waters flowed east as far as Lincoln, Saxilby church was one of the few dry places in the village, and there families lived for three weeks. The flood danger is greater now than in times past; the conversion of woodland, through which rain drips gently on to deep humus, into well-drained arable fields, and the covering of thousands of acres of land with macadamised roads and slate roofs, has given rain water a quicker run off than it had in Saxon or medieval England. Anyone who feels that George Eliot in the *Mill on the Floss* was using a novelist's license to heighten effect should read the statements made in 1858 about the flood of 1795, when Trent flood waters poured over their ancient course to the Lincoln gap. "Mrs. Mary Millins, now living at Skellingthorpe, in the same house in which she was born, is 93 years of age, remembers the Spalford bank breaking. The water came through the wood with a roaring noise like the report of thunder." The risk of losing a crop or of having cattle drowned was no different for the farmer on the Trent-side or in the Fens than a wet summer in Cumberland dales, when hay cannot be got in, or a disastrous snowstorm in which sheep are lost by the score. No such misfortunes have ever broken the patience and persistence of human effort. In the Fens proper, the problem of flooding has been enormously sharpened by man's own efforts; the very effectiveness of drainage in the past two centuries has dried out the peat to such an extent that it has shrunk in a spectacular fashion, and it is wasting owing to chemical action which goes on now that it is no longer waterlogged. The surface soil is so fine that in the dry springs that eastern England often gets, the soil—and with it the newly sown sugar-beet seed—blows away. It is only because of the great depth of the peat that no one seems to be concerned at the problem of erosion. The best crops are grown, and erosion is least serious, where the black peat has been clayed—mixed with the strong clay which underlies it. So the rivers, on their beds of unshrinking silt, are every year raised higher above the lands they drain; the pumping away of river waters calls on each generation to find more powerful machinery, and the strength of the river banks becomes a more critical matter.

Those who tried to describe the Fens before they were drained invariably dwelt on what seemed to them the squalid and precarious mode of life of the people, and the strange and unattractive qualities of the landscape. This is the other difficulty to which

I have already referred, in this way of appreciating how much wealth was to be won from these unusual parts. The oldest comment of this kind comes from the poem about St. Guthlac, the founder of Crowland:

Wide is this waste
Its exiled seats are many,
Hidden homes
Or miserable sprites;
They are the faithless ones
Who these cots inhabit.

The story of Hereward the Wake is filled out with legends but it has a solid core of truth. In May, 1070, a Danish fleet sailed up the Ouse to Ely, and the men of the Fenland joined it there to help in the Danish reconquest of England. Their leader was Hereward, a Lincolnshire thane, and after the Danes withdrew he led the futile resistance until the Isle of Ely was overrun by Normans, and Hereward disappeared. He seems to have made his peace with William the Norman, but the Fens may well have remained the home of displaced persons or political refugees. It is strange that the small castle of Ely, now known as Cherry Hill, was never enlarged by William the Conqueror's successors, for more than one group of political malcontents picked on the Isle as a base for rebellion.

It was in the seventeenth century particularly that the Fens began to receive attention—from poets, travellers, and landlords with capital to invest. One could fill pages with quotations from writers of that century and the next who tried to fix on paper their impressions of the land and the people. One of the travellers was Pepys, visiting poor relations near Wisbech: "With much ado through the fens along dikes where sometimes we were ready to have our horses sink to the belly we got by night with a great deal of stir and hard riding to Parson Drove—a heathenish place. I was bit cruelly by gnats." We need not take much notice of a Londoner's remarks on bad roads and lonely cottages, but in the gnats he had found a real disadvantage of fenland life. All the writers comment on ague, which we should call malaria; it was endemic in the Fens up to fifty years ago. A writer in 1636 suggested that "high and mighty Croyland sack" was the only remedy for "the devilish stinging of their humming gnats". Those who could afford to do so slept under mosquito nets, but the remedy within the reach of ordinary folk was opium, or, if you preferred, the following recipe: "Nail three horse shoes to the foot of the bed, and tap them with a hammer, saying:

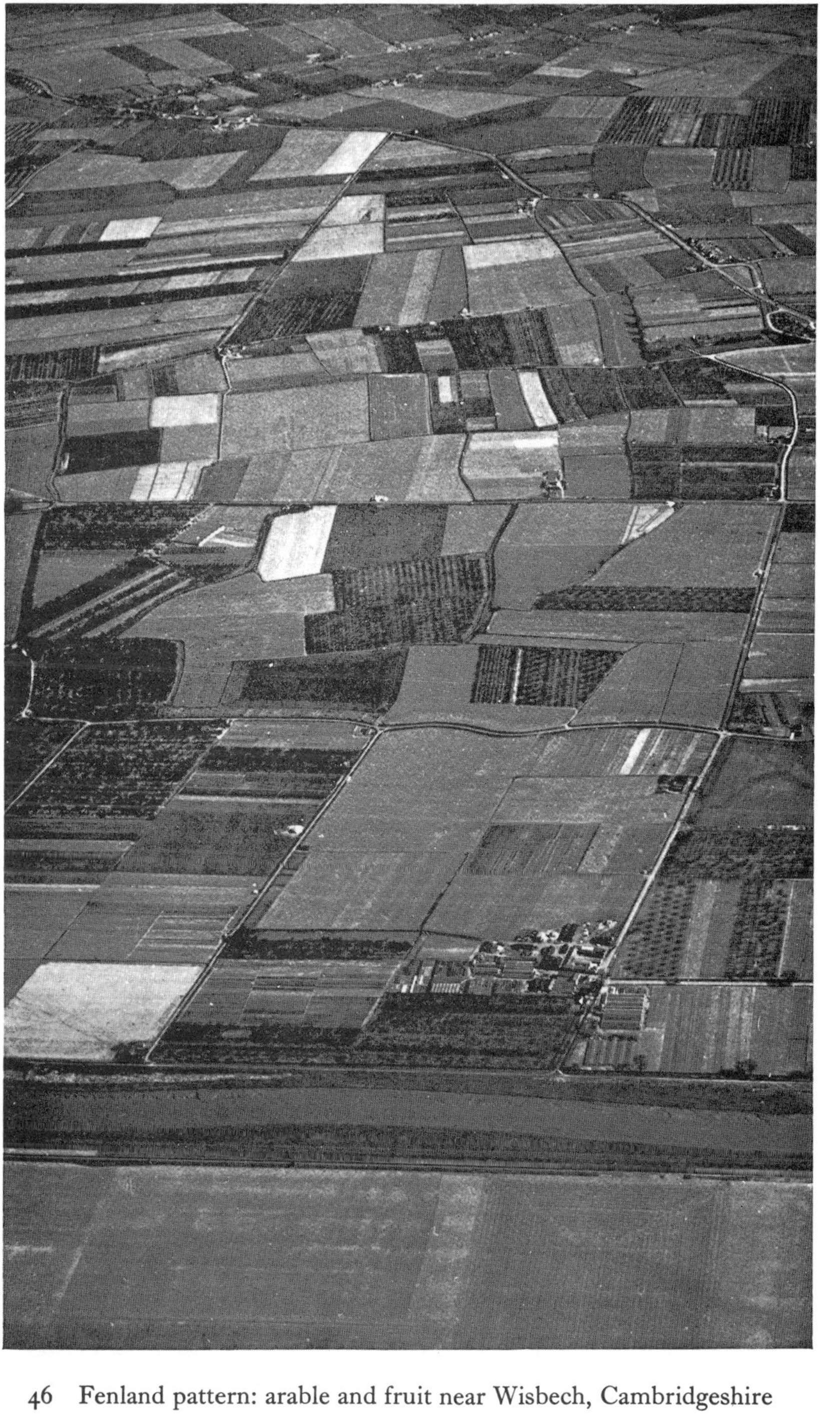

46 Fenland pattern: arable and fruit near Wisbech, Cambridgeshire

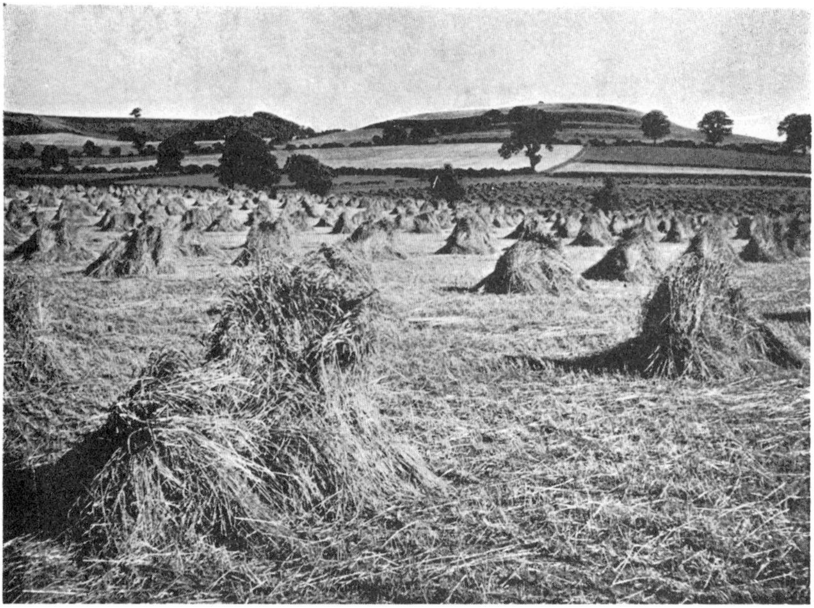

47 The edge of the Wolds near Scamblesby

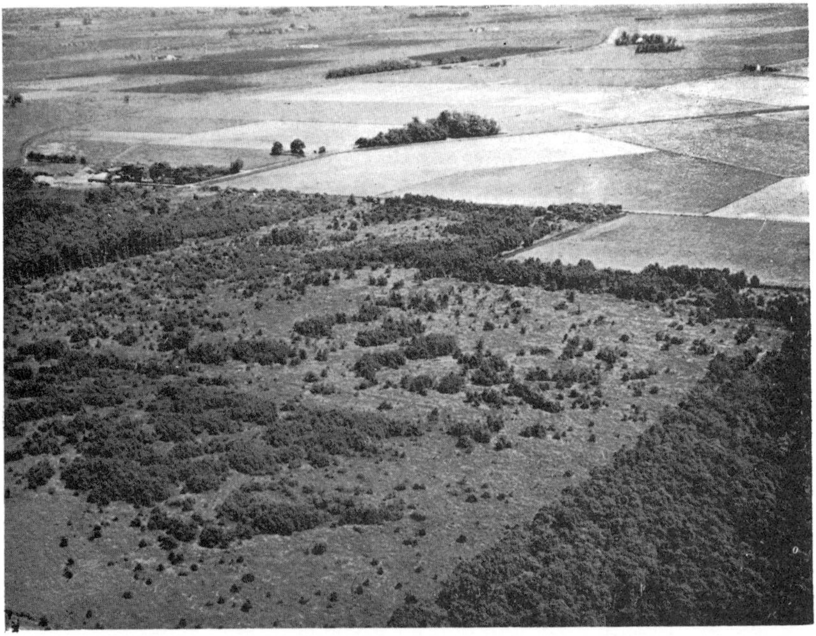

48 Holme Fen, near Peterborough: Fenland reverting to natural scrub

Feyther, son and Holy Ghost,
Naäle the divil to this poäst,
Throice I strikes with holy crook
Won for God and one for Wod and won for Lok.

In the last century quinine and medical attention were more effective than opium, or this broadminded appeal to a Christian God and Woden and Lokki. The habit of taking opium remained; Mrs. Burroughs in *Life as we have known it*, described the miserable slaves of opium and laudanum in Crowland in the 1850's.

Mosquitoes, like floods, are ills to which mankind has always been inured, and as I have said, such misfortunes must not blind us to the wealth of the Fenland. We take it for granted today and we must be ready to believe it of the past. Its wealth in Roman times we are hardly yet in a position to demonstrate, because although aerial photographs have revealed a dense occupation of parts of the Fens, we cannot yet interpret completely the maze of crop marks they reveal (8). The signs are the most plentiful on the silt fen south of a line from Spalding to Wisbech, on the valley gravels of the Ouse and the Welland, and on the margins of the Fens near such villages as Market Deeping, Thorney, and Chatteris. It has been suggested that we must think in terms of a large-scale pasture farming by peasants planted there by the imperial authorities.

One of the puzzles is the absence of evidence of occupation of the silt belt from Boston north-eastwards, and of the northern margins of the Fens. Towards the end of the Roman period a fall in the level of the land began to make life more difficult; to transform the rich farming area into the "wide waste" of St. Guthlac's time, and to form the countless meres which were to be a source of wealth for a thousand years. Embanking and reclamation must have begun in the Dark Ages, and the map of the Fens today, as Major Gordon Fowler has shown, is a palimpsest of young rivers and old; new cuts and washes and diversions no longer used; ports and havens which have long since lost their place on the sea. His map, which is printed in the National Trust's guide to Wicken Fen, is the most remarkable demonstration of what man has done to the Fens since the distant, but still unknown, days when the Roman Bank was built.

Man has destroyed the *natural* wealth of the Fens, and how much we have lost, partly through greedy exploitation and partly as a consequence of drainage, the records of the past can reveal. The growth of deep-sea fishing has meant that we no longer care for our freshwater fish, though whether cod and haddock are really better than Ancholme eels and Witham pike few have had a chance to judge. Those who like eels, and look in vain for them in the fishmonger's shop, will regret the passing of the days when rents paid in the Manor of Ely (the name means "eel-district") included 3,036 sticks of eels, and a further 14,500 eels in Lent. The monks of Ramsey, before the Conquest, were receiving each year 60,000 eels from one fenland manor, and the other rivers of Lincolnshire and of the Isle of Axholme were no less fruitful.

The meres and dikes were also the home of water-birds in numbers that the twentieth century can scarcely conceive. In the Middle Ages they must have formed part of the diet of common folk, as well as finding their way by purchase and gift, or as customary rents, to the tables of the rich. In the sixteenth century the household of the Earl of Northumberland in East Yorkshire consumed not only wild fowl such as mallard, teal, and widgeon, but also seagulls and terns, and a great variety of birds of the sea-shore and marsh; plovers, curlews, bustards, cranes, reeves and bitterns, knots, dotterels, stints, seapyes (oyster-catchers), redshanks and shollards (spoonbills); birds that some of us have never seen and none have eaten. Some of the supplies consumed at Wressle and Leconfield may have come from the Isle of Axholme and the Humber-side. In Elizabeth's reign the corporation of Lincoln presented the Lord Treasurer with one dozen godwits, five dozen knots and a dozen pewits. In the past two centuries so much destruction of wild life has gone on in Europe and North America, and to a less extent in the other continents, that it has reduced some species to extinction, and others to a rarity that makes observing and photographing them an esoteric sport. In no part of the world has man reduced wild life more drastically than in the Fens. The ruff was already so rare in the seventeenth century that it was taken young and fattened in captivity; it fetched a high price. Commercial exploitation reached a peak in the seventeenth and eighteenth centuries; nearly all the forty or so decoys which once existed in this area date from that time. The best known is that at Borough Fen near Peterborough which was made in about 1670, but the greatest number was in the Friskney neighbourhood, between Skegness and Boston. The ten decoys there in the eighteenth century, before the enclosure and draining of the East Fen, are said to have sent as many as 31,000 mallard, widgeon and teal to the London market. There was a famous family of decoymen at Friskney named Skelton; George Skelton, born about 1760, built decoys in Norfolk; Thomas his grandson, died in 1918 at the age of 85. All that remains of the decoys there now are the clumps of trees which surround the sites, an unexpected break in the expanse of ploughed land. The management of a decoy, with its six or so pipes down which the wild birds were led by decoy-ducks, and driven by terriers, required a subtle skill, unlike the stupid practice of driving the meres with boats in the moulting season, or in the nesting season before young birds could fly. The drainage of the meres put a stop to the source of supply, as it did to many another occupation. The East Fen near Friskney produced throughout the eighteenth century thousands of pecks of cranberries, and East Anglian and Yorkshire men and women knew the taste of cranberry tart better than they do now. The Isle of Axholme never produced such a spectacular wealth of fish or fowl, but in the seventeenth century Hatfield Chase still carried large numbers of red deer, and they were hunted as greedily as the wild fowl of the Fens.

Any description of the Fens in the past which dwelt overmuch on its wealth of natural resources would be misleading, and this is a fault in some writers of the past. Tradition says that Boston Stump was built of wool, and whether we imagine that to have a literal or a metaphorical basis, the wool itself was real enough. From beginnings which were easy on the line of silt encircling the Wash, and on islands like Ely to the south or Stickney to the north, a mixed agriculture developed which was wider in its variety than that of the uplands. The first and best evidence of its wealth is the great churches which began to be built in the Norman period, already larger in scale than in any other part of England, and the wealth of the fenland monasteries.

Ramsey, the rich of gold and of fee,
Thorney, the flower of many fair tree;
Croyland, the courteous, of their meat and drink,
Spalding the gluttons, as all men do think:
Peterborough, the proud, as all men do say,
Sawtrey, by the way—that old Abbey
Gave more alms in one day than all they.

There are plenty of descriptions of medieval manors and farms which show that the core of an estate, here as elsewhere, was arable land; arranged not in two or three large open fields but in a smaller number of fields probably in separate ownership. The piecemeal reclamation added steadily further areas privately held and separately enjoyed. Beyond the arable and meadow lay the undrained fenland which, like some of the meadow, was often flooded in winter and thus enriched each year, or islands which could only be reached by boat. Many of the commons in the Fens were so large that there was no stint to the grazing rights; each commoner could turn out as much stock as he liked. Sheep must have been numerous; in the fifteenth-century lists of English wool, that from Holland ranks next to Welsh border and Cotswold in quality. In the peat fen the commoner could cut peat to warm his house and even to build its walls. The woad mill at Parson Drove, near Wisbech, which stood until about 1900, was built of turves laid herring-bone fashion; and it may have preserved this building tradition of the Fens in this material. Timber was one of the few scarcities in the Fens, though bog oak could be used, provided it was split or sawn as soon as it was dug out of the peat. Turf served as fuel for the salt-pans which existed near most of the silt villages; round Bicker Haven, in Pinchbeck Marsh, on the Norfolk margin, and elsewhere, there are rows of mounds which show by their size how long this industry, using the salt-impregnated silt, must have gone on.

It is a sound antidote to Macaulay's notion of "a half savage population" and Samuel Smiles' picture of "an amphibious race largely employed in catching eels" to quote the twelfth-century monk, William of Malmesbury.

> The marshes themselves abound in trees, tall and without side branches, reaching up to the stars. The plain as level as the sea delights the eye with its flourishing growth. It is so smooth that nothing interrupts the view of travellers, nor is the slightest part of it left uncultivated. Here apple trees rise, and there the ground is clothed with vines, either trailing along the earth or supported on poles.

This description of the site of the abbey of Thorney is exaggerated, but it helps to redress the balance. We need also to correct the picture of "Fen slodgers" as a wild and lawless race, confirmed by their isolation in their resistance to improvement. The Fenland suffered from isolation no more than many other parts of England before the age of macadam. Causeways connected the silt villages and the islands in the past; Ely was linked with the uplands to the south, and Sibsey with Boston and the Wolds. In the Isle of Axholme the paved causeways can still be found flanking the roadway that is now metalled; they once carried strings of pack-horses taking Lincolnshire wool to the West Riding, and the merchant with his wool weights hanging by his saddle. Even if these causeways were difficult to maintain and their many bridges frequently defective, the waterways were alternative routes; until the railways came they provided long-distance communications, and the lesser dikes and lodes were as much used for everyday travel and transport as the canals of Venice. The comparison may seem far-fetched, but it is after all a defect of the romantic view of history that it elevated the Venetian gondolier and turned the fenman into something slightly less than human. The peasant shared with his fellows in the uplands the obligations of ploughing, harrowing, and harvesting; in addition

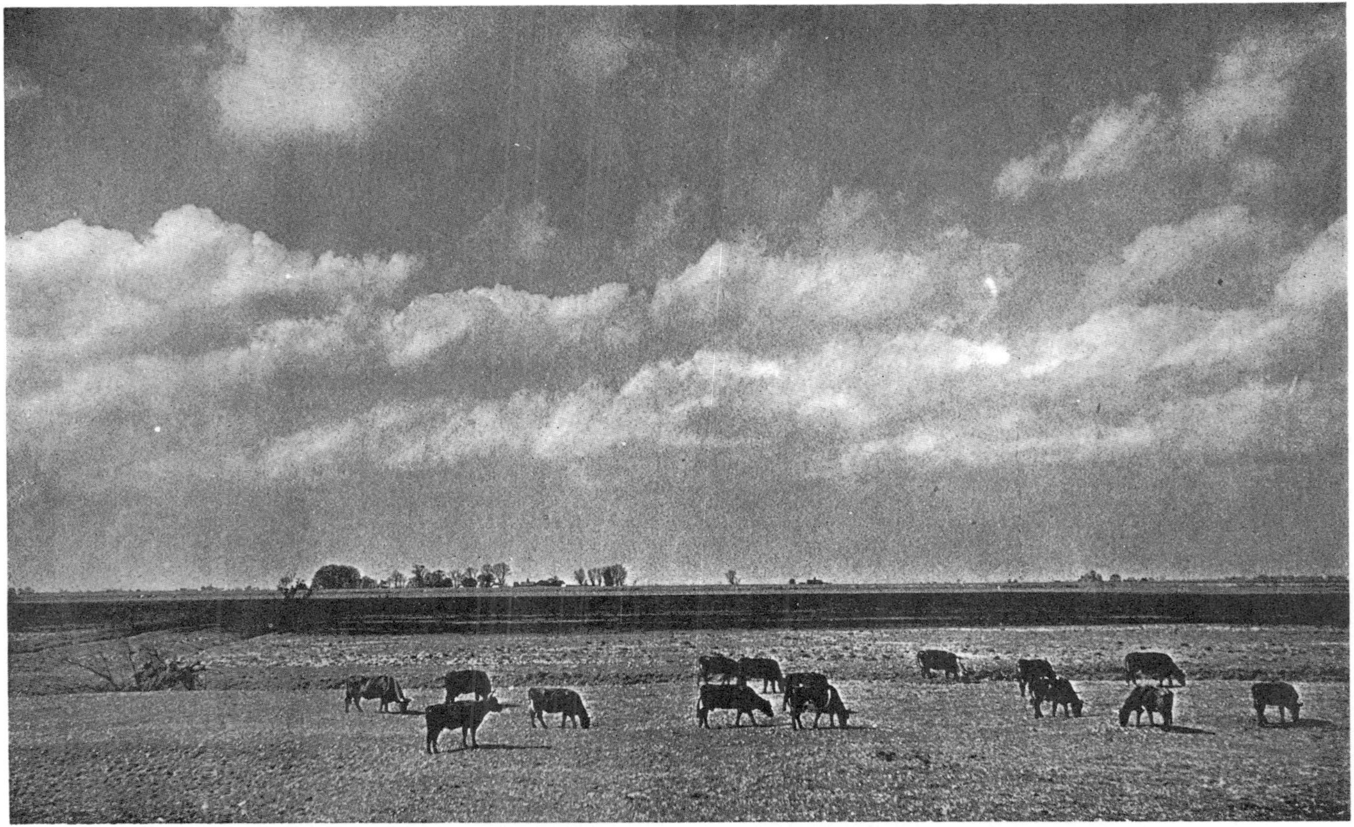

49 The Lincolnshire Marshland

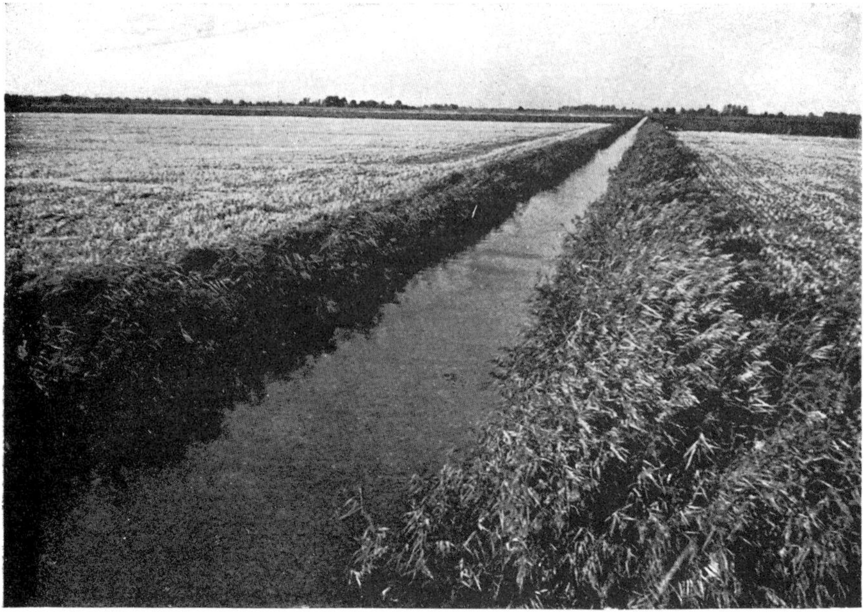

50 September: rushes flowering in Mildenhall Fen

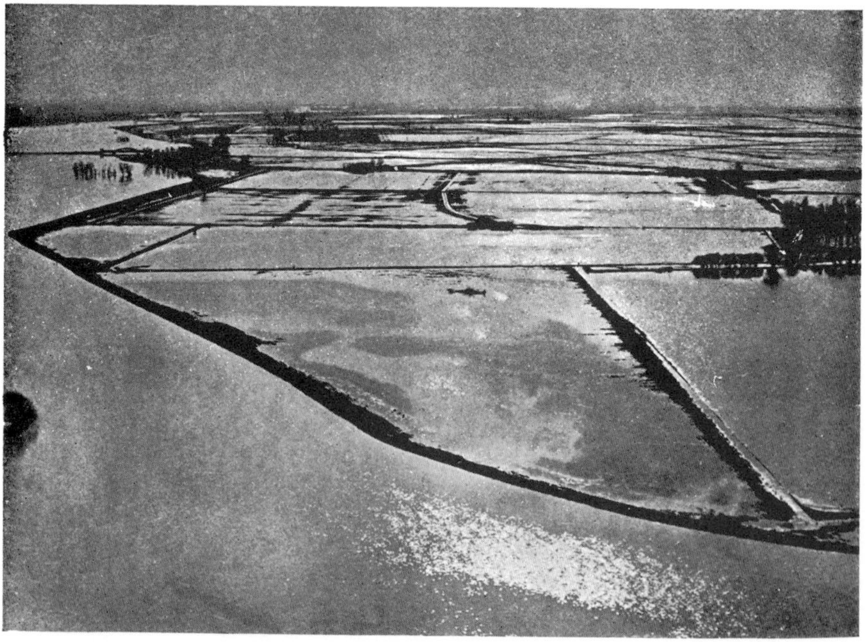

51 March (1947): the Ouse in flood near Ely

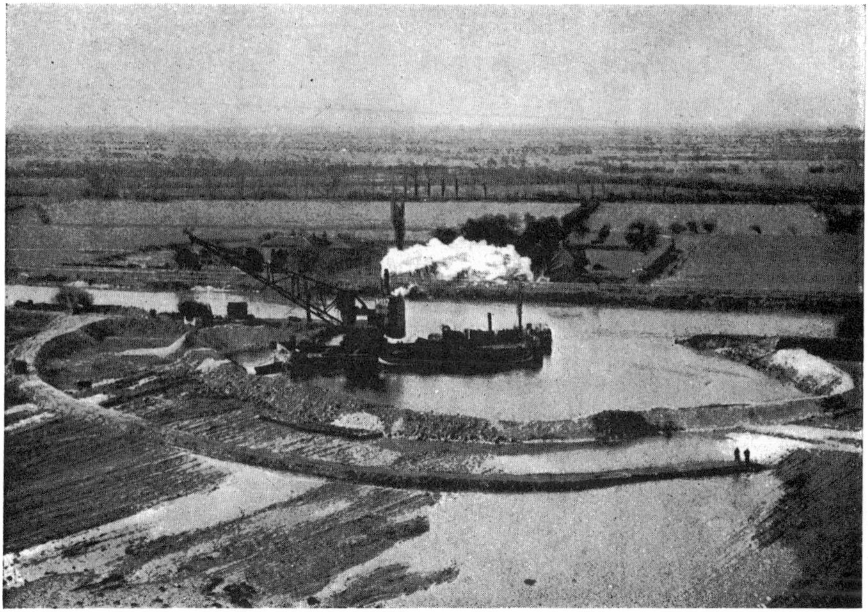

52 Closing the breach in the Trent bank at Morton, 1947

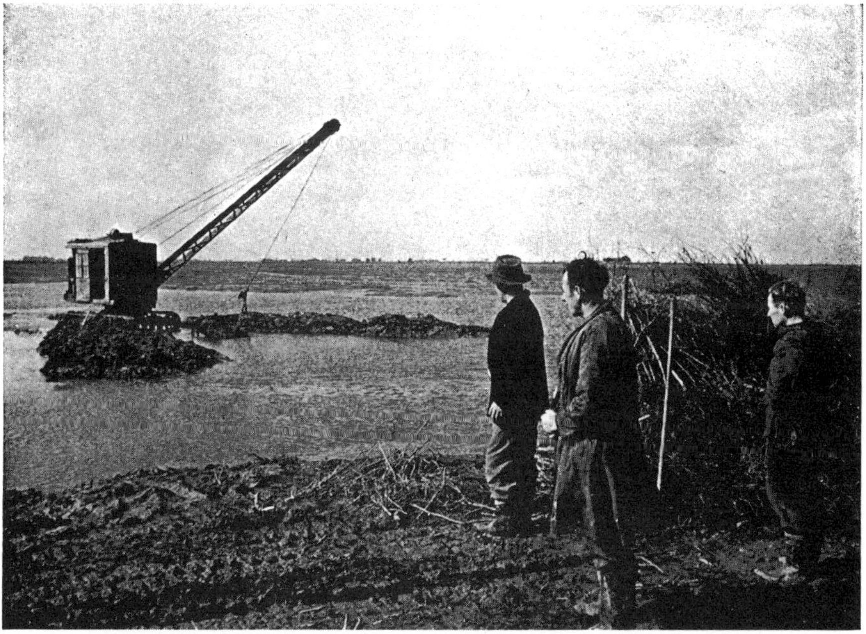

53 Reclamation from the Wash near the mouth of the Welland

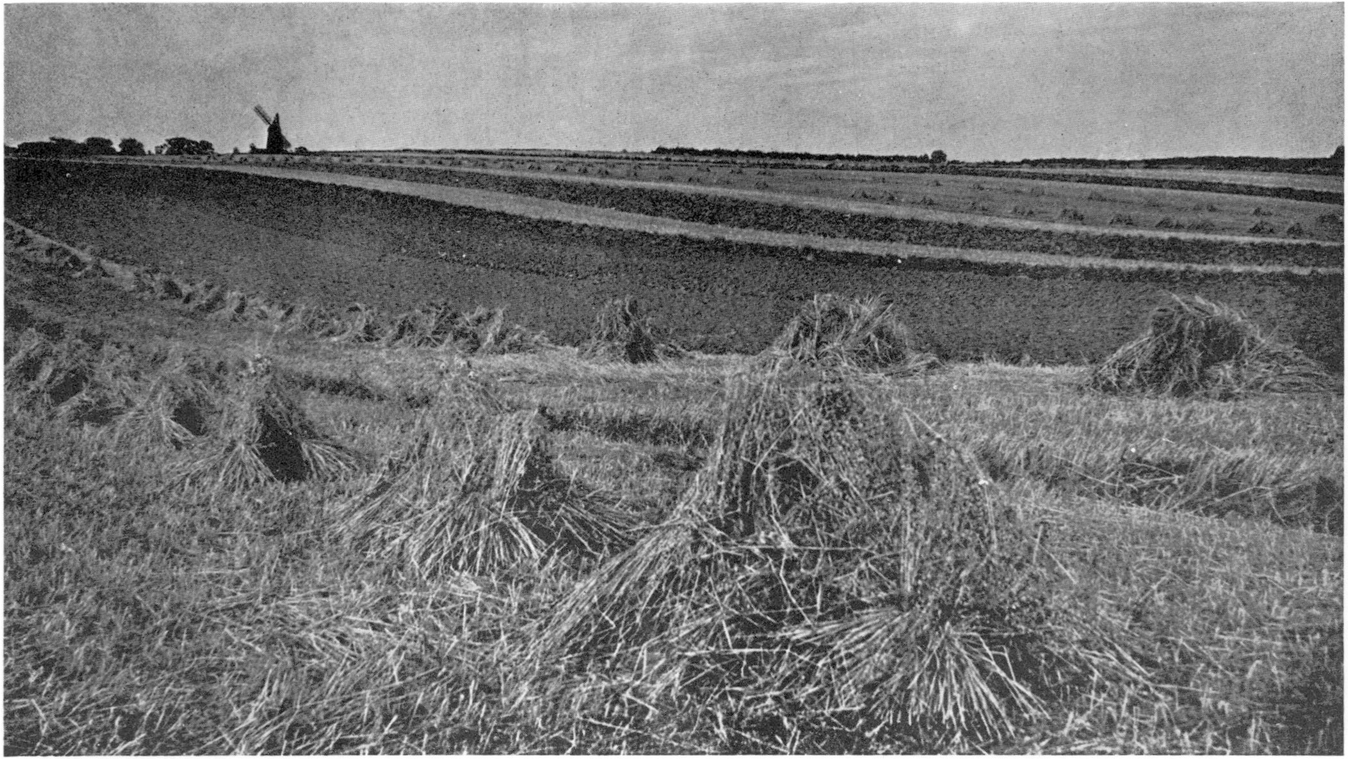

54 Epworth: medieval open fields in the twentieth century

he was often bound to provide boating services. On the Wisbech manor of Ely the fourteenth-century tenant had to "find at any visit or departure of the Lord, a boatman as far as Somersham, Ely, Brandon or elsewhere to the nearest manor, by freshwater, with the Lord's food". At Coningsby in 1200 there lived a fisherman named Geoffrey; he paid rent for his cottage by finding a man (doubtless himself on most occasions) to carry his landlord anywhere on the non-tidal waters of the Witham. The commoners had to take their part in the common task of maintaining banks and cleaning dikes. Just as some upland villages kept a common plough, specially large to draw drainage furrows, so some Fen villages kept a specially large pair of shears for cutting reeds; they were kept in the church when not in use. Victorian writers from overmuch reading of seventeenth- and eighteenth-century pamphlets and books, imagined the fenman as a wild and lawless creature, unused to obeying the law and incapable of co-operation. When the Adventurers arrived, he refused to co-operate in the destruction of his mode of living, but the degree of control that he had already acquired over the Fens depended on a minute regulation of their use. Just as the open-field villages had to make bylaws governing the use of the arable meadow and common, and to appoint bylaw men to enforce them, so the economy of the Fens depended on agreed practices and customary obligations, and on the dike-reeves or fen-reeves to maintain them. There is a long series of by-laws drawn up for Spalding, Moulton, Weston and Pinchbeck in 1591. They were to be read openly in the churches yearly by the fen-reeves, before the manor court meeting. The inhabitants were thus reminded that all fishers and swanherds were to be ready to help the fen-reeves to break ice when the dikes were frozen; that none were to catch any fowl in breeding time; that all such as proposed to lie in the fen all night fowling should be there by 8.0 p.m. and stay until 2.0 a.m. These and scores of other minute requirements maintained the safety and the prosperity of the community. One might argue that the Fens required a higher degree of social consciousness than the life of the upland villages, because great areas like the East and West Fen, Hauthuntre Fen, and the stretch of peat fen between Bourne and Wisbech were common to a number of villages. The name Hauthuntre Fen, originally given to Holland Fen, shows that it was used by a number of villages regarded as making eight Domesday hundreds. Several times a year men on foot, on horseback, and in boats spent days and nights rounding up all the stock so that they could be counted, the brands of the various villages checked, and intruders discovered. Such a practice required a larger view than in the uplands, where a man from the next village was, in the words of a by-law at least, a foreigner. Disputes there were, no less than in any other medieval community, but many of them were provoked by the attempts of the feudal lords, and particularly the monasteries, as the largest landowners in the area, to define boundaries in the common fen which hitherto had scarcely needed definition, or to enclose a piece of common for private use. Such disputes, recorded for us by the litigious bent of medieval England, were no different from the issues which excited riot or lawsuit in any other part of England. If the disputes seem sharp and protracted it was in part because the issues were of great value.

It was this manifest wealth, and the inviting possibilities of large-scale drainage and reclamation suggested by the modest effort of medieval landlords and local communities, that attracted the gentry, and ultimately the Crown itself in the seventeenth century. So started a struggle which lasted for centuries, in which the 1,500 square miles of the fens of Lincolnshire, Cambridgeshire and Norfolk, and the 180,000 acres of the Isle of Axholme and Hatfield Chase, were gradually brought under the mode of cultivation which we see today. The conflict between the improver and the commoner had indeed begun in the Middle Ages; in 1360 the Mowbrays in the Isle of Axholme had been checked in attempts at "approvement", and had been compelled to recognise the rights of their tenants to dig turf for fuel and for walling their houses; to dry flags to thatch them with; to dig up bog oak to repair the banks of the Trent; to rate hemp in the dikes, and to possess dogs to hunt in the moors. But this medieval conflict was only a foretaste; the agreement was to serve as a valuable defence for the commoners when they were defending their rights and their mode of life against the "Adventurers" as they were called. The name reveals their nature; the project for draining the Isle which was planned by the Dutch expert, Cornelius Vermuyden, in 1626, with the full backing of the impecunious Charles I, was a capitalist undertaking of the kind common in the Elizabethan and Stuart periods, and was expected to yield a profit fantastically large by modern standards.

We need not be surprised that, in a century when the East India Company's profit averaged one hundred per cent, and the Africa trade in slaves never produced less than a modest fifty per cent and frequently as much as three hundred, plenty of capital should be available for an undertaking which promised to put two-thirds of the land drained into the possession of the Crown and the undertakers, leaving the local freeholders and owners of common rights with the remaining third. Vermuyden completed his plan in five years, at a cost of £55,000. But neither he nor the other participants prospered in their venture. The attempt to drain some 77,000 acres by manipulating the rivers Don, Idle, and Torne, was a failure, because land hitherto dry was now drowned, and the participants had to spend a further £20,000 in making Dutch River to the Ouse at Goole. Although he had bought the king's third to add to the third he was awarded by the contract, in 1639 he was in gaol for debt. His adventures in land-drainage (and lead-mining in Derbyshire) brought him first a knighthood, but then only lawsuits, debts, and imprisonment; he disappears from history in 1656 a poor man. The Dutch gentry and the peasants who had come from Holland with him, and the French Protestant refugees, were no happier. Their lands were flooded in 1639 in the riots which were to continue intermittently for eighty years. The struggle of commoners against grasping landlords became merged in the issues of the Civil War; the famous John Lilburne associated himself with their cause.

All that Charles I had offered was to get hemp for them, so that they could live by making ropes and sacks; the commoners asserted that they had as much right to defend their commons with swords as Protector Cromwell had the government he had taken upon him. The French and Dutch settlers had their homes burnt, their mills destroyed, and their church at Sandtoft desecrated; they drifted away to America, or returned to the Continent. A sort of guerrilla warfare went on, waged particularly against Nathaniel Reading, collector of rents for forty years. He fought more than thirty set battles against what he called "a generation of vipers"; though they failed to kill him, and did not drive him away, he too died in 1713 a poor man. Perhaps his wife Arabella, sister of Sir Winston Churchill and aunt of the Duke of Marlborough, imbued her husband with some of the determination of her family. There was no clear-cut victory for either side; the improvers revolutionised the mode of life, without altering the social structure of the villages, and the Isle became a stronghold of small freehold farmers. They paid a high price for their freedom; much of the land is of poor quality, and when Archdeacon Stonehouse compiled his *History and Topography of the Isle of Axholme* in the 1830's he described the greater part of the freeholders as "very poor, and far worse than the generality of day labourers". Drainage rates were high, and the process of warping, which enriched much poor land with Trent alluvium, and was widely adopted in the nineteenth century, is today regarded as too expensive. Only the Trent-side from Althorpe to Adlingfleet is as rich as one assumes fenland to be, and was specialising in growing potatoes a full century before south Lincolnshire began to do so. The crop went down to the Trent, and by water to the West Riding, to feed the woollen towns.

In the Fens, the story ran differently only insofar as the land was richer. In 1598, Lord Willoughby wrote to the Earl of Essex expressing his opposition to a bill for draining the fens, because "now a multitude of poor men enjoy it as common, and the bill would dispose of it to owners, the engineer, and *some* commoners. Some land is only drowned in winter, and to drain that would not help the general poor but undo them, and make those that are already rich far more rich." His comment went to the heart of the matter, but he was wasting his breath. Most men of Lord Willoughby's standing had an eye to profit rather than welfare, and Parliament could be convinced by the claim that the land to be drained was eminently suited for growing cole-seed and rape-seed "which is of singular use to make soap and oils with". That was a cogent argument two centuries before the discovery of petroleum, and indeed an important function of the Fenland after drainage was to provide England with soap. The Protestant temper of the seventeenth century resented the existence of "a rude and almost barbarous sort of lazy and beggarly people"; they were barbarous because they were content to live a different life from the rest of England, and lazy because they had not acquired a way of thinking of work as something to be done every day. In the first half of the seventeenth century landowners were busy in the valley of the Ancholme, where Sir John Monson led the way because the foreign undertakers were too expensive; he was allotted 5,827 acres as his share. Lord Willoughby's son, the Earl of Lindsey of Grimsthorpe, undertook in 1634 the drainage of the Lindsey level, between Kyme Fen and the river Glen; he spent about £50,000, and acquired 14,000 acres of common land. In the East Fen, Sir Anthony Thomas carried out in 1631 a scheme which partially drained that area; he probably cut the Maud Foster Drain and made the Maud Foster Sluice in Skirbeck, and gave his name to Anton's Gowt, above Boston. Farther south was the area where Vermuyden's work had touched off this local emulation. The greatest English undertaker, the Earl of Bedford, gave his name to this level, but within it the memory of Dutch experts and investors is preserved in Vernatt's Drain and Bevill's Leam; names like Adventurers' Land and King's Land, between Peterborough and Wisbech, still mark the undertaker's reward and the royal perquisite. The area between the Witham and the Wolds was least affected at this time perhaps because there, as in the Isle, the commoners were fortified by a code of laws for the use of the East, West, and Wildmore Fens drawn up in 1548. Everywhere the outbreak of the Civil War was the signal for the destruction of sluices, banks, and fences, and the commoners' cattle and geese invaded the land; the activity of Lindsey, Monson,

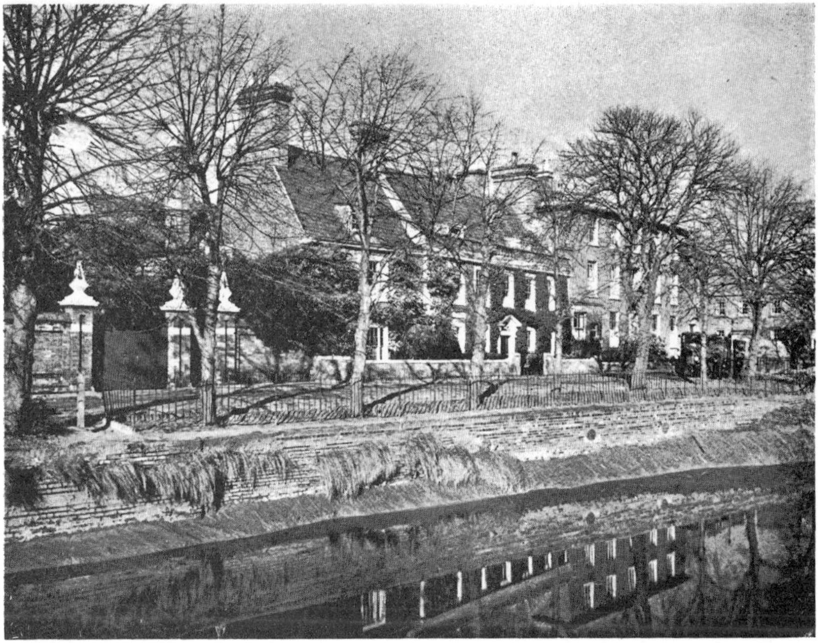

55 Houses by the Welland at Spalding

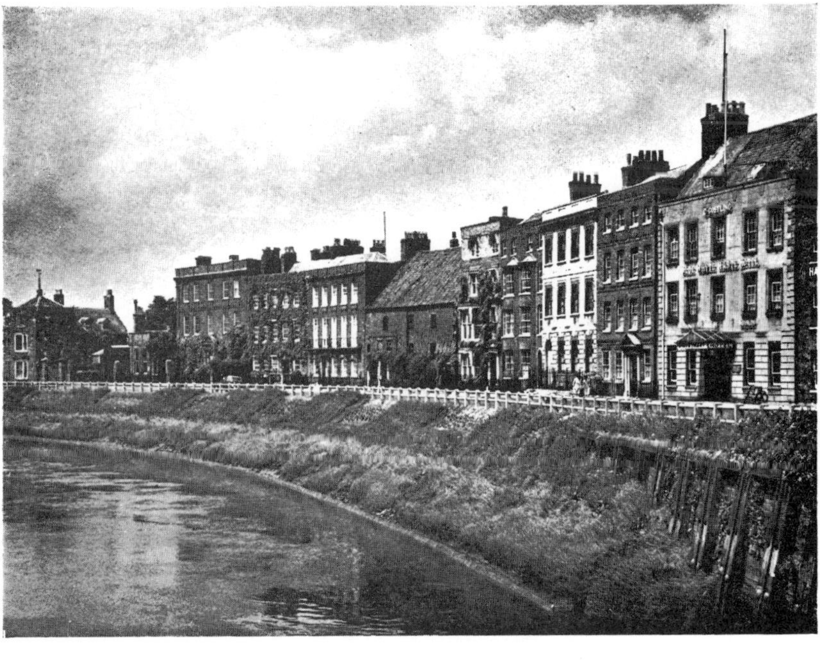

56 The Brinks at Wisbech

GEORGIAN BUILDING IN FENLAND TOWNS

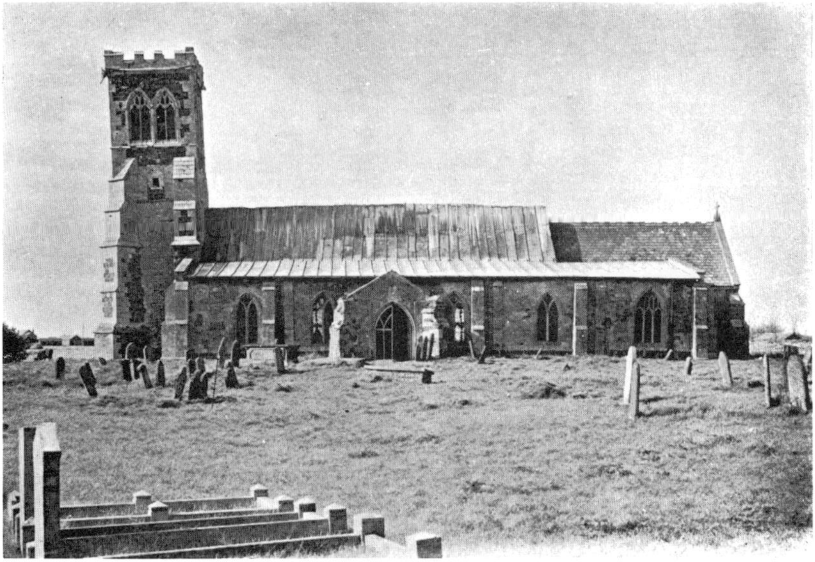

57 A Marshland church: Saltfleetby All Saints

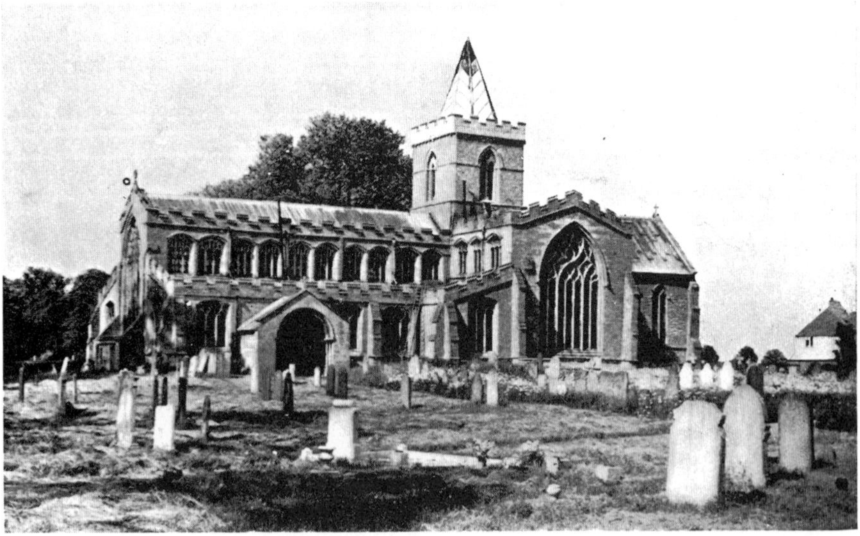

58 A Fenland church: Algarkirk

Thomas, and Vermuyden, with royal backing, had helped the men of the Fens to decide which side they were on, and their war was waged within sight of their homes. They soon found that there was nothing to choose between King and Commonwealth; both believed in private property and the right of the undertaker to his reward. The fact that the struggle was protracted—the East Fen was not enclosed and drained until 1810, and major cuts were being made in the middle of the nineteenth century—meant in fact that the process of adjustment was allowed to take two centuries. The amount of land dry enough to plough was gradually extended, and on the land which was still drowned from time to time the flocks of cattle and the droves of geese grew steadily, so that the prosperity of the area was scarcely checked. But the transition time was a bitter one for many, and the habit of resistance with violence, of hamstringing sheep, burning crops, and shooting men as they lay in bed, lasted into the nineteenth century.

Under the impact of the new religious and political ideas, and the attack of the new capitalists, the men of the fens and valleys found their own particular answers to the moral and political problems of the day. There is no more appropriate point than this to speak of the growth of Nonconformity, and the debt which Britain and the English-speaking communities all over the world owe to Lincolnshire. It is no accident that Gainsborough, in the time of Shakespeare and Ben Jonson, should have been the home for a time of John Smyth, the father of the Baptist movement, and of one of the first Congregationalist churches under John Robinson, which drew its members from adjacent villages in Lincolnshire and Nottinghamshire. Smyth's congregation went to Amsterdam in 1608, and most of its members eventually joined the Dutch Baptists, but Helwys of Nottinghamshire returned to London and the Baptist movement in England. Robinson's congregation, after betrayal at Boston in their first attempt to escape to Holland, sailed again in 1608 from one of the lonely havens of the Humber. The famous John Cotton, vicar of Boston, was one of these Puritans who tried, for longer than Smyth or Robinson, to remain within the Established Church; even the bishop of Lincoln admitted that he was "of great gravity and sanctity of life, a man of rare parts for his learning and eloquence, and well spoken". The chancellor of the diocese heard him deliver three sermons, each about two hours long. There is a clear picture of Boston on the eve of the Civil War in the description of his Sunday afternoon services in the Stump; they lasted for five hours—a two-hour sermon, followed by a public catechising of the young people. "There was as many sleepers as wakers, scarce any man but sometime was forced to wink or nod", but Cotton, through those long Sunday afternoons, was helping to shape a frame of mind which has contributed much to the character of England on both sides of the Atlantic, old and new. From 1620 onwards the many ships which left for the New World carried yeomen and burgesses from Lincolnshire villages and towns, men of some substance, who could afford to buy at least their passage, and often grants of land in the plantations. One of the first was William Blaxtone of Horncastle, who left England "because of the Lords Bishops", and later left Boston, Massachusetts, "because of the Lords Brethren"; he disliked any religious discipline and found for the rest of his life a peaceful isolation on Rhode Island. Other parsons were John Wheelwright, vicar of Bilsby, who went to New Hampshire, and Samuel Whiting, rector of Skirbeck. In the 1630's there left Lincolnshire several parties of men and women connected with Cotton and with the families of the Earl of Lincoln and Lord Saye and Sele. Among them were Hough and Leverett, aldermen of Boston, and Richard Bellingham, formerly member of Parliament for that town. Many of these Lincolnshire men were destined to play leading parts in the affairs of the New England communities; men from Boston, England, were governors of Boston, Massachusetts, for most of the years between 1641 and 1686.

Not all the leaders of Nonconformity left England. One of the foremost figures among the Baptists was Thomas Grantham, their ablest writer. He was baptised at Boston in 1653; became pastor of a congregation at Halton Holgate near Spilsby; was in prison at Lincoln and Louth under the Restoration, and lived to see the Revolution of 1688 and toleration for Nonconformity. He was zealous in creating new groups in the Fens, where the Baptists were in any case strongly established. The same is true of Axholme; the very early Baptist churches at Crowle, Epworth, and Butterwick may be the result of the work of Smyth early in James I's reign. Similarly, Quakerism took a firm hold; its greatest strength seems to have been in the Trent valley; the Gainsborough monthly meeting has been in existence since 1667. One of the most attractive buildings of its kind in Lincolnshire is the meeting house at Brant Broughton; the doorway, flanked by a mounting stone, has the date 1701. While William Warburton, Pope's friend and first editor of his works, was sitting in his rectory writing on the necessity of the *Alliance between Church and State*, equally serious-minded men and women met near by to arrange and maintain a form of life and belief which contradicted every line he was writing.

The last and greatest contribution of Lincolnshire to Nonconformity, John and Charles Wesley, came from Epworth in the centre of an area which, by 1730, had a strong tradition of independent religious thought. John Wesley's upbringing there, and his first parochial work at Epworth and near-by Wroote, must have had some influence on him. After the development of Methodism, Epworth saw John Wesley frequently, and his round of Lincolnshire usually included Alkborough, Barrow and Grimsby on the Humber-side, and Horncastle and Louth in the Wolds. Ever since his time, Lincolnshire has been one of the strongholds of Methodism, as were also Cornwall and Lancashire. When Horace Walpole heard John Wesley preach, he thought him "as evidently an actor as Garrick"; his performance was marred by "very ugly enthusiasm". This judgment comes from another world than that of the tiny chapel in a Wold hamlet, or the camp meeting of the Primitive Methodists in a natural arena such as the Ancaster valley. Methodism was a source of strength and a means of expression at a time when life in the village called for endurance and offered no other outlet.

It is the last phase of the undrained fens, or the half-drained fens, which is best recorded. There were geese by the thousand in Holland Fen, plucked two, three, or five times a year for their down, and marched up to London in enormous flocks to feed the capital. Scotch cattle were fattened by the thousand; the driving of them over the Dam at West Walton was a wild affair, reminiscent of modern America or Australia. Women hustled children indoors and shut the gate while the herd charged past, and mounted drovers kept them moving. Great numbers of sheep were kept everywhere, but particularly in Wildmore Fen; they did so well that the heavy losses from rot in wet seasons were no discouragement. Horses ran almost wild on the West Fen, and the Wildmore Fen produced its own breed, the Wildmore Tit, which was highly regarded. More than one writer marvelled at the number of cattle near Ramsey, or in Deeping and Spalding Fen; and at the heavy crops of corn, beans, mustard, hemp and cole-seed that could be seen everywhere on the drier land. The last remnants of the undrained fens were the East Fen, between the foot of the Wolds and the silt villages from Leake to Friskney; boats could go from one to another of the twenty meres, by the havens or rows which connected them; the water was so clear that pike could be watched and fat bream speared with a hay-fork.

Farther south, Whittlesea Mere was only the largest of several. In 1774 the Earl of Orford made a voyage on "the narrow seas" of Lincolnshire which was as nice a piece of affectation as his uncle's Strawberry Hill. His fleet of "four sail of the line, three tenders, a bumketch and a victualler" pretended to explore this foreign land; the party behaved like most Englishmen of their age.

Bridges too low for their boats to pass were removed (and restored); the places they found were named (Orford Bay in Whittlesea Mere); the natives were described as unflatteringly as if they were Indians. When one member went ashore and his return was overdue, the alarm of the party was recorded, "the late accounts from New Zealand making us apprehensive on his account". Occasionally they dropped the pretence, and got some variety from fishing by going to the races at one of the near-by towns, or seeing a play at Peterborough. Whittlesea Mere was the scene of many regattas in the eighteenth century; hundreds of boats took part, and Yaxley club feast took the form of boating-parties on the mere. When it was drained in 1840, its first crop was an astonishing collection of objects dropped into it over the centuries, including the well-known medieval silver-gilt censer and incense boat which had once belonged to Ramsey Abbey and are now in the Victoria and Albert Museum. After that it produced equally remarkable crops of roots, and the finest corn in Huntingdonshire, but the days of village sports on the water were gone, and while the Dutch still have their meres, the English have only the Norfolk Broads. Those who wish to see Fenland as it was in the Middle Ages must go to Wicken Fen, between Ely and Newmarket, where the National Trust keeps a large area in something like its virgin condition (74). When the Adventurers took over their allotments, they left Wicken Sedge Fen for the commoners to get sedge for thatching and peat for fuel, and since it has not been drained, it is now many feet higher than the surrounding fields. It is not indeed natural fen; the present type of vegetation, and the characteristic birds, animals and insects depend on the land being kept in its half-tamed condition. Drains and dikes must be kept open, and the sedge cut regularly; otherwise Wicken Fen would grow first bushes and then deciduous trees.

Another phase of fenland life came to an end with the railway age. The wealth of the eighteenth century is visible to us in the handsome houses that line the Welland at Spalding (55) and the Nene at Wisbech (56); the large three- and four-storied Georgian warehouses at Spalding and Boston were filled with agricultural produce; Wisbech in 1775 had seven mills for pressing kolza oil, the commonest source of oil before the tropical oils became plentiful and petroleum was discovered. Humber keels came down the coast and smaller boats travelled many rivers and dikes which do not see them now. Denver Sluice, the beginning of tidal water on the Ouse, was full of lightermen in their fur caps and sleeved waistcoats of blue or red plush with glass buttons. They were the last characters in a procession that had lasted for four to five thousand years, during which peaceful trade had eventually found freedom from invading Bronze Age folk, English pirates, Danish raiders, and discontented feudal barons. Along those rivers had passed an unbelievable range of people and commodities. In Roman times, corn for legionaries in the north; in the Middle Ages, wool for the Low Countries, building stone from Northamptonshire and Lincolnshire for churches and monasteries in the Fens; in the fourteenth century, a party of Cambridge undergraduates going to York for the Christmas vacation and Durham monks on their way home after shopping for their abbey at Boston fair; in the fifteenth century, a bailiff of Tattershall going about his business. In the sixteenth and seventeenth centuries, sea-fish bought at Stourbridge fair and carp and pike from Crowland were taken on their way to Belvoir and Grimsthorpe for those large households. From the seventeenth century onwards it was increasingly coal from Newcastle, going as far as Bedford, or Nottinghamshire coal for Lincolnshire villages; but there were also such unexpected things as the medieval glass from Tattershall going down the Witham and up the Welland to Stamford. In the nineteenth, there was that strangest of all Cambridgeshire products, coprolite. The bones and fins of prehistoric animals, found in phosphatised form in a seam a foot thick some twelve to twenty feet down, were mined and ground up for farmers who were then prosperous enough to afford such an expensive fertiliser. Now the coprolite industry has ceased, and on many of the rivers that were once so busy there are no boats to be seen. Potatoes are taken from the Fens to Yorkshire in lorries that rush through the narrow medieval streets of Stamford and Grantham. The twentieth century has turned the lighterman, whose life, "though hard, is attended by no dangers that a prudent temperance will not remove", into the lorry-driver, whose life is equally hard, not much less lonely, and a great deal more dangerous.

Although the Fens are now drained, the struggle against the water has not been won. Now that the upland water reaches the Fens in two days instead of a week, and the silt fen is ten feet higher than the peat fen behind it, new cuts and more powerful pumping stations are required. The windmills (or wind-engines as they were called) have gone out of use, and the last of them has fallen down; there were once thousands of them, and fifty in Whittlesea parish alone, but unlike the Dutch, we have not bothered to preserve one as a museum piece. They were only tenanted from autumn until early summer, but in those months the tenant had to be ready at all hours to work round the great head with its thirty-six-feet sails, or to get in the canvas if the wind rose to a gale. The steam engines have gone the same way; in Pinchbeck Marsh there is a beam engine, installed in 1833 and still working perfectly; it gives greater satisfaction to the eye than the kind of electric pump which will replace it in another year or two. The drainage work, like everything else in the twentieth century, is now centralised, and much depends on the great pumping stations at Wiggenhall St. Germans and Black Sluice, Boston. To stand in the latter station, as I have done, and see the water being sucked out of the South Forty Foot Drain, is tremendously impressive. Another demonstration of the ease with which modern man can accomplish the merely mechanical is to watch a new channel being made to carry the river Welland round the town of Spalding. Vermuyden used hundreds of men, and the Earl of Bedford added five hundred Dutch prisoners of war. We use two excavators to cut a two-mile channel in a single summer, and this is a trivial undertaking compared with the projected scheme for the Ouse, which will provide a new thirty-five-mile long channel, skirting the southern Fens, and all the consequent road and railway bridges. When such works are done, we still have to follow the Dutch into considering such subtle problems as the optimum level of water in the dikes and drains for grassland and different kinds of crops on varying types of soil. The challenge to human ability is endless.

The last and greatest change in the Fens has happened in the last seventy years or more. The stories of cattle by the thousand and commons white with sheep seem as incredible now as the accounts of the original wild life, for there are fewer livestock than in any other part of England, and every field is under the plough. The fenland farmer has found his solution for the changed status of English farming in growing potatoes and sugar-beet, flowers and fruit; he has added frost to the hazards he has to contend with; but that is preferable to the uncertainty of world market prices and international politics.

Chapter

VII

Country Matters

A COUNTY which has produced so much of the nation's food has naturally had its own ideas of what to eat and how to eat it, and I will not dispute the Lincolnshire man's good sense in what he chose to sell to others and what he kept for himself. The origin of the Lincolnshire breed of sheep, the Lincolnshire long wool, is lost in antiquity, but no one valued this large-boned animal for its meat until the eighteenth century. The wool itself has always been sought by the world's users of fine wool. In the Middle Ages it was Florentine merchants, riding round from monastery to monastery; in the seventeenth century it was merchants from Yorkshire and East Anglia. The Yorkshire men crossed over the Trent from the Isle of Axholme, or used the Roman road from Doncaster and ferried across at Littleborough; Massingberd of Ormsby, at the other end of the county, was visited every year by clothiers from Ipswich, Hadleigh, and Boxford in Suffolk. Fifty years ago men from the Argentine and Australia came to the famous ram sales at Riby, near Grimsby, on the farm of Henry Dudding of Riby Grange, recognised as the premier farmer of England; they paid prices which will never be equalled for the products of the Lincolnshire Wolds. The mutton was good enough for Londoners: in Defoe's time Lincolnshire and the midlands "furnished the City of London with their large mutton in so incredible a quantity". Lincolnshire horses were no less in demand; Horncastle fair was, until a couple of generations ago, probably the largest horse fair in the world; its streets for three weeks in the year were jammed with horses and horsy men. Lincoln Fair was only a little less famous, and from these fairs went horses for farmers and for the draymen of the towns of Victorian England. Alford Bull Fair is still, along with Lincoln Fair, the chief one for Lincoln Red cattle.

The one animal that the county produced, which could not be driven to London, and was valued not for its bristles or its skin, but simply as good food, was the pig. Even geese could be plucked four times a year, and shod for the long trek to the capital; fish could be taken alive, as Defoe describes, in great butts carrying tench and pike, perch and eels for their Cockney consumers. But no one devised anything better to do with pig than to salt it down.

In the darkest days of the agricultural depression, bacon was the only meat that the farm labourer and the struggling freeholder could afford, and pig-killing has remained in Lincolnshire an occasion when, for once, gifts to neighbours could be generous and goodwill could take real form. The very name for the immediate products of the killing—"pig cheer"—shows how much it has meant; it is still part of the traditional gesture that the dish in which the fry or the sausages are given should be returned unwashed. The Lincolnshire breed of pig, the Lincolnshire Curly Coat, is going out of fashion, in favour of smaller breeds; it is not suited to specialised pig-production and the bacon factory. Lincolnshire sausages and pork-pies are famous, and brawn and haslet are well enough known, but the real indication of a Lincolnshire upbringing is a liking for scraps, small pieces of fat crisped in the rendering down, or an ability to eat bacon in which there is no more than the thinnest trace of lean in four inches of fat. The bacon was no mere breakfast dish; it appeared at dinner in an egg and bacon pie, and at tea as cold bacon or in a bacon cake. Those who were brought up in the county recall such dishes with a sentiment which may now be deceptive, but there is no doubt in my mind of the quality of Lincolnshire plum cake, or the unsurpassable taste of home-made bread eaten hot from the oven and spread with treacle. It is more difficult to commend the Lincolnshire vegetable, mercury, marquery, or Good King Henry, whatever name you choose; Poor Man's spinach it is, and much less pleasant than its cultivated cousin.

Lincolnshire has never been eminent among fruit-growing counties, but like every part of England, it produced in the past its own varieties of apples, which were particularly suited to the local soil. Most of them are disappearing now, in this age which can only think in terms of Bramley's Seedling and Cox's Orange Pippin. Lincolnshire has naturally suffered a large invasion from Nottinghamshire of that much overrated apple, Bramley's Seedling, and the Holland Pippin, which was a better apple at the same season, is unknown. A near relative is the Lincolnshire Holland Pippin or Striped Holland Pippin. The Squire's Pippin was raised at Wigtoft; it looks like a small Blenheim Orange. The Stamford district has produced more than one apple of note: Lord Burghley, one of the finest russet dessert apples, was bred at Burghley House; Brown's Seedling and the Stamford Pippin came from a nurseryman at Stamford. From the Fens as well as Kirton Pippin came Sleeping Beauty, and Shepherd's Pearmain is claimed by both Lincolnshire and Norfolk. Until recently there was Schoolmaster, a fine large, long-keeping, cooking apple, of which a tree stood, appropriately enough, in Stamford Grammar School. In Victorian

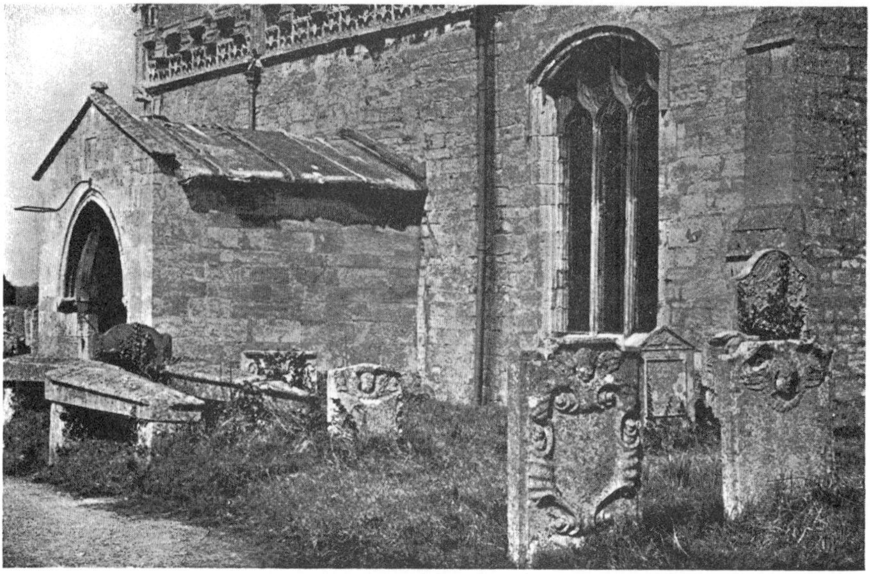

59 Typical headstones at Ancaster

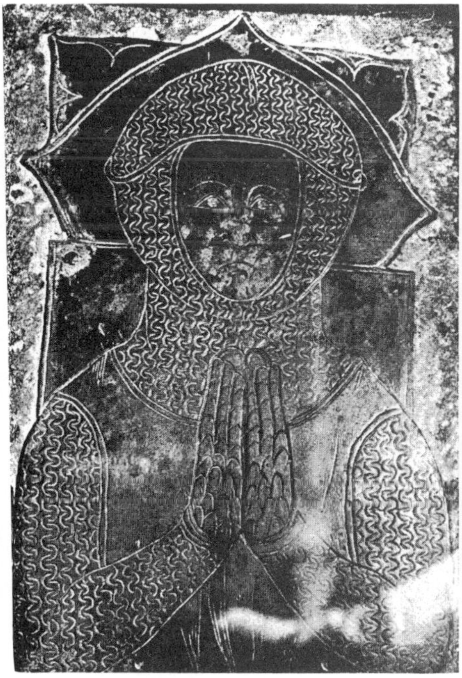

60 Brass to Sir Richard de Boselyngthorpe (*c.* 1275)

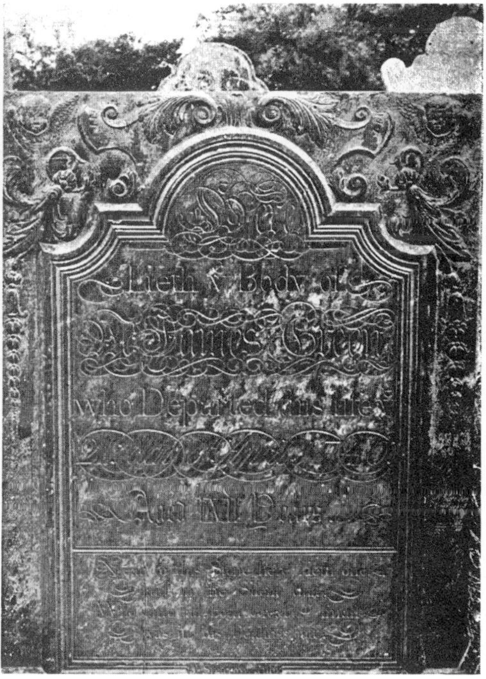

61 Slate headstone at Foston by James Sparrow

LINCOLNSHIRE MEMORIALS

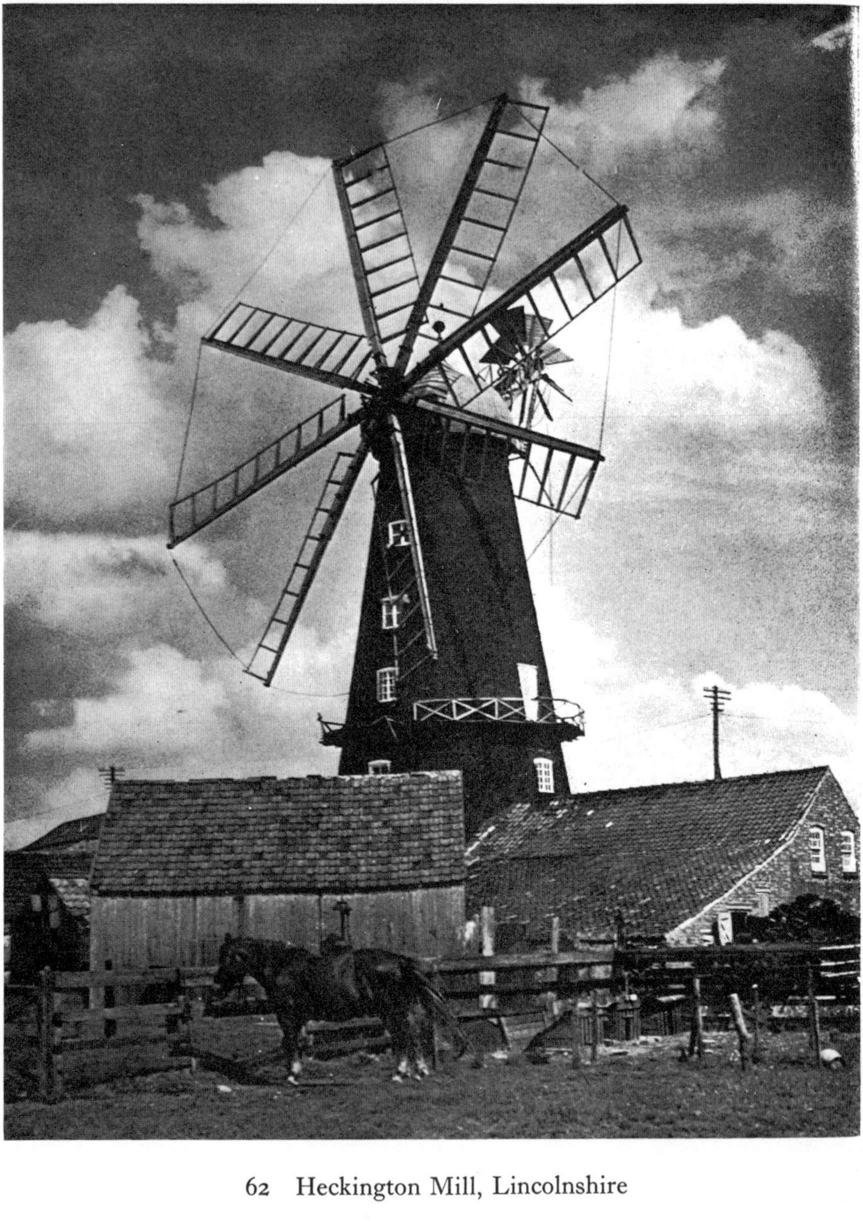

62 Heckington Mill, Lincolnshire

days Lord Lennox was much grown round Lincoln itself.[1] It is a pleasant change from the twentieth-century fruit-shop, which merely sells "good eaters" which will taste like turnips or cotton-wool, to savour the names of Lord Lennox, or Sleeping Beauty, or Lincoln Codlin; it is even better to search the old orchards and find the apples still treasured and their qualities remembered. The only sad thing is that the trees on which they hang are thirty years or more old, and the young trees which are taking their place have been bred for every reason but a good one—for their colouring, or uniform size, or because they crop regularly, but not because they have the best flavour when they are at their prime.

The wide expanses of Lincolnshire, which have grown so much corn, have naturally been famous for their windmills, and the county still has more working mills than any other in England (62). Some of them seem oddities because they have five sails, like the Maud Foster at Skirbeck, Boston, or six, like Myer's mill at Alford; in fact mills with five or six sails are more efficient, and the craftsmen who built mills were an ingenious race, always looking for improvements and devising their own. Lincolnshire windmills for grinding corn have been of two types. The oldest is the post mill, and most of the surviving specimens are eighteenth century, though Foston Mill, which stands by the North Road between Grantham and Newark, and is now derelict, has the date 1636 inside. Several were demolished in the 1930's—Carlton-le-Moorland and Kirkby Green, for instance. The smock mill with a tower of wood, common in south-eastern England, was not strong enough for Lincolnshire winds; the typical mill is the great tower mill of five or more stories. Nearly all were brick, though there were several stone towers on the limestone belt and there was one built of chalk at Waltham north-east of the Wolds. They invariably had a wooden ogee-shaped cap covered with vertical boarding and with the automatic fan-tail for turning the sails balancing the sails themselves behind the curved white cap. Too often now all that one can see is the dark brick tower, beheaded and useless, and one automatically writes of windmills in the past tense. The village of Haxey is ringed with disused towers. With them a whole vocabulary has gone from our language: the glossary in Rex Wailes' book on windmills is full of such delightful words as the windshaft and the wallower, the great spar wheel, the quants and the runner stones. The achievement of our age has been to build greater power mills at Lincoln and Hull, and to make the fortunes of the Ranks and the Whittons, when quite simple and much less costly improvements such as the use of roller-bearings

[1] I am indebted to P. Morton Shand for my information about these old apples; it is pleasant to be able to state that he has recovered most of them.

would have made windmills efficient enough to survive. If Victorian England had had less capital for railways and steam mills, would we be worse off today? Along with the windmill has gone the Lincolnshire wagon which used to carry corn to the mill and the market town; it was an enormous wagon, carrying four tons and pulled by four horses. It had no particular refinements of ornament or construction, but it was fitted in capacity to large farms and wide cornfields.

The same process has driven the Humber keel from the Humber and the Trent. The large mills are to be found on the Brayford at Lincoln and at Gainsborough and Hull; they grew up because they were fed by water-borne cargoes, but today there is no one surviving specimen of that ancient type of craft which carried the corn to them. It was a sea-going vessel, akin to the Tyne and Norfolk keels; all were descended from the viking boat, and they had changed little since medieval days at least. Because of the shallow waters it used, the Humber keel had movable keel boards slung over the sides, but the characteristic feature, to one not acquainted with details of construction, was the square rig. The best place in which to see it, twenty or thirty years ago, was on the Foss Dyke near Drinsey Nook; the square sail drifted slowly through the fields, and seemed more at home there than on the wide waters of the Humber.

A different type of mill which deserves to be recalled was the woadmill. Woad is indigenous to Britain, as every schoolboy knows, but when it was first grown on a large scale in the Fens I cannot tell. Certainly it was well established by the end of the eighteenth century when publicists like Arthur Young began to describe farming practices in detail, and it only ceased to be grown between the great wars. It was a very exhausting crop, and only the best land was sown with it. The leaves were gathered from the growing plant in the autumn; they were then crushed in circular mills turned by several horses, and after draining were rolled into small balls. The process of allowing the balls to dry and then to ferment, and finally of grinding them into the powder which was used for dyeing, went on over the winter. The last mill to work was at Parson Drove, and Rex Wailes has done a good service in recording this mill and the details of the industry.

The woad industry was insignificant before the eighteenth century; its growth was a by-product of the industrial revolution and the great expansion of the cloth industry. Lincolnshire was too far away from the centres of industrial development to play more than a trivial part in that; it has only been reached in the past seventy years by the spreading tentacles of large-scale mining, and hardly knew the earlier phase when industry was growing out of craftsmanship. The only pottery-making in the county was when William Billingsley, a well-known maker of china and a celebrated flower painter, established himself at Torksey. He had worked earlier at Pinxton and Mansfield, and moved to Torksey in 1803, where there were clay deposits which had not been used for pottery since Roman and Norman times. But he was of a roving disposition, and soon moved to South Wales; his best work was done at Swansea and Nantgarrow, and his Torksey china is a rarity. The same forces which were leading to the extension of china and porcelain manufacture were responsible for the establishment of linen-weaving at Appleby, near the Humber. The villagers made fine linen for the table, bed hangings and similar things, but the industry died out a century ago. It is perhaps odd that cheese-making as a rural industry has not survived in the county; there was no Lady Beaumont to make the happy discovery of a Lincolnshire equivalent to Stilton. In the seventeenth century most Lincolnshire farmhouses made a hard cheese, for cheese presses figure very frequently in the inventories which I mentioned earlier. Cheese-making lasted longest in the Trent valley, and the cheese was marketed at the cheese fairs at Gainsborough and Newark.

One of the curious aspects of English social history which is still unexplained and largely unrecorded, is the habit which made its appearance between 1600 and 1700 of placing headstones to mark burials in a churchyard. The more pretentious monuments of the feudal nobility and the gentry, who could afford a burial within the walls of the church, have been well studied, but no one has paid sufficient attention to the stones which in the last two centuries have filled the village churchyard. There are a few medieval headstones; the curious will find two in Grantham churchyard—small stones with a rounded head in which a simple cross is incised. But headstones carrying a date earlier than 1700 are rare; the number of eighteenth-century examples shows that the habit—indication of rising pretentions, if not of a rising standard of life—spread rapidly. Kesteven churchyards, and those of the fenland villages south of the Wash, are full of fine memorials (60, 61). The common material is Ketton stone; Ancaster was much less used. Although the material was, so to speak, imported, it came by waggon in uncut slabs which were then carved by local masons. It is seldom possible to find the name of the mason, even if he put it on originally; and the stones in Spalding churchyard, for instance, should be looked at individually for the combination of the fashionable forms of Baroque ornament with a vigorous and not over-tutored imagination which can be seen through the lichen and the mask of weathering. One of the masons who can be rescued from oblivion was William Sands of Spalding. He was described as "architect and carver in stone" when he was admitted a member of the Spalding Gentlemen's Society in 1745; there is in Weston church a delightful wall tablet, with the inscription carved on the wavy shield surrounded by acanthus scrolls popular at the time, and Sands may have carved the two similar tablets which are fixed to the outside of Spalding church. Such masons aspired to be architects, and even if they found the step difficult to take, they could pave the way for the next generation. Several of the fine Georgian houses in Spalding built alongside the river Welland between 1750 and 1770 are ascribed to a Sands who was probably William's son.

In Kesteven there is variety of a different kind. The village masons here evolved a local type of monument, which was carried out in Ancaster stone; perhaps the form owes something to the qualities of the material. It consists of a very substantial slab or ledger, tapered towards the foot and usually plain on top, supported on two vertical slabs so that the ledger is raised about a foot from the ground. Sometimes the end face of the ledger is ornamented, and a brief inscription is carved on the support below. These memorials are to be seen in most of the churchyards between Leadenham in the north and Grantham in the south; they are unsigned, and one can only suggest from the distribution of them that they were made by masons working somewhere near the Ancaster quarries. They are too substantial to have travelled far from either the quarry or the mason's yard. Another material which was less bulky, and therefore travelled much farther afield, was Swithland slate, from Charnwood Forest in Leicestershire. It was used only for headstones, and not in Lincolnshire for the everyday purposes that Dr. Hoskins has described in *Midland England*, but its use began in the early years of the eighteenth century. Most of the slate headstones in Kesteven date from after 1800, when the Nottingham–Grantham canal was open, and the slate slabs no doubt became much cheaper when they could be brought by boat. But a century earlier small Swithland headstones were being erected at Grantham and near by which had been engraved by local craftsmen. There are a few examples—at Ropsley, Great Gonerby, and Sedgebrook, for instance—which have a cherub engraved at the top in markedly archaic fashion; they belong to a style common in the Vale of Belvoir and must have been engraved there. This need not cause surprise, because after about 1750, when these headstones are usually signed, James Sparrow of Radcliffe-on-Trent near Nottingham (61), and George and Francis Lamb of Bottesford sold many headstones in Lincolnshire. Sparrow's son George moved to Grantham and set up business there, and from 1760 or so until 1825 his workshop and that of other masons such as George Neale were producing many slate headstones in which the fashionable styles of the time are paraded. The earliest are simple works; the hard slate permitted either carving in low relief of a cherub's head, skull and crossed bones, an hour-glass, or other simple emblems of man's mortality; or, alternatively, only engraved lettering in the various styles—gothic, roman, or cursive italic—of the writing masters' copy books. James Sparrow introduced into Lincolnshire, in the 1740's, the full range of Baroque and Rococo fashions with richly carved acanthus sprays that threaten to turn into Gothic crocketed pinnacles. Then comes the more dignified and poised ornament of the Adam period—urns on columns, and festoons of foliage that are shallow and verging on the mechanical. The element of popular art is indeed dead by 1790; the only interest in the later headstones lies in the variety of the lettering, and by 1825 or so that too is lifeless and automatic. Many of us when walking through a churchyard, try not to see the wilderness of stone, white marble, grey and pink granites, and the like, brought far from the places to which they belong to shout down the quiet monuments of an earlier age. The whole story of craftsmanship in modern society is there, if we can bear to read it: the village craftsman working on local material, and making out of the limited range of his experience something that becomes art because it is more than merely useful; the same craftsman stimulated by the impact of architectural fashions, but eventually robbed by them of his own personality, and driven to catch a customer with the bait of a new material, the like of which had not been seen in the churchyard before.

These villages which could perpetuate the dead in their own way, could entertain the living too, and there is the same pattern of development in this side of village life. The community made its own entertainment, and when the world at large gave forth suggestions, they were embodied in the rural pattern; but eventually the suggestions became a barrage of commands which rural minds could only obey. I suppose the oldest evidence of village amusements are the turf mazes, of which the county had at least four examples, and still has one. I visited Alkborough, an isolated village in the angle of Trent and Humber, again in 1950, and the maze, though still visible, is sadly in need of recutting. There used to be another at Appleby, which was known as Troy Walls; those at Alkborough, Horncastle, and Louth all bore the name Julian's Bower. They must be of medieval date—the Louth one is mentioned in 1544—and one would rather think of them as the site of traditional games than as penitential paths for confessed sinners trying to find the way to salvation.

The turf mazes are not peculiar to Lincolnshire, but an entertainment which belongs more to this county than any other is the Plough Jag play. There are a few villages, such as Carlton-le-Moorland, where the play is still performed, but this is perhaps no more than a self-conscious clinging to tradition. In most places the annual performance is now a hazy recollection of the oldest inhabitants; the plays died in the nineteenth century when, in E. K. Chambers' words, high farming brought about "the ultimate degradation of the farm labourer". Before that there must have been very few villages which had not their own Plough Boys, or Plough Jags, Bullocks, or Stots. The name indicates that once the plough which was taken round was actually pulled by oxen. Preparations began early in December, and performances were often started before Christmas, but the play belonged properly to Plough Monday—the first Monday after Twelfth Night—and not to Christmas. Plays vary a good deal, but the variation is not from place to place so much as from period to period; each generation wrote in new lines and introduced topical characters. The oldest surviving texts are full of reminiscences of folk-songs and of plays and ballads of the sixteenth and seventeenth centuries; plays performed more recently have taken in the Napoleonic Recruiting Sergeant, and one of the tunes commonly used was the hard-worked Victorian melody best known as "Villikins and His Dinah". Though the village borrowed from the strolling player and the printed ballad, or even from the music hall, the play was always village property, and the occasion a high one. No women were included in the cast, and young men taking the party of the Lady or Dame Jane were keen enough to let their hair grow; at Alkborough, where the tradition was very strong, the most precious beads, brooches, and watch-chains in the village were borrowed to adorn the top hats of the four Hat Men. When my grandmother was a child there, her mother was reluctant to let the team come into the kitchen, because of the dirt they brought in, but the children offered to scrub the floor afterwards, so that they could see the play, and be allowed to handle the heavy and sparkling top hats. The children watched the oddly dressed party: the Hobby Horse with pins and fish-hooks in his tail; Besom Betty, who came last to sweep out the clods carried in by the actors; they laughed at Beelzebub, with his frying-pan, and the Doctor who claimed to cure

Hipsy, pipsy, palsy, gout,
Pains within and pains without,
Heal the sick or cure the lame,
Raise the dead to life again.

One wonders whether they were frightened when the Indian King or the Fool was killed in the mock duel; they did not know that here was the core of the ceremony. On this dark day in January after the end of the Christmas holiday, the death of the old season was confirmed, and the miraculous resurrection of the Indian King was the same magic ceremony as had been performed in these villages for a thousand years to promote the revival of the earth without which spring ploughing would be ineffective. This pagan ceremony, common to peasants in Ireland and the Balkans and Lincolnshire, had survived not because the Christian Church failed to suppress it, but because, along with so many other heathen notions, the Church sanctified it with a wise approval. The special plough used in the ceremony was kept in the church in medieval times; the collection customarily made in each cottage and farmhouse kitchen was taken over for the maintenance of a light in the church. There are many bequests in medieval wills to the plough light, along with the yeomens', the weavers', the maidens', and the young men's lights; and at Thimbleby there was a Plough Gild. In some places on Humber-side, such as Barrow and Grimsby, the Plough Stots performed a sword dance, as they did in the Whitby area of Yorkshire; it is curious that the ceremony took this particular form in the places where contact with the Scandinavian world was closest and long retained.

The songs sung on these and similar occasions have vanished, or have survived only by adopting Victorian guise. Forty or fifty years ago, Percy Grainger and others were just in time to collect the songs which accompanied rural sports and occasions. In Bourne workhouse they found Philip Gray, once a shepherd, who sang a sheep-shearing toast which he had learned at a shearing from a wool-winding man. In the north of the county, they found George Gouldthorpe at Barrow-on-Humber. He had had a hard life, but "a life of drudgery, ending in old age in want and hardship, had not shorn his manners of a degree of humble nobility and dignity, nor could any situation rob him of his refreshing Lincolnshire independence". He sang with a gaunt simplicity "Six Dukes went a-Fishing", a fifteenth-century ballad recording the murder of a duke of Suffolk—William de la Pole, whose family had made a fortune as merchants and bankers in fourteenth-century Hull. One wonders if it is more than coincidence that this song should have continued to be sung on Humber-side. There was Joseph Taylor of Saxby All Saints, who at the age of seventy-eight still had a ringing tenor, and a style full of rhythmic contrasts, ornaments, and slides. Another singer was George Wray of Barton. He had started work in a brickyard at the age of eight; went to sea, returned to brick-making, and then carried coals to the Humber-side villages in his own boat up to the age of seventy-three. He had been a great dancer in his time, and his brother played the fiddle for dancing. It was Percy Grainger who heard one of these men sing a fragment, all that he could recall, of a song which began:

It was on the fifth of August, the weather hot and fair,
Unto Brigg Fair I did repair, for love I was inclined.
I rose up with the lark in the morning, with my heart so full of glee,
Expecting there to meet my dear, long time I'd wished to see.

There was no more than that; not enough, fortunately, to make a song for the concert platform, but it has become well known in the rhapsody which Delius made out of it. Tunes such as this, or "Broomfield Hill", which Mabel Peacock heard a servant girl from the Isle of Axholme sing, are much older than that best-known Lincolnshire song, "The Lincolnshire Poacher", which belongs to the eighteenth century and the age of the Game Laws; these older ballads tell a story common to many parts of Europe, and express feelings which are timeless and universal. Not that the oldest songs are necessarily the best; even in the eighteenth century the growth of the Greenland whale-fishing from Hull gave rise to this:

No shoe nor stocking I'll put on nor comb go in my hair,
Nor any lamp or candle light burn in my chamber bare.
Nor shall I lie with any young man until the day I die,
Now the cold, cold coast of Greenland has torn my lover from me.

It was thus that the hardest things in life, the death and the cruelty, the separation of lovers and the violence of the laws, were expressed and relief found, before the days of the cinema and the radio, which now provide cheap daydreams and vicarious singing. The songs have gone with the things that figured in them—the mill and the miller's daughter, the sheep-shearing, the fair, and the whale-fishery. The descendants of Joseph Taylor and George Gouldthorpe are still spoken of in their villages as great singers, but they no longer sing the songs which were an essential part of everyday life up to a century ago.

One of the few genuine survivals is the Haxey Hood—another Plough Monday ceremony, once performed in several villages in the Isle of Axholme. The hood is still thrown up for everyone to struggle for, under the eyes of the Plough Boggans, and finally carried by the victor to his favourite pub. Perhaps it has survived because the open field of medieval Haxey, on the hill-top near the church, is still open; the game would have become impossible

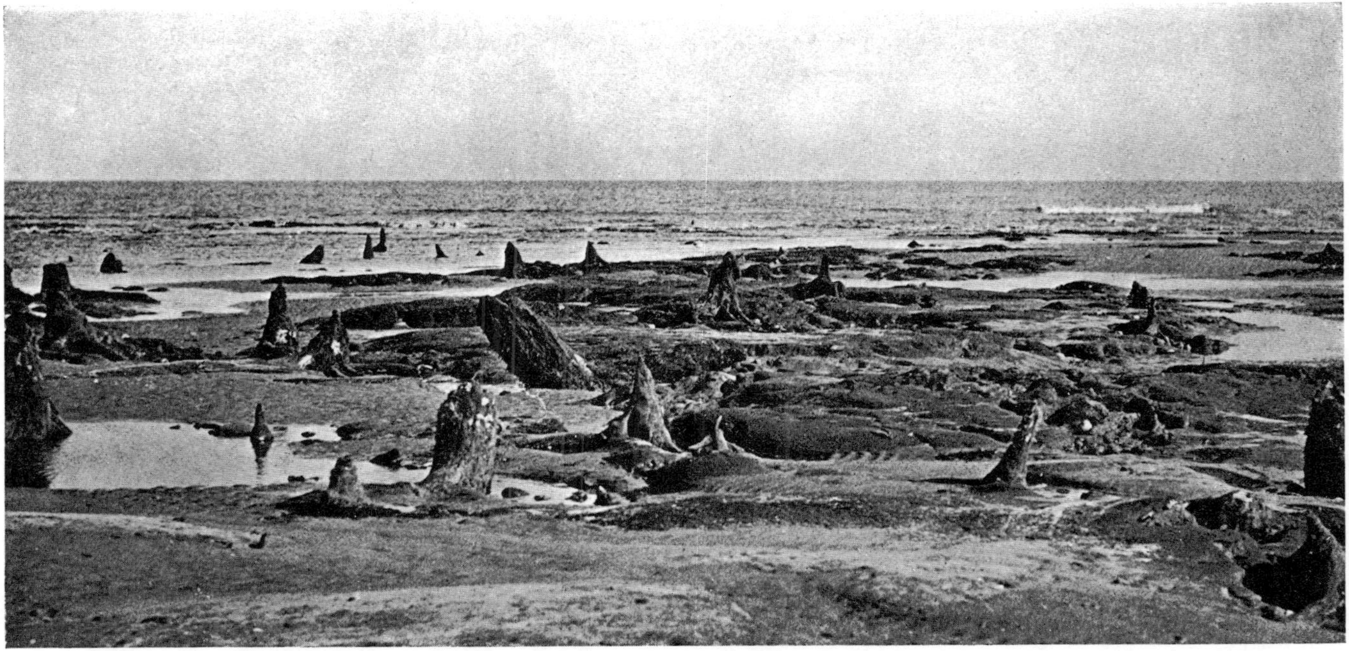

63 Low tide at Mablethorpe: the submerged forest

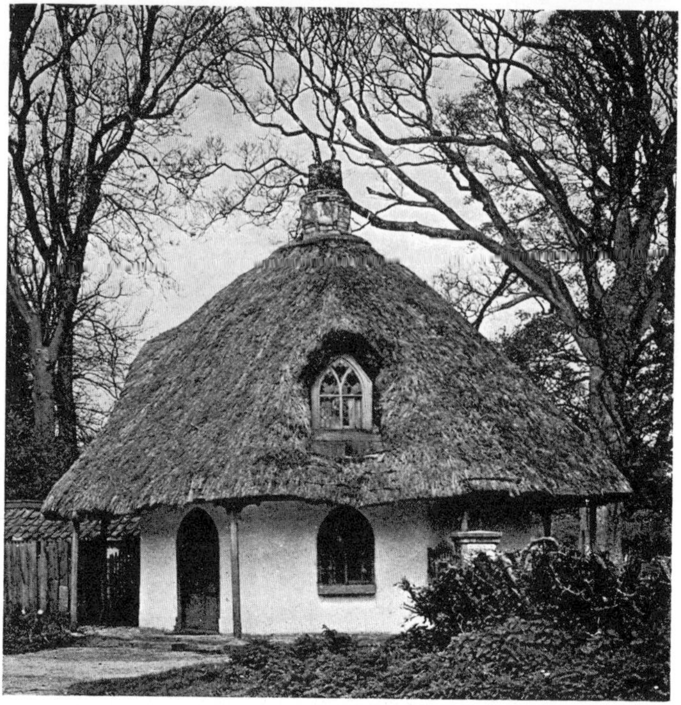

64 Estate cottage in Picturesque style at Langton by Spilsby

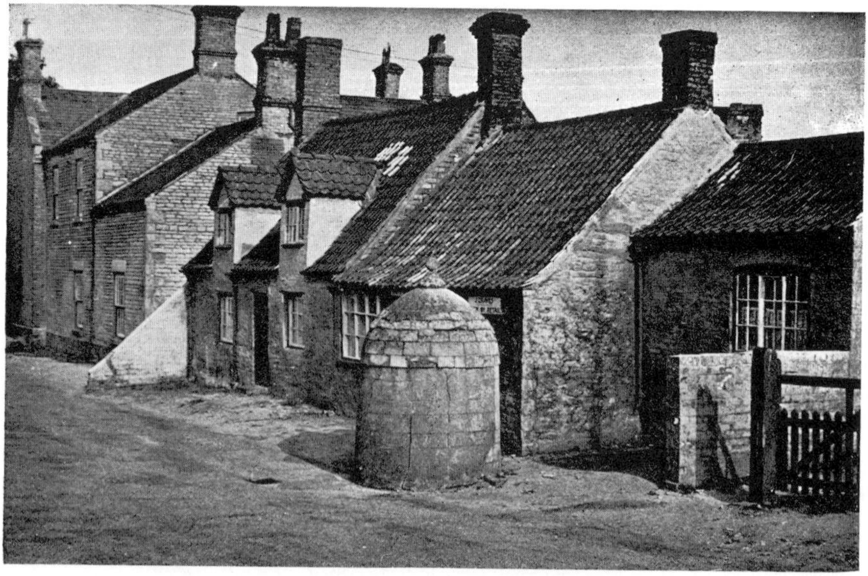

65 Stone cottages and a well cover at Digby

among hedges and through field gates. Today it is a spectacle for visitors from Sheffield, and the windmill which once turned nearby has given way to a great concrete water tower, but the survival may serve as a reminder of the enduring homogeneity of the Danelaw, to which the Plough Monday ceremonies, whatever their local form, appear to belong.

Chapter

VIII

Town and Country Today

LINCOLN has been and still is a city with several facets. Its oil engines and excavators are used by men who have never heard of the cathedral; we who think of it as a cathedral city forget that it has been a port and a centre of the cloth industry. Its two periods of greatest prosperity have been from the Danish settlement to the Black Death (1349), and in the last century.

In the first phase it ranked with Southampton, Lynn, Boston, and York among the wealthiest provincial cities, and it did not outgrow its medieval size until the nineteenth century. From this first phase Lincoln has kept a greater wealth of buildings than any other city in England. The list starts with the Minster, of which only the towers are later than the thirteenth century. There is an indication of the wealth of the county and of the astonishing effectiveness of medieval coastal and inland shipping, in the twelfth-century font imported from Tournai in Belgium (there is a second in Lincolnshire at Thornton Curtis near the Humber), and in the use of Purbeck marble for the nave piers(21). The list includes a thirteenth-century Greyfriars and three churches south of the Witham in the suburb of Wigford, all containing good Norman and Early English work. The tale of secular buildings is even more impressive: an early Norman castle, two of the gates into the walled cathedral close, and the ruins of the thirteenth-century bishop's palace; a stone bridge over the river, two Norman houses in the upper city, and a Norman guildhall in Wigford. Forty medieval churches have disappeared, and some of them we should regret, but most of them were insignificant buildings. Defoe described them as "the meanest to look at that are anywhere to be seen". Much more to be regretted is the loss of many medieval houses. It is doubtful whether any provincial city in the thirteenth century had as many stone-built houses; more than one observer in the eighteenth century commented on the relics of them. This very early prosperity depended more than anything else on Lincoln's place in the Scandinavian world; when that world disintegrated England made new ties with the Low Countries and the Baltic, and Boston and Lynn prospered in their turn. Lincoln had the cloth industry and the cathedral to live on;

witness the rebuilding of the Stonebow in the sixteenth century (78) and the surviving timber-framed merchants' houses in the upper city(79) and along the riverside. Round the cathedral are the houses of the members of the cathedral chapter, some medieval but most of them rebuilt after the Royalists sacked the close during the Civil War.

Stamford has had three phases of prosperity. The first, as with Lincoln, covered the early Middle Ages, and it has left us three churches (St. Mary's, All Saints, and St. George's) and a priory (St. Leonard's) outside the town walls. The second phase Lincoln did not share; it covered the fifteenth century, when Stamford, like the Cotswolds, was the home of wealthy wool merchants(70). In that age St. John the Baptist's was built, and St. Martin's across the Welland in Northamptonshire; the older churches were improved and richly furnished; the generosity of Merchants of the Staple of Calais, like William Brown, has given the name "callis" both to his fifteenth-century hospital and others founded later. The third phase covered the eighteenth century, and was due more than anything to the growth of traffic on the Great North Road; it gave Stamford a town hall, an assembly-room, and a theatre, while private citizens built those houses which are as fine as any outside the Georgian spas.

As well as two of the finest inland cities, this part of eastern England had two of the largest medieval ports. Cambridge and Lincoln could not hold their own against the towns at the river mouths, and Lynn and Boston took their place, just as Hull supplanted York. Here, away from the stone belt, the merchants must have built timber houses, and today Georgian brick houses stand in their place, but there are in both towns incomparable monuments of many centuries. Of the two Lynn is perhaps the richest in variety, but its parish church, though of fine scale, cannot compare with the famous Stump. The two churches are differently conceived: St. Margaret's, Lynn, is a small cathedral, with its cruciform plan and twin west towers; Boston Stump, with its tremendously spacious interior, is a preaching hall, inspired by the friars in the thirteenth century, and incidentally perfectly suited to the Puritan preacher in the seventeenth century. All the wealth of the town went into the one building, but Lynn had two medieval churches to share the generosity of the benevolent. Both towns were international centres in their heyday; merchants from Norway, the Hanseatic towns, Italy, and the Low Countries met (and sometimes fought with) English merchants from all parts. Monks from Durham, Ely, Bardney, and stewards of feudal nobles were there to replenish the pantry and restock the cellar of their houses. The Hanseatic merchants brought furs,

Swedish iron, soft woods, pitch and seal oil; the Dutch, fish for the Lenten season and manufactured goods from Flanders; the Italians, cloth. All these were paid for with English wool and foodstuffs, for we were then able to export corn and bacon, butter and cheese. Lynn and Boston were the only ports apart from London where the Baltic merchants of the Hanseatic League had their own precincts, and at Lynn their timber-framed houses in St. Margaret's Lane still stand; at Boston nothing of the Steelyard remains. In such wealthy and cosmopolitan towns the friars were quick to see an opportunity for preaching; Lynn has the graceful tower of the Greyfriars and gateways of two other friaries; Boston has the Shodfriars Hall, an almost unrecognisable restoration of the Dominicans' building. The social life of a medieval town was interwoven with its religious observance, and the halls of the guilds were clubs and social centres, where merchants met and discussed their ventures, hobnobbed with the nobility and arranged charity for the poor. This was a class-conscious society even though the divisions were not so great as in the eighteenth century. Boston has preserved the hall of one of its fifteen guilds —St. Mary's, a handsome brick building of the fifteenth century. Round the corner from it are the medieval warehouses of the Spain family; William de Spaigne was more than once alderman of the Guild and mayor of Staple. The other guildhalls at Boston have gone, but at Lynn two have survived; the hall of the Trinity Guild, with its handsome chequered front of freestone and flint (66), which later became the town hall, and St. George's Guildhall, a large fourteenth-century building of brick. This latter became a theatre in Elizabeth's time—not so different from its medieval purpose—and it is said that Shakespeare's company played in it. When last I saw it, it still had its link with the theatre; it was being used as a store for scenery and properties. Now it has happily been restored and is the property of the National Trust; it is said to be the largest medieval building of its kind, since the destruction of the guildhalls in London and York by German bombs.

Between the medieval prosperity and the Georgian revival there were, for most of these towns, years of depression and decay. Lincoln seemed to one observer in 1637 "a corpse of a city". Boston was a "decayed and ruined port". Such remarks were often exaggerated, especially when made by corporations seeking relief from taxation, but they have a substantial core; cloth of Lincoln green, says of Louth, and Stamford blankets were things of the past. The towns fell back on the more enduring support of the countryside; behind the great wealth to be got from the cloth industry, or trade with Norway and Holland, there was

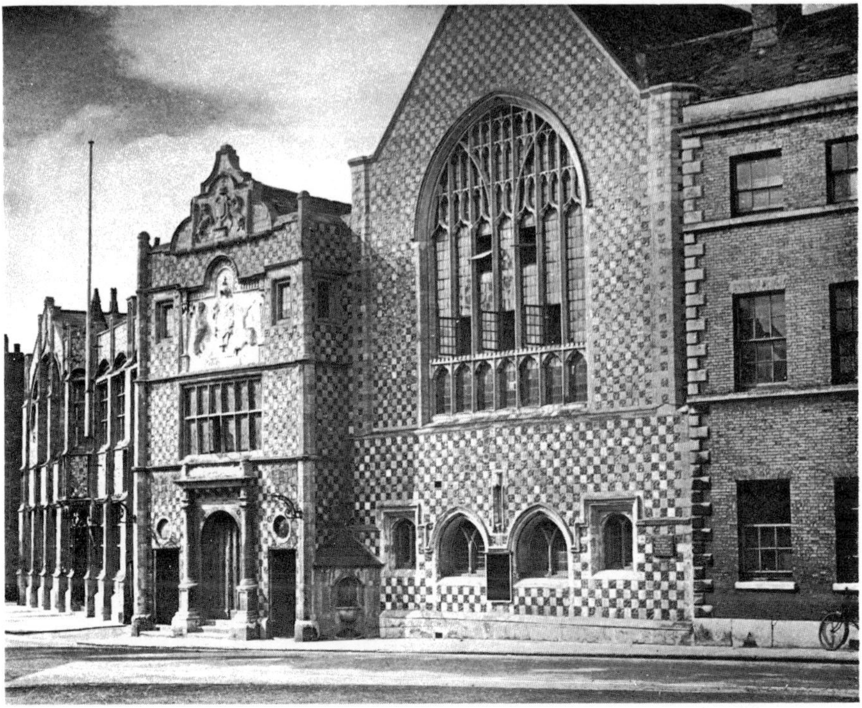

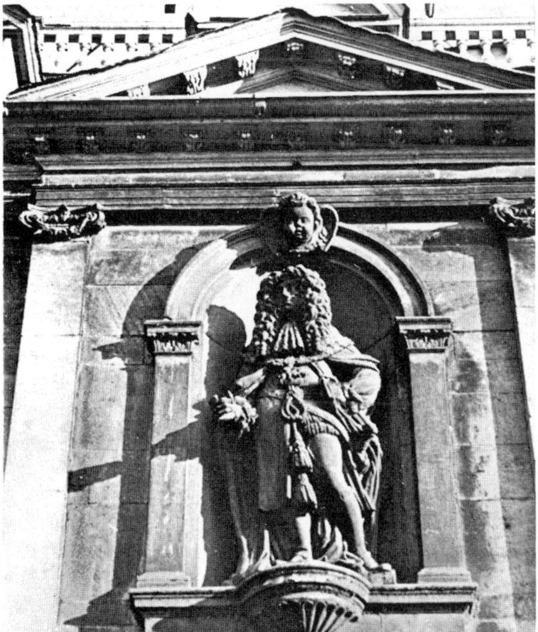

66 (*above*) The fifteenth-century hall of the Trinity Guild, now the Town Hall

67 Figure of Charles II on Henry Bell's Customs House (1683)

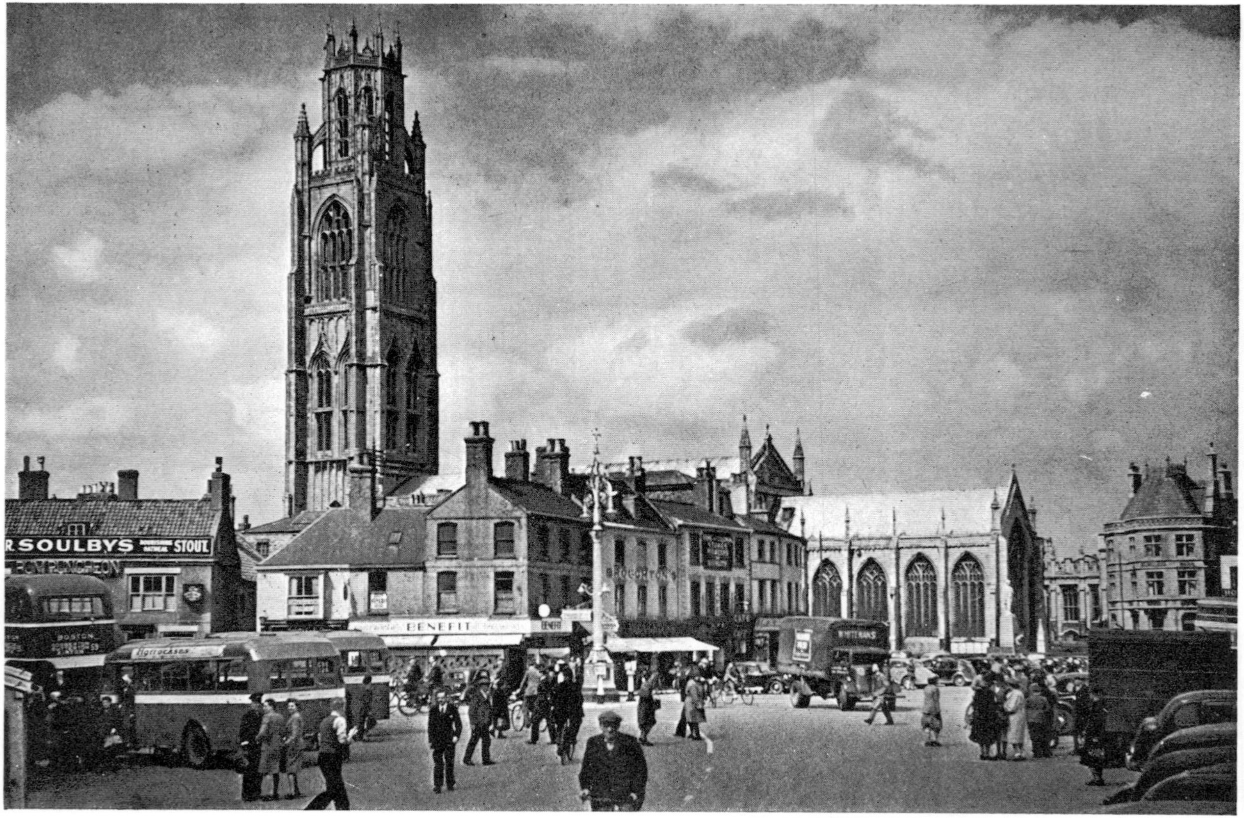

68 Boston: the Stump overlooks the busy Market Place

always the steadier if less spectacular function of providing the countryman with a market for his surplus and shops in which to buy what he could not grow or make. Here was stability. The Middle Ages discovered, and we have had to learn over again, that a town which puts its eggs in one basket can fall on hard times if the basket collapses.

With one exception the towns of Lincolnshire and the Fens are ancient ones, but some of them have gone through several incarnations. The newest are Scunthorpe and Grimsby, and it is hard to find kind words to say of them. The ironstone deposits of north-west Lincolnshire were only discovered in 1858 (or re-discovered; they were worked in Roman times), and Scunthorpe has grown from 250 to 53,000 in much less than a century; it has destroyed three other villages in the process, and made nothing out of them but an agglomeration of houses. The town has no centre that I have been able to find, and the only things to look at are the powerful ranges of steel furnaces and the graceful but curiously unnatural shape of cooling towers. Round about the countryside is devastated: from the Trent the limestone scarp is spotted with the random colours of modern houses; to the east the surface-mining leaves a deep waste behind. Thirty years ago the overburden was moved by men with barrows who sifted every shovelful for the flint implements, bronzes, and Roman pottery that ancient man had left behind; Scunthorpe Museum has some of the most magnificent prehistoric implements of any museum in England. Now the mines are deeper and the mechanical excavators save nothing. In time these wastes may be cultivable, or at least capable of afforestation, but twentieth-century town-planning will never be able to give Scunthorpe a shape; the havoc of Victorian private enterprise is irrevocable.

Grimsby is no easier to like. Of the earlier incarnation of this ancient port there is now little trace; it has grown in a century and a half from a population of 1,500 to be the largest town in the county, and the new town bears small relationship to the old. Indeed, there can have been little of the old to preserve, because between the old port and the new there were long centuries of decay and poverty, owing to the silting-up of the haven. An Icelandic saga speaks of Grimsby as a great resort "of men both from Norway, the Orkneys, and from Scotland and also from the Southern Isles", and today it is closely tied again to that northern world, but in the centuries of depression between, one of the two medieval churches disappeared; the other was much reduced in the impecunious eighteenth century and largely rebuilt in the richer nineteenth. Grimsby is now one of the largest fishing ports in the world; its fishermen's homes are not romantic cottages, but terrace-houses in mean streets, typical of Victorian England. It was the steam trawler which made Grimsby; deep-sea fishing is an industry which produces fish by the thousands of tons, and has, as well as docks, coal wharves and ice factories. The romance is hard to find; one must dwell on the sight of the Humber mouth on a cold spring day when the air is a clear hard blue and the wave-crests are white, and the east wind at Cleethorpes makes one realise how much colder it will be in the White Sea, for which the trawlers are heading as they pass in front of Spurn Lighthouse. Grimsby's pride is that while Hull supplies cod for most of the fish and chip shops of the industrial midlands and north, most of the finer quality fish comes from the Lincolnshire port.

An upstart town like Scunthorpe, or a renewed town like Grimsby, has little visual quality to commend it; there is nothing but the evidence of private fortunes and public ineptitudes. But we must not imagine that only the last century has robbed us of legacies from earlier ages; we often overlook the changes wrought on our medieval towns in the Georgian period because they put in place of medieval buildings others that we now admire. At Spalding all that is left of the very wealthy priory is a range of brick buildings of the fifteenth century; the plan of the priory is completely buried under the eighteenth-century Spalding, and only records tell us that its history is different from that of Wisbech. There the Norman castle has gone, and in their turn the episcopal palace built by Bishop Morton of Ely in the fifteenth century, and the house built by Secretary Thurloe during the Commonwealth. A modern Georgian house occupies the site, and only the plan of the Georgian development shows the distant influence of the military origin of the town. At Lincoln the medieval city has survived only because the industrial Lincoln of the last century or so, of agricultural implement-making, and now of oil engines, pumps and excavators, grew in the valley bottom where the railway ran, and left the hill-top site alone.

Some towns have reverted to the village status out of which they grew; they are discouraged places, where every house seems to show sign of a shrinking of life and interest. I think of Folkingham, which in the coaching days was a busy place, and has a fine open centre, surrounded by Georgian houses and inns, with a fine large church at one end and a stone manor-house of *c.* 1670 at the other. The buses which now stop there bring no travellers to the Greyhound; the Georgian frame is still intact, but it is empty. I visited Folkingham in the summer of 1950 and could not get a meal at the Greyhound or anywhere else. The House of Correction, built in 1826 on the site of the Wake's castle, is a rural slum; the children playing round it and the cart-horses standing on top of the castle mound were the liveliest things I saw. Barton-on-Humber is another town which has dwindled in the last hundred years; it had been for seven centuries or more the southern point of the Humber ferry and in coaching days it was the beginning of the long drive to London for people from Hull and eastern Yorkshire. There is nothing now to show that Barton (24) was one of the county's medieval ports, as well as a ferry terminal, except the two fine churches; the flavour of the town is Georgian, and it still has some good houses. Wainfleet, too, was once one of the many thriving ports of this long coast; it was granted a charter and endowed with a grammar school by its best-known son, William of Waynflete, when he was Lord Chancellor of England. Now it is a tiny market town of plain Georgian buildings; the two medieval churches have gone, the fine fifteenth-century brick building of the school remains rather incongruously and lonely, and the mouth of the haven is miles away across the salt marshes.

Still another lost town is Torksey; at the time of the Norman Conquest it was more populous than Nottingham, and it had later three parish churches and two religious houses. Now it is a tiny village with a very small, though not uninteresting, parish church. It declined when the Foss Dyke silted up, and there are green fields where buildings once crowded in the angle between the Trent and the canal; the ground is strewn with fragments of pottery made there in the twelfth century, and the stone of a lost church. The reopening of the canal in the seventeenth century did not bring the town back to life, and even the Elizabethan manor-house was never rebuilt after the Civil War. This and many other medieval ports of the Lincolnshire coast, the Trent, the Humber, and the Wash—a list of them would include almost all the riverside and coastal villages of today—were the predecessors of Glasgow, Liverpool, Cardiff and Bristol, in the centuries when Europe was the civilised world and England lay on the fringe of it; they declined when England turned about and began to face the Atlantic. Several have disappeared completely from the map; others are now miles from the sea and one can scarcely imagine them as ports for sea-going vessels.

There are market towns of two ages in Lincolnshire. Both had their happiest age in the century before 1850, but in that time they differed widely. There were first of all the many small towns whose population was not far from 1,500 one way or the other, and had grown very little for centuries. They are the ancient markets, resorts for men and women who did not expect to have to walk or ride, man and wife together on a farm-horse, more than about five miles. There were thirty or more of them: small and intimate towns like Caistor (72) and Alford, Epworth in the Isle, Bourne on the edge of the Fen, and Kirton-in-Lindsey on the Cliff. The market-place is no great ranging open space, but small enough for modest buildings to enclose, and for the church to overlook without dominating. The proportions of such towns were, and still are, excellent, although now the market may be dying and the market-place either grass-grown or stained with oil from standing cars and buses. I think particularly of Caistor because the town has not grown enough for the market-place to be dwarfed by later developments. It stands up above the Ancholme valley on a spur of the Wolds, planted on the site of a Roman town part of whose walls, with a semicircular bastion, is still visible south of the church. The site has had its occupants for two thousand years without a break of any length because several springs provide a good water supply. Round the small market-place are pleasant Georgian houses, and the Butter Market, with the Sessions House over it, built in 1662. Farther down the slope are the church and the seventeenth-century grammar school in warm brown stone; the building that stands over the town is the Victorian Methodist chapel, commemorating John Wesley's conquest of this Wold community.

Lincoln, too, had its Butter Market, an early eighteenth-century building flanking an equally pleasing church; both have been pulled down for the sake of motor traffic. The butter market was for women to sit in and gossip. The countryman who had ploughed on the Wolds could stand a few more hours in the open air; he needed the whole square to be sure of meeting all his friends and the pavement was his club. So it is still, and the shops at his back are little altered. The best are the saddlers and ironmongers; in them you can find the traditional tools and the implements tested by time. Some of them are still being made at the back of the shop, and if you have special needs they will often make what you want.

Such shops give us the last meagre glimpse of what was, up to a century ago, a remarkably complete community. The evidence of it can be found in any old directory, such as those which William White of Sheffield began to produce early in the nineteenth century. He was not afraid of a really comprehensive title page, and his directories are indeed *Historical Statistical and Topographical Descriptions* of all *the Wapentakes, Hundreds, Sokes, Liberties, Boroughs, Towns, Ports, Parishes, Townships, Chapelries, Villages, Hamlets, Manors, Fens and Unions.* There is no better way of seeing what has happened to the English countryside and country people than by comparing the volumes issued in 1826 and 1842 with those for the later years of the nineteenth century.

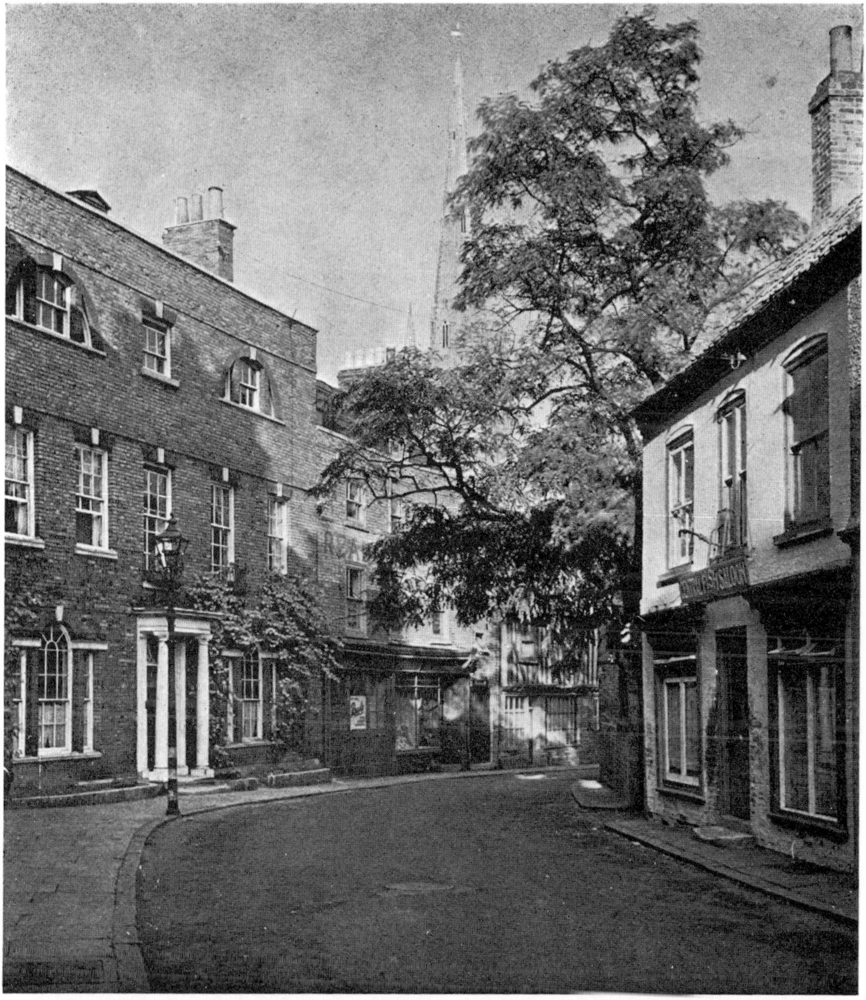

69 A perspective in Grantham: fourteenth-century spire, sixteenth- and eighteenth-century houses

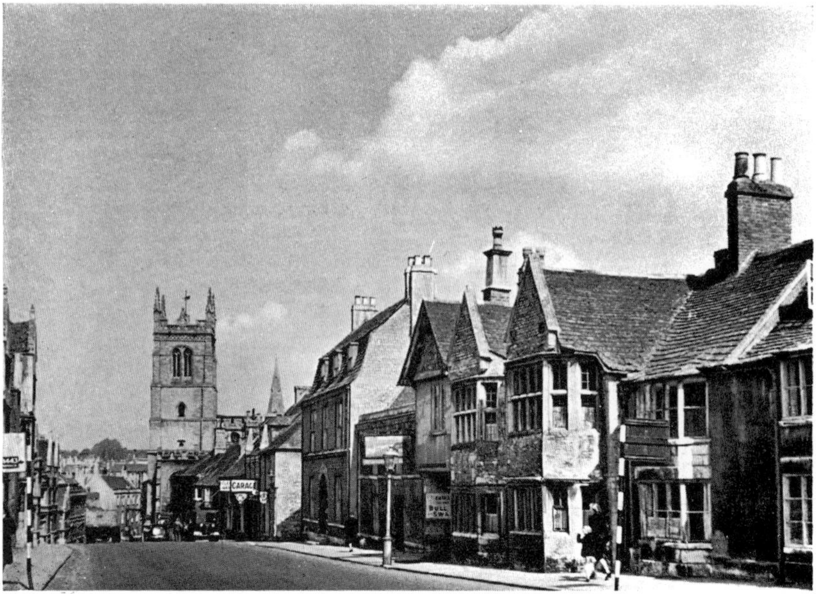

70 The approach from the south: Stamford Baron

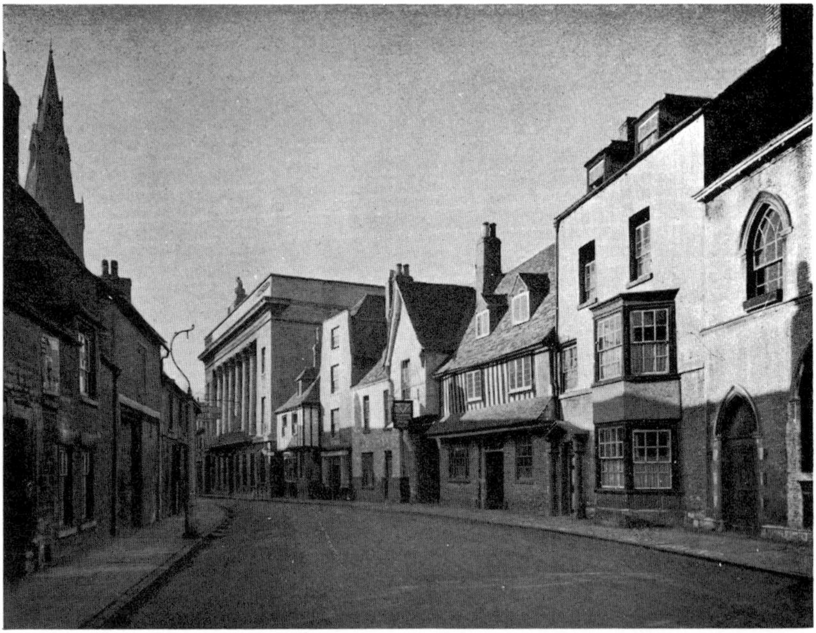

71 Seventeenth- and eighteenth-century houses in St. Mary's Street and the Stamford Hotel (1810)

STAMFORD

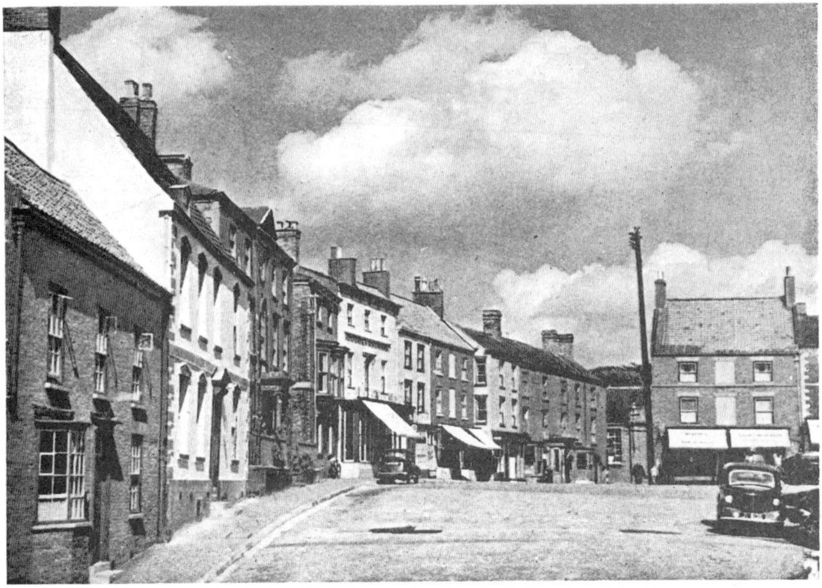

72 The Market Place at Caistor in the Wolds

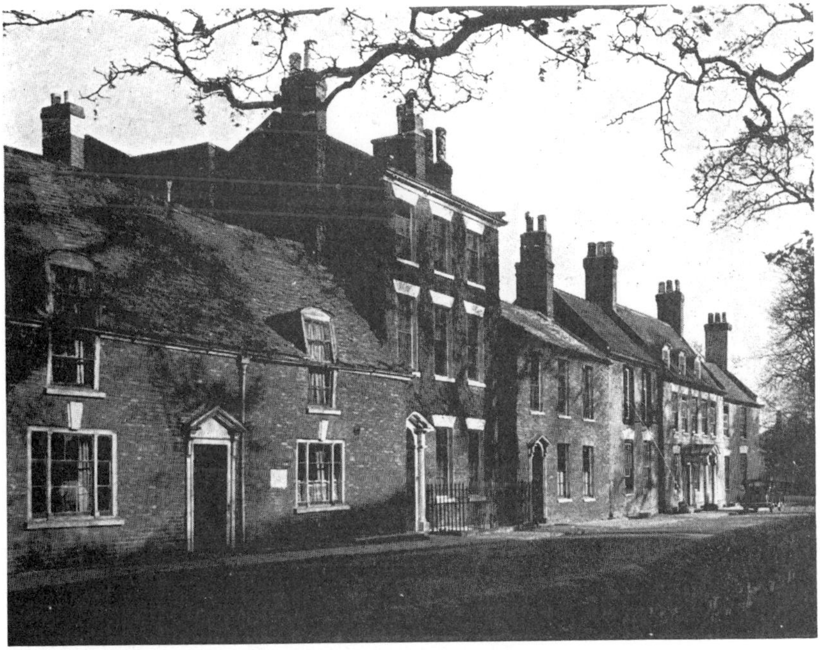

73 Georgian houses by the churchyard at Spalding

LINCOLNSHIRE MARKET TOWNS

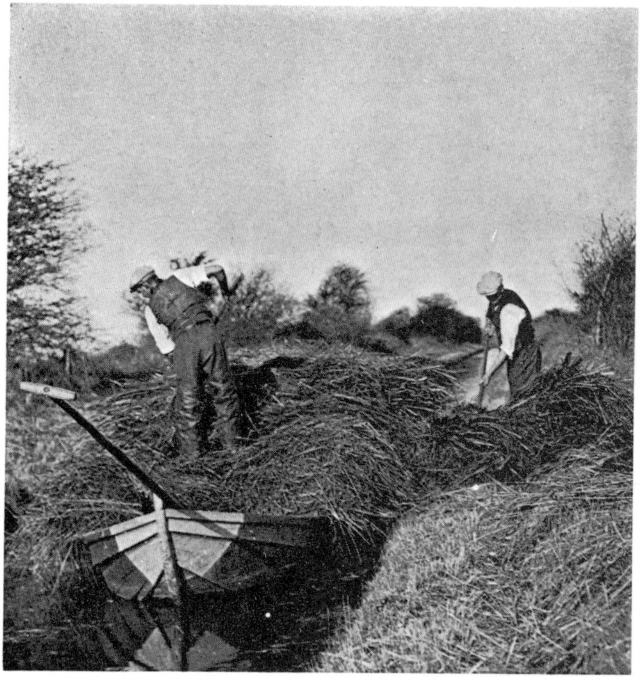

74 Loading cut sedge in Wicken Fen, Cambridgeshire

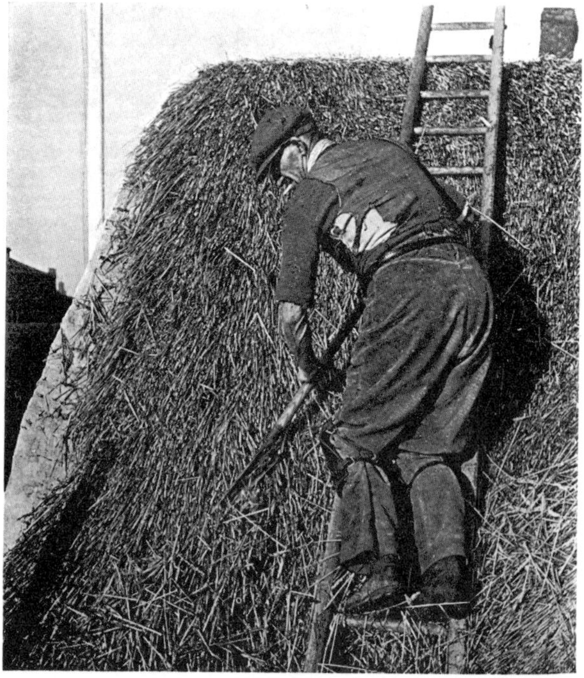

75 Thatching at Spalding, Lincolnshire

I have before me the 1842 directory; I see that Louth had 18 bakers, of whom 4 milled their own flour; 3 basket-makers, 12 blacksmiths, 3 boat and sloop builders, 2 bone-crushers, 7 booksellers, binders and printers; 30 shoemakers, 3 brass and iron founders, and 5 braziers and tinners; 9 brewers, 14 bricklayers, and 6 brick-makers; 28 butchers; 27 cabinet-makers and joiners, 5 chair-makers and turners; 2 carvers and gilders, a carpet rug and blanket manufacturer, 4 coach builders and 3 clog and patten makers. So the list goes on; coopers, curriers, druggists, dyers, fishmongers, furriers, gardeners and seedmen, glovers, grocers and gun-makers. The guns you can still find occasionally, hung in a farmhouse kitchen, or poked among the rafters in the barn; ancient muzzle-loaders or not so ancient pin-fire guns, the barrels sometime beautifully chased and the triggers, hammers, and lock plates magnificently engraved with scenes of the chase. There were hatters, ironmongers, lime-burners, linen-drapers, machine-makers, maltsters, mariners, nail-makers, painters, paper-makers, plumbers, poulterers, rope-makers, saddlers, stonemasons, straw-hat makers, tailors, tallow chandlers, tanners, tobacco pipe makers, watch- and clock-makers. The clocks have become heirlooms and are still ticking on in farmhouse kitchens and on landings; the paint is a little faded, but the round sun on the face still shines, and the deliberate sound is still a background to the quiet of winter evenings by the fire or of hot summer afternoons when flies buzz in the window. The long parade of craftsmen ends with wharfingers, wheelwrights, and whitesmiths. They are gone now; the last to go were those who worked with local materials, such as the rope-makers, using hemp grown in the Isle of Axholme and the Fens, or the basket-makers, whose willow-holts can still be found in the Trent valley. A recently published book on rural industries[1] is illustrated with photographs of rope- and basket-making in Lincolnshire, but they had not been taken these twenty years, and I doubt whether the subjects could be found today. There is a covered ropewalk at Morton near Gainsborough, a long wooden shed roofed with pantiles; it is no longer used.

I have spoken so far only of the smaller market towns which have scarcely grown in size in the last five hundred years; but in the eighteenth century some of them were already being picked out by historical forces and cast for larger roles. By 1800, in addition to Lincoln, Stamford, Boston, Wisbech and King's Lynn, which each had populations of 4,000 or more, there were Spalding, Grantham, Louth and Gainsborough, which were nearly as large. They gained at the expense of the smaller, just as today Nottingham and Leeds have robbed them in their turn

[1] *Rural Crafts in England*, London, 1949.

of their local primacy. But while their culture flourished it was a fine thing. Stukeley commented, after sixteen years in Stamford, that "that is true life, not the stink and noise and nonsense of London". Each of these towns had its theatre with repertory seasons: a medieval manor-house at Gainsborough and a medieval guildhall at King's Lynn; at Sleaford a plain stone box of a building in a back street, and at Stamford an imposing building in the centre of the town. Louth was described in 1792 as one of the gayest towns in Lincolnshire; it had frequent assemblies and concerts, and "even masquerades", which must have been the height of Georgian pleasure. Alford had its assemblies and its players; the races went on for three days each year. Here the Lincolnshire Stuff Ball was first organised in 1785 by the Friends of the Society of Industry. It was a masquerade in which men's clothes and women's gowns had to be made of Lincolnshire cloth, in a well-meant effort to revive a dying industry. At Grantham (69) in 1787 the old guildhall was enlarged, and the Duke of Rutland and Lord Brownlow contributed the cost of adding a room large enough to serve as an assembly-room. Crabbe, who was vicar of two nearby parishes, describes the monthly meetings, spoiled by the local bore:

Yet cares he nothing what we judge or think,
Our only duty's to attend and drink.

At Boston, the Assembly Rooms, built in 1820, still serve as an admirable foil to the view of the Stump from the south. Rennie's bridge over the Witham has been rebuilt, but one or two of his iron footbridges over the Maud Foster Drain still survive. Boston's most fashionable pleasure was to visit Vauxhall Gardens, laid out in 1815 by the owner of Vauxhall Gardens, London, with "an elegant saloon, a very ingenious maze, and also a marine grotto and a cosmorama". Traces of them can still be seen in the garden of Vauxhall House, and I am told that a mural painting in the drawing-room shows the gardens as they were.

This age made Stamford (70, 71) into one of the most beautiful towns in England. Round the medieval churches, and especially the incomparable tower and spire of St. Mary's, the streets rising up from the Welland are full of stone houses of the period from 1650 to 1850. The vernacular Gothic of the seventeenth century, of mullioned windows and steep gables, rubs shoulders with the elegance of sashed windows, ordered fronts, and mansard roofs. The vigour of the life of the town, whether it was the polite balls and assemblies, or the vulgar and brutal sport of bull-running, is recorded in the pages of the *Lincoln, Rutland and Stamford Mercury*, England's oldest provincial newspaper.

The gentry were developing a taste for picnics, which they later passed on to the community at large; there were meetings one evening each week on the newly enclosed Heath at Dunston Pillar, for tea and cards. But life was not all masquerades and cards; Maurice Johnson started the Spalding Gentlemen's Society in 1709–10, which still survives and fulfils its original purpose. It was founded partly to give the local gentry an opportunity to read the *Tatler* and the *Spectator*, but Maurice Johnson had an antiquarian bent, as did some others of the early members, such as Stukeley and Beaupré Bell; they gave it a bias which turned it into one of the most famous local antiquarian societies. The rules from the first minute book are printed in Professor Stuart Piggott's life of William Stukeley; they give us a clear picture of the meetings: candles, snuffers, and a good fire; a pot of coffee and another of bohea tea (and a chamber-pot); twelve clean pipes and an ounce of best tobacco; Latin and Greek dictionaries to support learned discussion, and a tankard of ale to round off the evening. At Stamford, Stukeley tried to found a like club, which he called the Brazen Nose Society, after the knocker which had been taken from Brasenose College, Oxford, in the thirteenth century when students migrated there and tried to found a third English university. But neither here nor at Peterborough did these imitations last for more than a few years.

Most of these larger towns are on navigable rivers, and none of them are far away from one; the spectacular growth of trade, much of it water-borne, gave them a spurt which put them ahead of quiet towns in the Wolds or on the limestone. Gainsborough, Boston, Spalding, Wisbech, and King's Lynn were the first to gain, and after them Louth and Grantham, and to a less degree Horncastle, Caistor, Brigg, and Sleaford. At Gainsborough and the fenland towns the industrial products of the midlands and the foodstuffs of the Fens were transhipped from river boats to coasters; London devoured most of them. There are great warehouses by the rivers, and the merchants' houses, "tight boxes, neatly sashed", are not far away. The Dutch ingeniously got the best of both worlds in Amsterdam by having a road on either side of the canal with the warehouses underneath them; English merchants had more room and spread themselves generously. The result is that Wisbech and Spalding, along with Louth and Newark, are the finest brick towns of eastern England. Boston has not taken enough care of its Georgian inheritance to be ranked with them, and Lynn's character depends on the fine quality of buildings of more than this one age, and particularly on Henry Bell's work (67). At Wisbech the late Georgian building round the site of the castle has the smooth look of metropolitan Georgian;

it was the work of Joseph Medworth, a London speculative builder. The development alongside the artificial waterway which forms the backbone of the town is its best feature (56). Riverside building began early both here and at Spalding—Willesby Hall at Spalding is an Elizabethan brick house. The reason was that the banks provided sites well above flood-level, and for the same reason Dutch villages crowd along the top of the dikes. Most of the surviving houses and warehouses belong to the second half of the Georgian era (55). At Spalding, too, many of the houses have been spoiled by added bay-windows and the like, and worse, Welland Terrace has been cut in half by a monstrous cinema. Wisbech has fared better, and the Brinks are a splendid sweep of prosperous building (56). Boston has the same elements in its plan—a market-place and the two roads flanking the Witham. Round the Wide Bargate the houses are decayed and shabby, or transformed into offices and shops; down the riverside the Customs House, built in 1819, is slipping into the water, but beyond it South Square, containing the medieval guildhall, the Elizabethan grammar school, Fydell House (built in 1726) and completed with great six-storey warehouses, is a very satisfying ensemble (77). Fydell House has been ascribed to Henry Bell of King's Lynn, but there is no evidence to support the claim, and Bell died in 1717.

When the rivers were improved, the farmers' rising profits poured into those towns favoured with a link with the waterways. The directory fills out with the attorneys who dealt with their land purchases, the fire and life offices which insured their new buildings, the coach-builders who sold them carriages for their wives, and the academies which educated their sons and daughters. Sailing-vessels and steam-packets went up and down the Trent and the Witham, calling at all the villages on the banks between Gainsborough and Hull. We do not realise in these days how natural it was, a century ago, to make the journey from London to Gainsborough in a coasting vessel to Hull and then the packet to Gainsborough, as a new vicar of Gainsborough did in 1842. My grandmother recalled going from one of the villages of the Ancholme valley to Hull in a market boat. Now the rivers carry only corn and fertilisers, oil and gravel; the staithe has gone at Burton Stather; you can sit in the riverside inns and look at the river, but you cannot take a boat on it.

The autobiography of Thomas Cooper, Chartist and Victorian popular lecturer, gives a remarkably vivid picture of Gainsborough in the early years of the nineteenth century: the ferment in the streets when the postman rode in with news of Wellington's victories; the river crowded with brigs, sloops, keels, and

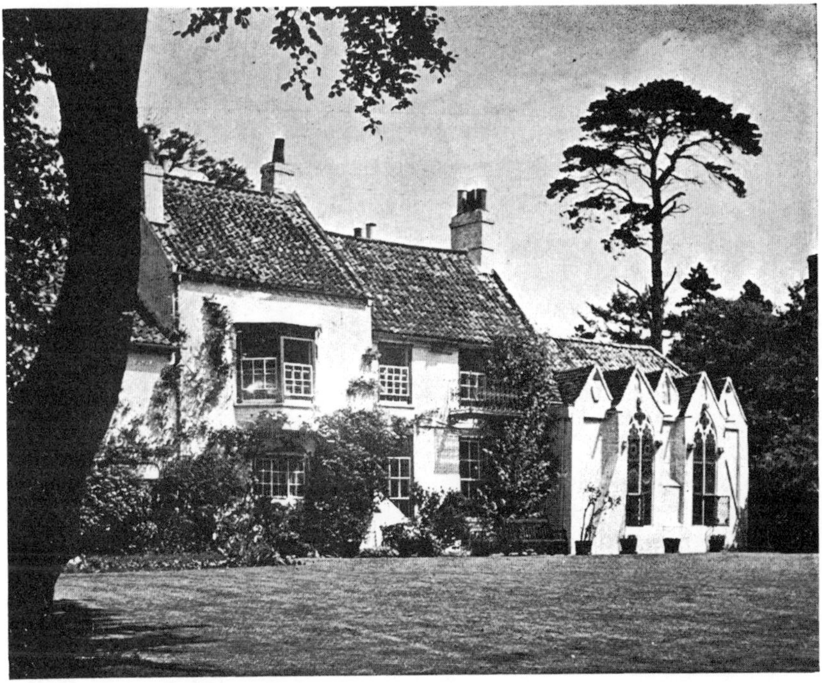

76 Tennyson's birthplace: the old rectory at Somersby

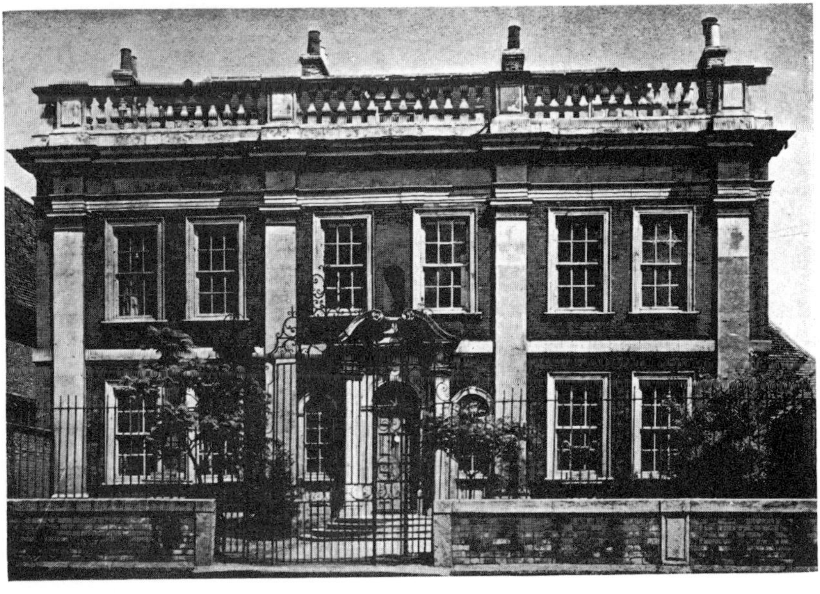

77 Fydell House, Boston (1726)

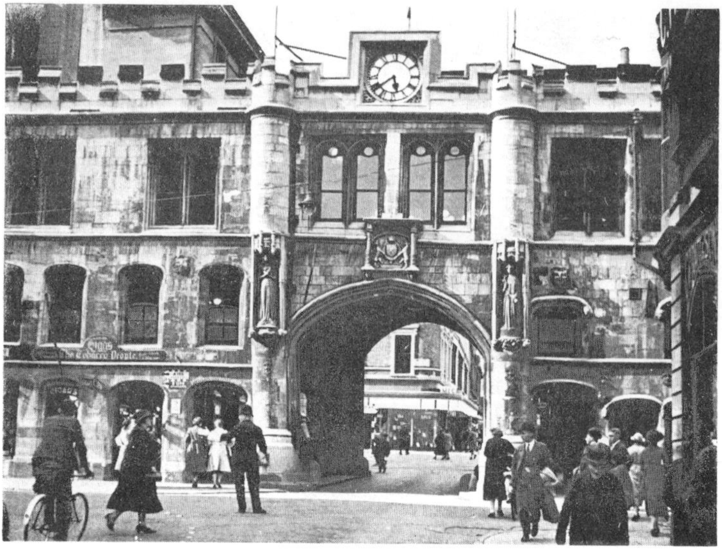

78 (*above*) The Stonebow with the Guildhall over (finished *c.* 1529)

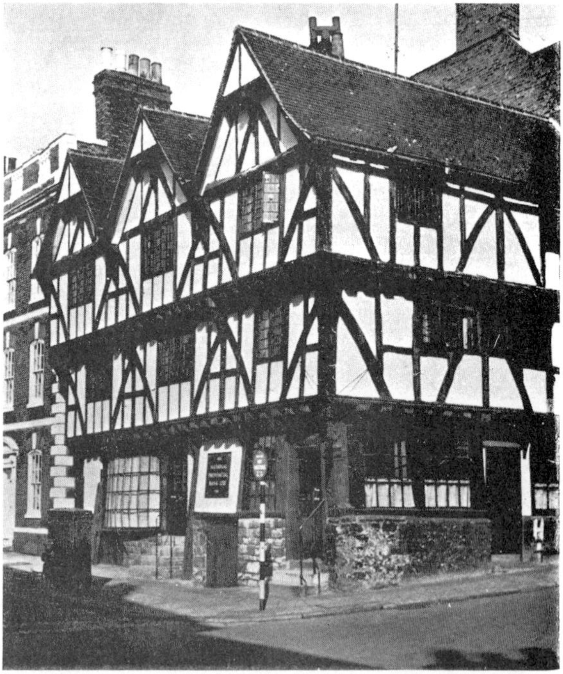

79 Houses on Castle Hill (sixteenth century)

LINCOLN

flat-bottomed ketches from Staffordshire, and the lively noise of sailors in the streets. But Cooper himself belonged to another Gainsborough; the Gainsborough of back streets in which people lived on barley cakes when wheaten flour rose to six shillings a stone, as it did while Wellington was on the field of Waterloo. His widowed mother dyed cloth in the kitchen, and made cardboard boxes which she hawked in country markets and at farmhouses and cottages. It is difficult to realise, when one's mind is filled with a picture of these modest communities, successful in so many senses of the word, that the gulf between rich and poor was growing, and was about to reach its widest. The countryside was being revolutionised. In nearly every village the larger landowners were canvassing their neighbours for support for a Parliamentary Bill to enclose the ancient "open fields, commons and other waste grounds". (Note the word "waste"; it would never have occurred to cottagers to describe the common as waste in our sense of the word.) The smaller freeholders and cottagers, even if they could foresee the difficulties ahead, could scarcely hope to put their feelings into words that would weigh with a committee of the House of Commons. Then came the surveyor, tramping the windy expanses of the open fields with chain and note-book, putting in pegs to mark where hedges would have to be planted and drains cut. After that it was only a matter of making fences to protect the young quicksets, digging the drains, and last of all paying the bill—the cost of lawyers and commissioners and surveyors, of labour on roads and drains, and of fences for the tithe allotments. It sounds a typically English affair, leaving every village to find its own way, through the traditional Parliamentary procedure, of solving the nation's problems of feeding an additional quarter of a million mouths each year. Lincolnshire's contribution was a notable one: to grow corn and rear sheep on the chalk wolds and the limestone uplands which had been fit for nothing but hunting the fox and coursing the hare, or at best for large rabbit-warrens to supply the Brigg market for rabbit-skins. Tennyson, in his young days at Somersby, knew the men who were doing it; he wrote of the "Northern Farmer" who had cleared Thurnaby waste:

Dubbut looök at the waäste; theer warn't not feeäd for a cow;
Nowt at all but bracken an' fuzz, an' looök at it now—
Warn't worth nowt a haäcre, an now theer's lots o' feeäd,
Foorscoor yows upon it, an' some on it down i' seeäd.

But Tennyson was comfortably reared in a beautiful village where the charm of the surroundings hid the poverty and the struggles which made men Chartists; he could see the quaintness of old-fashioned farmers and the social pretensions of the newer generation, but he could not see the other side of the medal which Victorian England struck to self-help and enterprise. There was no place in the new enclosed village for anyone but farmers with capital and farm labourers; farming for an independent existence was nearly gone, and agriculture in Lincolnshire was well on the way to being the great industry it now is. I suspect that one concession only was made to the cottager: the wide verges of Lincolnshire country roads, especially in the Wolds. Nowadays they are dense with sheep's parsley in the summer, but until recently the grazing of them was let each year, and the tented herd of cows kept the herbage down. The village neatherd of the Middle Ages turned into a boy leaning on a stick, and now he too has vanished—into the village school. The villages were changed in the process no less than the landscape. In those owned by a single landowner no new houses were built, for fear the occupants if unemployed would be a burden on one man alone. The open villages such as Winterton, where land could be had for building and where no one man monopolised the houses, were crowded with labourers who rode miles to their work on donkeys. This is difficult to believe but it is recorded in the cold words of a nineteenth-century report. On the large farms seasonal work was done by gangs of women and girls in conditions which roused the indignation of Victorian moralists. You can read an almost incredible description of such a gang, working round Crowland in *Life as we have known it*; the writer Mrs. Burroughs, joined at the age of eight a gang of which she was the *eldest*; they walked several miles to one large farm or another in the fens between Crowland and Peterborough, and worked for fourteen hours a day. There is nothing lacking—not even the overseer's whip—to make this account as terrible as that of any Lancashire cotton mill, and this was at the date when such atrocities had already been stopped in the cotton industry. A measure of life had been drained out of the village, and the dregs were squalid.

The life had gone in one sense with the loss of village institutions and the disappearance of ancient ties within the community, and in another sense it had departed with the young men who emigrated, either abroad, or to the industrial midlands. The sea attracted some of the most adventurous; Matthew Flinders, a doctor's son from Donington in Holland, has a high place of honour in the story of Australian exploration, along with George Bass, son of an Aswarby farmer; they gave their own names to half a dozen places in Southern Australia and names of Lincolnshire towns and villages to many others. The young commander of the sloop *Investigator* which charted the Australian coast in 1801 had in his crew several Lincolnshire men, including as midshipman his fourteen-year-old cousin, John Franklin, who was for nineteen years governor of the island they discovered, and later disappeared in that attempt, successful but fatal, to discover the North-West Passage. His statue adorns the market-place at Spilsby, where he was born. He was one of the greatest Arctic navigators and explorers of the nineteenth century; there is a direct link between Captain James Cook, the eighteenth-century navigator, and Sir John Franklin in the person of Sir Joseph Banks of Revesby, who went as botanist on Cook's first expedition to the South Seas, and later encouraged Matthew Flinders. From Elizabeth's day until the time of Napoleon the colliers and coasters and Baltic traders had been the nursery of the English navy, and Lincolnshire's contribution is worth remembering.

From the ancient ports and riverside villages young men found their opportunity at sea; the life of the villages on the inland side of the county drained away into the industrial cities of Yorkshire and the midlands. Gainsborough is the only town in the county which belongs to that New England; behind the medieval High Street, which is only separated from the Trent by mills and warehouses, there is another wider road, flanked by bay after bay of engineering workshops. The boiler-making which could be heard reverberating through those walls, has stopped now; twentieth-century Gainsborough lives not by steam-engines but by tractors and wrapping machines. The adjustment was a hard one for the town: it shows today in old names on shop fronts peeping through the new cheap paint put on in the 1930's when bankruptcies were common and businesses changed hands often. In the transition the older town of substantial Georgian houses fared very badly and the Victorian town around it became very shabby; but Gainsborough is probably more secure now than in the past. Steam-engines and tractors may be outmoded, but the insubstantial luxuries of this age must have their wrappings, whatever the contents.

The Lincolnshire men and women who fled to the industrial towns found a livelihood but not a life worth living, and out of the conditions made for them there grew Lincolnshire's newest industry: providing for the thousands who could escape, once a year, from their urban prison to the sea-coast. When the spa alone was fashionable, among the middle classes, Lincolnshire could not compete. There were one or two springs at such places as Aswarby, Stainfield, and Braceborough which had a transient local popularity. Woodhall Spa was the accidental result of a boring for coal; it grew up in the Victorian age when spas had lost their social importance, and the pleasures of the open air had been discovered. Its attraction lies not in its buildings, but in gardens and the moorland country of pine trees and heather round about. The pleasures of sea bathing were slow to be appreciated, and they were first tasted at places which we now leave on one side. Frieston Shore, between Boston and Skegness, where the Georgian hotel still stands behind the sea bank, has always been a favourite resort of Boston people, but the midland folk who once came to bathe (and drink the sea water) and to contemplate the Norfolk coast, now prefer the headier joys of Skegness. Skegness ought to be added to the list of towns which are enjoying a second incarnation; when Leland came this way in 1540 the old port had just been "clene consumid and eten up with the se"; when Byng, the next tourist, came in the 1790's, he found one inn and not much else. He said of Skegness that "if a good house was built here, with a clever landlord, it would draw much company". That was a forecast of what Mr. Butlin was to do, when he opened his first holiday camp at Skegness in 1937; the forecast could not be realised until the industrial workers of the midlands began to get time to escape from the steel works or the hosiery mill. The Saturday half-holiday in Nottingham dates from the 1860's; that and the Bank Holiday Act of 1871 brought Skegness and Cleethorpes within reach of the railway excursion. Cowper's lines of two centuries ago have been reinforced by time:

But now alike gay widow, virgin, wife,
Ingenious to diversify dull life,
In coaches, chaises, caravans and hoys,
Fly to the coast for daily, nightly joys,
And all impatient of dry land, agree
With one consent to rush into the sea;

the only effect of time is to put motors in the coaches and to plant the caravans in every other field behind the sand-hills.

What can one say of Skegness, and Cleethorpes or Mablethorpe? There is a pier, be it long or short; there are the inevitable flower-beds and boating lakes and miniature golf courses. Those who think that some question of taste is involved will prefer Scarborough or Weymouth, but two things distinguish these Lincolnshire resorts. The first is that they possess a large share of the essence of the county; the clean freedom of a windy world whose edges are as far away as they can be under a sky which dwarfs the most ambitious buildings. Two families can fill a Dorset cove; these Lincolnshire sands are still clear and empty when half the population of the midlands are planted down there, and a great sense of release blows into everyone. The other thing is that here was built the first factory for the mass-production of happy holiday-makers. It is easy to poke fun at Butlin's holiday camps, but they are the best solution so far to the problem of family holidays for the millions, and unquestionably better than the alternative of multiplying indefinitely the squalid, chaotic scatter of bungalows and caravans.

While the townsman was building up his claim to holidays, the countryman was living through sixty years of depression in which holidays had no part. Census figures show that the Lincolnshire village doubled its size throughout the first sixty years of the nineteenth century; more land under crops meant more work. The village was largest in the 1860's, before the impact of foreign competition and the effect of mechanising agriculture began to be felt. This, too, was the height of prosperity for the country house. The rent-roll of the Massingberds of Ormsby, a typical family of ancient descent and modest status among the gentry of the county, had risen to a peak of £3,800 in 1812, during the wartime inflation, and again to £3,500 in the third quarter of the century. Round Grantham, Harlaxton Manor, Easton Hall and Stoke Rochford were all rebuilt in neo-Tudor or neo-Jacobean style. The largest estates in the county were Brocklesby, Belton and Grimsthorpe. Grimsthorpe Castle was maintained on 24,000 acres of Lincolnshire land, which brought in half Lord Willoughby d'Eresby's income of £74,000, the other half coming from 100,000 acres in Wales. The estates of Lord Brownlow were mainly in Shropshire, but included 11,000 acres in Kesteven. The Brocklesby foxhounds could run for many miles in the northern Wolds before they left the Earl of Yarborough's 57,000 acres. Under such patronage foxhunting flourished; the first steeplechase was run and a new sport invented. It is said that at Brocklesby it was the custom until recently for the butler, after the port had circulated, to announce: "The horses are bedded, my lord." The gentlemen then trooped out to the stables to satisfy themselves that their horses were comfortable.[1]

Sir Osbert Sitwell, in his fascinating autobiography, remembers Christmas at Blankney, which then belonged to his grandfather the Earl of Londesborough, as "a place in which to kill everything you saw except horses and dogs. Horses were enthroned in a state which even Caligula never dreamt of for his favourite." The village of Blankney has no place in his recollections, for such houses did not form part of a community; they were communities in themselves, filling and emptying with the sporting seasons, the ranks in them bound by no ties but those of personal service.

[1] This story is told by Mr. Christopher Hussey in his account of Brocklesby in *Country Life*.

Most of them have melted away, and the villages which fringed them are poorer because they cannot learn again even in a generation the habits of independent thought and action which the country house had taken away. But the decay of the country house, which is one of the momentous changes in the English countryside in the present century, is less marked in Lincolnshire than in many other counties. The rent-rolls of the gentry never swelled so large, and the fall is not so great. Gunby Hall, on the edge of the Marshland, a beautiful red brick house of 1700, is now the property of the National Trust. Stubton Hall, a pleasant Regency house in the upper Witham valley, is about to become an educational institution. Apart from these, I cannot recall any other houses of consequence that are not still privately occupied.

However many small farms were swallowed up in the making of such estates, Lincolnshire is too large to be dominated by a handful of landowners, and there are large parts where the small- and medium-sized farmer survived if he had a fair share of innate qualities. The story of the struggle is told in Blue Books, and it is as moving as that of the conditions in the industrial towns. In terms of statistics it meant that the heaviest land, and the poor soil of the middle wolds, and the under-drained land in the Ancholme valley and elsewhere, became derelict, and remained so until after 1939. Wheat could not be grown successfully in face of American competition and production declined by a half; although barley and cattle productions increased, the total result was that this rich county did much less than it had done to fill the nation's larder. The Norfolk four course rotation, based on sheep and turnips, became impossible as the price of mutton and wool collapsed. In terms of human disappointment and discouragment, it meant that the mortgage with which the farm had been bought, at the peak price of 1870, could not be paid off, even if the whole family worked fourteen of more hours a day and accepted standards lower than those of farm workers, which were low enough in all conscience. The freeholders in the Marshland seldom saw on their own tables a cut of the beef fattened in their own fields, and dried cow dung was again used as a fuel—infallible sign of utter poverty. The innate qualities I spoke of were intelligence enough to seize whatever profitable courses there were in a world which offered very few to food producers, and determination to stay on the land, whatever the personal deprivation. Determination to stay meant being willing to sell the farm to Lord Yarborough, as a great-grandfather of mine did, and to remain on the family holding as a tenant.

Over much of the county ingenuity and determination could often hold the farm together, but in the Fens and the Isle of

Axholme they could do more. There the high prices of the 1860's had induced large owners to sell out in small lots, and the class of small freeholders had been strengthened. Their case was bad when the depression came, but they were saved by three crops. One was the potato, already widely grown and a secure crop (apart from weather risks) because, fortunately for the small farmer, it could not be imported. If potatoes helped to save the Irish, they also saved the small farmer in Lincolnshire. The second crop was bulbs. When Wilson Fox toured the Fens in 1892, collecting evidence for the Royal Commission on Agriculture, among the many freeholders struggling to keep a grip on their few acres, working fourteen or fifteen hours a day and just managing to pay interest on the mortgage, he found one man at Wainfleet who was making money. He was growing bulbs—snowdrops and daffodils then, not tulips—and it paid. Fox could have found others round Spalding, for bulb growing had begun there in the 1880's. Soft fruit, the third crop, had already become important; the first orchard in the Wisbech area had been planted in the 1850's. Woad and flax, sheep and cattle disappeared as the grassland was ploughed up; flowers, fruit, and vegetables took their place alongside potatoes and wheat, and the twentieth century has added sugar-beet. By 1914 the economic tide had turned in the Fens; the rest of the county had to wait until the onset of another war. The sight of a prosperous countryside is something this generation has scarcely known, but it shows itself in the Fens, not only in the intensely efficient look of every farming operation, but in lofty glass houses for seed potatoes, new barns and loading bays, freshly painted houses, and most of all in neat and cared-for farm gardens. We had come to expect that a farmer was a person who had neither time nor energy to attend to his own front garden, and neglected fruit trees and the wilderness of vegetable garden have been the usual frame to derelict barns and shabby farmhouses. The Fens are a heartening contrast because of the patent self-confidence as well as the prosperity. Over the rest of the county the change has begun, but has yet to make a marked difference. The Fens are different in so many ways; they have the most stable farming population in the whole of England and the largest proportion of owner-occupiers, and those two things explain much. The rest of the county falls in with the national pattern of farmers who are three-quarters of them tenants on whose landlords the burden of restoration largely falls. At the other end of the scale is the great industrialist who farms a thousand acres; whose farm gate of characeristic colours can be seen in half a dozen parishes, who possesses more powered implements than his ancestor had horses, and employs the equivalent of a whole village. I call him an industrialist, but he is a farmer and not a retired steel manufacturer; I mean to infer that in Lincolnshire more than any other county, there are farmers whose daily operations involve the same grandiose manipulation of machines and men as any factory manager's, and on top of that they need more lively intelligence, because they are working not with inanimate ore, but with nature in a very chancy climate.

I wish I had space here to write of the people I know who live in the farmhouses and cottages I have tried to describe, who attend the churches and the chapels, organise the whist drives and dances and attend the educational classes in the schools and the village halls. They have been leaderless now for a century or more; it would have been expecting too much of the law of averages to hope that more than one community here and there could throw up a leader from ranks creamed off by emigration and industry. As someone has said, the would-be leaders have had political or social or sectarian axes to grind, and those who were capable of leading and had something to give too often felt that the village was not the biggest problem they could tackle. The village has never been democratic, except in the sense that it did once provide more or less equal opportunity; in the last century it has not done that in any sense at all, and as far as farming is concerned it never will again, short of a revolution in our society. But even if the commonwealth of the English village has been overthrown, the individual English countryman can still be found in every village. If you want to know the face of Britain, you must learn not from maps or pictures, but from the man who knows it, intimately, on every inch of the surface and below it. The townsman's wits are spread over the whole world as thick as the page of a newspaper; there is nothing he knows properly. The countryman's are expended on a small span of it; past generations are still standing by his side, and the whole depth of their experience and his is available at every moment. I am proud to count such men among my forebears, and I have known them as fellow students, huddled round the stove in a village school on winter evenings. They can illuminate the historian's generalisation, and dredge up for him much that has never reached the printed page. I hope that some of the things they have taught me have found a place in this book.

MAP

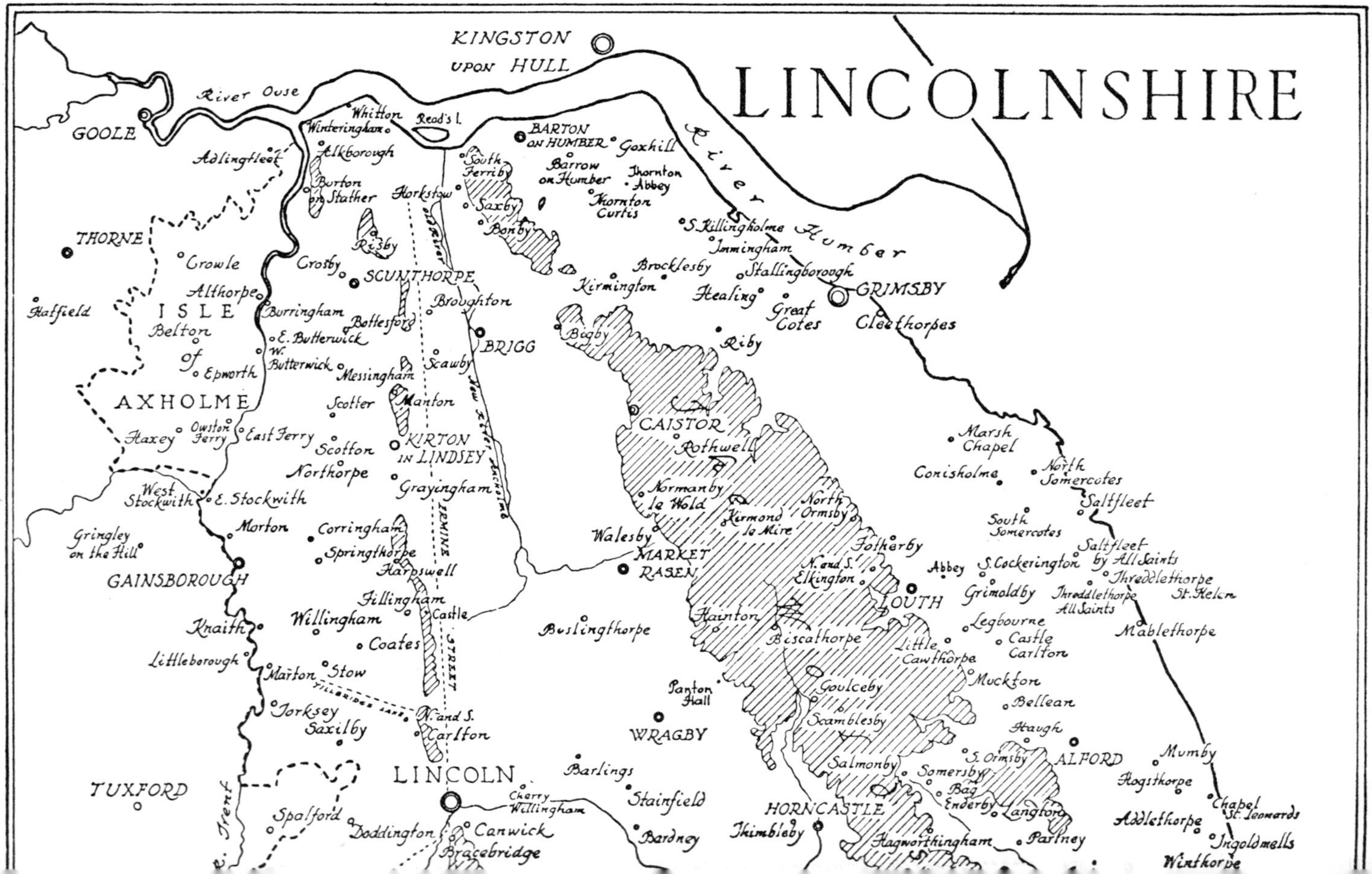
LINCOLNSHIRE
KINGSTON UPON HULL
River Ouse
River Humber
GOOLE
Whitton
Read's I.
Winteringham
Alkborough
Adlingfleet
Burton on Stather
Horkstow
South Ferriby
Saxby
Bonby
BARTON ON HUMBER
Goxhill
Barrow on Humber
Thornton Abbey
Thornton Curtis
S. Killingholme
Immingham
Stallingborough
GRIMSBY
Cleethorpes
Brocklesby
Kirmington
Healing
Great Cotes
Riby
THORNE
Crowle
Risby
Crosby
SCUNTHORPE
Broughton
Hatfield
ISLE of AXHOLME
Althorpe
Belton
Epworth
Burringham
Bottesford
E. Butterwick
W. Butterwick
Messingham
Scawby
BRIGG
Bigby
Scotter
Manton
Haxey
Owston Ferry
East Ferry
Scotton
KIRTON IN LINDSEY
Northorpe
Grayingham
CAISTOR
Rothwell
Marsh Chapel
Conisholme
North Somercotes
Saltfleet
West Stockwith
E. Stockwith
Gringley on the Hill
Morton
Corringham
Springthorpe
Harpswell
ERMINE STREET
New River Ancholme
Old River
Normanby le Wold
Kirmond le Mire
North Ormsby
Walesby
MARKET RASEN
Fotherby
South Somercotes
GAINSBOROUGH
Fillingham
Castle
Willingham
Coates
Knaith
Littleborough
Marton
Stow
Tillbridge Lane
Torksey
Saxilby
N. and S. Carlton
Buslingthorpe
Hainton
N. and S. Elkington
LOUTH
Abbey
S. Cockerington
Saltfleet by All Saints
Theddlethorpe St. Helen
Theddlethorpe All Saints
Grimoldby
Biscathorpe
Legbourne
Castle Carlton
Little Cawthorpe
Mablethorpe
Muckton
Panton Hall
Goulceby
Belleau
Scamblesby
Haugh
WRAGBY
ALFORD
Mumby
S. Ormsby
Somersby
Salmonby
Bag Enderby
Langton
Hogsthorpe
Chapel St. Leonards
Addlethorpe
Ingoldmells
Winthorpe
TUXFORD
LINCOLN
Barlings
Stainfield
Cherry Willingham
Canwick
Bracebridge
Doddington
Spalford
R. Trent
HORNCASTLE
Thimbleby
Bardney
Hagworthingham
Partney

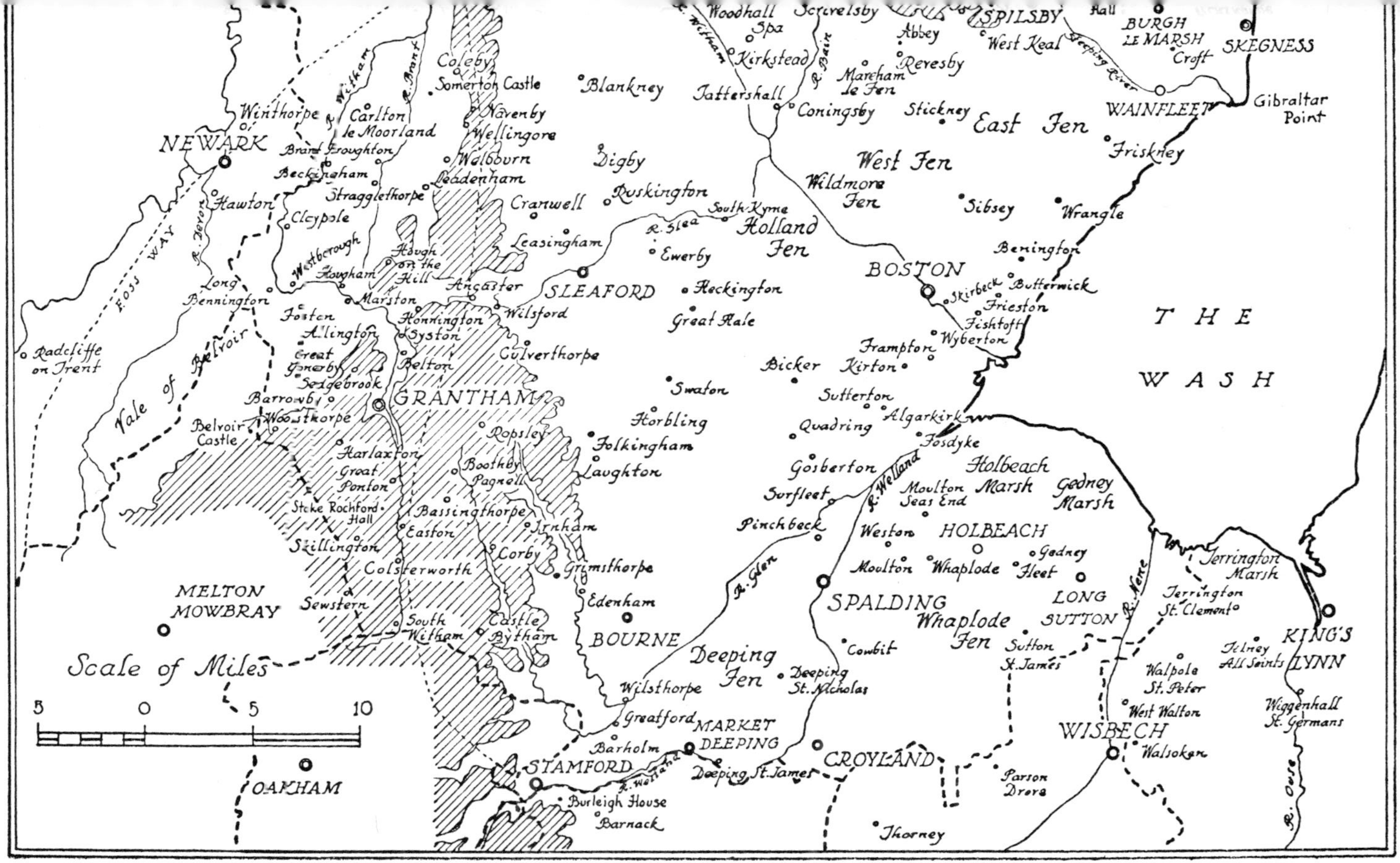
NEWARK
Winthorpe
Carlton le Moorland
Brant Broughton
Beckingham
Hawton
Claypole
Stragglethorpe
Westborough
Foston
Long Bennington
Radcliffe on Trent
FOSS WAY
R. Devon
R. Witham
R. Brant
Coleby
Somerton Castle
Navenby
Wellingore
Welbourn
Leadenham
Hough on the Hill
Marston
Honnington
Syston
Allington
Great Gonerby
Sedgebrook
Barrowby
Woolsthorpe
Belvoir Castle
Vale of Belvoir
Belton
GRANTHAM
Harlaxton
Great Ponton
Stoke Rochford Hall
Skillington
Colsterworth
Sewstern
South Witham
MELTON MOWBRAY
OAKHAM
Scale of Miles
5
0
5
10
Blankney
Digby
Ruskington
Cranwell
Leasingham
Ancaster
SLEAFORD
Wilsford
Culverthorpe
Ropsley
Boothby Pagnell
Bassingthorpe
Easton
Irnham
Corby
Castle Bytham
Grimsthorpe
Edenham
BOURNE
Folkingham
Laughton
Horbling
Swaton
Great Hale
Heckington
Ewerby
R. Slea
South Kyme
Holland Fen
Woodhall Spa
Kirkstead
Tattershall
Scrivelsby
R. Bain
Coningsby
Mareham le Fen
Revesby
Abbey
Stickney
West Fen
Wildmore Fen
East Fen
SPILSBY
West Keal
BURGH LE MARSH
Croft
SKEGNESS
Steeping River
WAINFLEET
Gibraltar Point
Friskney
Wrangle
Sibsey
Benington
Butterwick
BOSTON
Skirbeck
Frieston
Fishtoft
Wyberton
Frampton
Kirton
Bicker
Sutterton
Algarkirk
Fosdyke
Quadring
Gosberton
Surfleet
Pinchbeck
R. Glen
R. Welland
THE WASH
Holbeach Marsh
Gedney Marsh
Moulton Seas End
Weston
HOLBEACH
Gedney
Moulton
Whaplode
Fleet
LONG SUTTON
SPALDING
Whaplode Fen
Cowbit
Sutton St. James
Deeping Fen
Deeping St. Nicholas
Wilsthorpe
Greatford
MARKET DEEPING
Barholm
Deeping St. James
STAMFORD
Burleigh House
Barnack
CROYLAND
Parson Drove
Thorney
R. Nene
Terrington Marsh
Terrington St. Clement
Walpole St. Peter
West Walton
WISBECH
Walsoken
Tilney All Saints
KING'S LYNN
Wiggenhall St. Germans
R. Ouse

INDEX

The numbers printed in **heavy** type refer to the figure numbers of the illustrations.